Muddy Boots & Smart Suits

ISEAS – Yusof Ishak Institute (formerly the Institute of Southeast Asian Studies) was established as an autonomous organization in 1968. It is a regional centre dedicated to the study of socio-political, security and economic trends and developments in Southeast Asia and its wider geostrategic and economic environment.

The Institute's research programmes are the Regional Economic Studies (RES, including ASEAN and APEC), Regional Strategic and Political Studies (RSPS), and Regional Social and Cultural Studies (RSCS).

ISEAS Publishing, an established academic press, has issued more than 2,000 books and journals. It is the largest scholarly publisher of research about Southeast Asia from within the region. ISEAS Publications works with many other academic and trade publishers and distributors to disseminate important research and analyses from and about Southeast Asia to the rest of the world.

Muddy Boots & Smart Suits

Researching Asia-Pacific Affairs

Edited by
Nicholas Farrelly, Amy King,
Michael Wesley and Hugh White

ISEAS YUSOF ISHAK
INSTITUTE

First published in Singapore in 2017 by
ISEAS Publishing
30 Heng Mui Keng Terrace
Singapore 119614

E-mail: publish@iseas.edu.sg
Website: <http://bookshop.iseas.edu.sg>

*The responsibility for facts and opinions in this publication rests exclusively with the
authors and their interpretations do not necessarily reflect the views or the policy of
the publisher or its supporters.*

ISEAS Library Cataloguing-in-Publication Data

Muddy Boots and Smart Suits : Researching Asia-Pacific Affairs / Edited by
Nicholas Farrelly, Amy King, Michael Wesley and Hugh White.
   1.   Asia—Politics and government.
   2.   Pacific Area—Politics and government.
   3.   Asia—Civilization.
   4.   Pacific Area—Civilization.
   I.   Farrelly, Nicholas, 1982-
   II. King, Amy, 1982-
   III. Wesley, Michael, 1968-
   IV. White, Hugh.
JQ24 M941   2017

ISBN 978-981-4459-78-5 (soft cover)
ISBN 978-981-4459-79-2 (E-book PDF)

Typeset by International Typesetters Pte Ltd
Printed in Singapore by Markono Print Media Pte Ltd

CONTENTS

ABOUT THE CONTRIBUTORS

Julien Barbara is a Senior Policy Fellow at the State, Society and Governance in Melanesia Program in the Australian National University (ANU)'s Coral Bell School of Asia Pacific Affairs, and Convenor of the Centre for Democratic Institutions, both at the ANU. Prior to joining the ANU, Dr Barbara worked for the Department of Foreign Affairs and Trade and the Australian Agency for International Development (AusAID). From 2011 to 2012, Dr Barbara was Director of the Regional Assistance Mission to Solomon Islands (RAMSI) Machinery of Governance programme. His research interests include democratic governance, state-building and post-conflict development, with a focus on the Pacific.

Joan Beaumont is Professor in the Strategic and Defence Studies Centre at the Australian National University (ANU)'s Coral Bell School of Asia Pacific Affairs. Her publications include the prize-winning *Broken Nation: Australians and the Great War* (2013) and articles on war memory and heritage, including: "Contested Transnational Heritage: The Demolition of Changi Prison, Singapore", *International Journal of Heritage Studies* 15, no. 4 (2009); "Hellfire Pass Memorial Museum, Thai-Burma Railway", in *The Heritage of War*, edited by Martin Gegner and Bart Ziino (2012); "The Diplomacy of Extra-territorial Heritage: The Kokoda Track, Papua New Guinea", *International Journal of Heritage Studies* 22, no. 5 (2016); and "The Yokohama War Cemetery, Japan: Imperial, National and Local Remembrance", in *Remembering World War II*, edited by Patrick Finney (in press).

Nick Bisley is the Executive Director of La Trobe Asia and Professor of International Relations at La Trobe University. He is currently the Editor-in-Chief of the *Australian Journal of International Affairs*, Australia's oldest scholarly journal in the field of International Relations. He is the author of many works on international relations, including *Issues* *in 21st Century World Politics, 3rd Edition* (2017), *Great Powers in the Changing International Order* (2012), and *Building Asia's Security* (2009). He regularly contributes to and is quoted in national and international media including *The Guardian, The Economist*, and *Bloomberg.*

Peter J. Dean is a Senior Fellow in the Strategic and Defence Studies Centre at the Australian National University (ANU)'s Coral Bell School of Asia Pacific Affairs, as well as an Adjunct Fellow in the Pacific Partners Initiative at the Centre for Strategic and International Studies (CSIS) in Washington D.C. Dr Dean was the 2014–15 Fulbright Scholar in Australia–United States Alliance Studies. He is series editor of the Melbourne University Press Defence Studies Series and editorial board member of *Global War Studies* and the *Australian Army Journal.* His latest publication (with Stephan Fruehling and Brendan Taylor) is *Australia's American Alliance* (2016).

Nicholas Farrelly is the Deputy Director responsible for impact and engagement at the Australian National University (ANU)'s Coral Bell School of Asia Pacific Affairs. After graduating from the ANU in Asian Studies, Dr Farrelly completed his doctorate at Balliol College, University of Oxford, where he was a Rhodes Scholar. He also convenes the ANU's elite undergraduate PhB programme in Asia-Pacific Studies and is the Director of the ANU Myanmar Research Centre.

Evi Fitriani is the Head of the Department of International Relations in the Faculty of Social and Political Sciences, University of Indonesia (FISIP UI). She is the co-founder of the University's Masters in European Studies, and the FISIP UI ASEAN Study Center. She is also the Indonesian Country Coordinator of the Network of East Asian Think Tanks (NEAT). Dr Fitriani was trained in International Relations in Indonesia, the UK, the US, and Australia, as well as in Japan, Sweden, the Netherlands, and Hungary. She has obtained more than twelve international awards and grants. Her research focuses on Indonesian foreign policy, ASEAN, Asian regionalism, and Asia–Europe relations.

Cecilia Jacob is a Research Fellow and Director of Studies in the Department of International Relations at the Australian National University (ANU)'s Coral Bell School of Asia Pacific Affairs. Her work focuses on civilian protection, internal conflict and political violence in South and Southeast Asia, and international norms of sovereign responsibility and protection. Her books include *Child Security in Asia: The Impact of Armed Conflict in Cambodia and Myanmar* (2014) and (edited with Alistair D.B. Cook) *Civilian Protection in the Twenty-First Century: Governance and Responsibility in a Fragmented World* (2016).

Paul Kenny is Research Fellow of Political and Social Change in the Australian National University (ANU)'s Coral Bell School of Asia Pacific Affairs. Dr Kenny obtained his PhD in Political Science at Yale University and has taught at ANU since 2013. He was previously Assistant Professor of Political Science at Trinity College Dublin. His current research examines the causes and consequences of populism, xenophobia, and ethnocentrism. His first book, *Populism and Patronage: Why Populists Win Elections in India, Asia, and Beyond* is forthcoming.

Amy King is Senior Lecturer in the Strategic and Defence Studies Centre at the Australian National University (ANU)'s Coral Bell School of Asia Pacific Affairs. She specializes on Chinese foreign and security policy, China–Japan relations, and the international relations and security of the Asia-Pacific region. Dr King received her D.Phil in International Relations and M.Phil in Modern Chinese Studies from the University of Oxford, where she studied as a Rhodes Scholar. She is the author of *China-Japan Relations After World War II: Empire, Industry and War, 1949–1971* (2016).

Charles Miller is a Lecturer in the School of Politics and International Relations at the Australian National University. He received his PhD in Political Science from Duke University in 2013. His research interests include military effectiveness, public opinion and research methodology. His work has appeared in the *Journal of Peace Research*, the *International Journal of Public Opinion Research*, the *International Relations of the Asia Pacific*, the *Australian Journal of Political Science*, and the *Australian Journal of International Affairs*.

Greg Raymond is a Research Fellow in the Strategic and Defence Studies Centre at the Australian National University (ANU)'s Coral Bell School of Asia Pacific Affairs, focusing on Southeast Asian security. He is currently working on a Minerva Initiative-funded research project looking at Thailand's alliance with the United States amidst rising great power rivalry. His forthcoming book is on Thailand's strategic culture. Before joining the ANU, Dr Raymond worked extensively in the Australian

Government, including in strategic and defence international policy areas of the Department of Defence.

Michael Wesley is Professor of International Affairs and Dean of the College of Asia and the Pacific at the Australian National University (ANU). He has published on Australian foreign policy, Asia's international relations and strategic affairs, and the politics of state-building interventions. His 2011 book, *There Goes the Neighbourhood: Australia and the Rise of Asia*, was awarded the John Button Prize for the best writing on Australian politics and public policy. Previously Professor Wesley was the Director of the Coral Bell School of Asia Pacific Affairs at ANU from 2014 to 2016; the Executive Director of the Lowy Institute for International Policy from 2009 to 2012; Director of the Griffith Asia Institute at Griffith University from 2004 to 2009; and Assistant Director-General for Transnational Issues at the Office of National Assessments, Australia's peak intelligence agency, from 2003 to 2004. He gained his PhD from the University of St Andrews and his BA (Honours) from the University of Queensland.

Hugh White is Professor of Strategic Studies in the Strategic and Defence Studies Centre at the Australian National University (ANU)'s Coral Bell School of Asia Pacific Affairs. He studies Australian strategic and defence policy, and the regional and global security issues affecting Australia. He has been an intelligence analyst, a journalist, a senior staffer to Kim Beazley and Bob Hawke, a senior official in the Defence Department, and the first Director of Australian Strategic Policy Institute (ASPI). He was the principal author of Australia's 2000 Defence White Paper. His recent publications include the Quarterly Essay, *Power Shift: Australia's Future Between Washington and Beijing* and *The China Choice: Why America Should Share Power.*

1

INTRODUCTION TO RESEARCH IN ASIA-PACIFIC AFFAIRS

Michael Wesley

The study of the societies of Asia and the Pacific through Western methods of the humanities and social sciences has always been driven by the dynamics of wealth and power. The European study of Asian and Pacific societies and cultures was central to the colonial enterprise; originally as a fascination with other wealthy and powerful societies, then as part of a Western ideological hegemony determined to demonstrate that the societies of Asia and the Pacific were in decline, in contrast to the Europeans' own ascendancy (Anderson 1991, 163–64). The study of proud pasts and contemporary societies soon became part of dozens of independence movements across Asia and the Pacific, a vital ingredient of the intellectual emancipation of colonized peoples (Chatterjee 1993). With independence came a Cold War, a desperate zero-sum struggle between capitalism and communism that mandated the need in the rival camps to understand the particular character of the newly independent governments and the societies they ruled in Asia and the Pacific. "Area Studies", the deep research of Asian and Pacific societies, grounded in extensive fieldwork and advanced proficiency in vernacular languages, was born. Across the Western world, Asia and the Pacific were divided into regions and studied in their own departments. In establishing a national university in 1946, the Australian government mandated that one of four areas of global excellence the new university had to achieve was in Pacific studies (which at the time was intended to include Asian studies) — precisely because of the new and unknown world

1

of international relations that was to be ushered in by the independence of states to Australia's north and east.

The rapid economic ascent of Northeast and then Southeast Asian economies led to renewed attention to Asian societies. Debates arose over the causes of the Asian economic miracle: was it a question of culture, or institutions, or the peculiar legacy of war and colonialism (World Bank 1993; Johnson 1982; Amsden 2001)? These debates drew regional thinkers into the battle lines, as some advocated the catalytic role of distinctive Asian "values" in the stability and success of a lengthening chain of Asian economic success stories (Barr 2005). Others countered that there was in fact nothing distinctive about Asia's economic success; the stunning growth rates were a consequence of "perspiration" (meaning large infusions of investment and low-cost labour) rather than "inspiration" (meaning superior cultural values or institutional design) (Krugman 1994). Today, Asia and the Pacific stand at the cusp of the security consequences of the past three decades of their societies' remarkable economic rise, as economic prosperity has led to a deepening rivalry and the recession of American strategic primacy (White 2012; Wesley 2015). Speculation over a "post-American world" (Zakaria 2009), a "new Asian hemisphere" (Mahbubani 2008), or an "Asian century" (Australian Government 2012) has been rife, as an eagerness to peer into the future and understand the consequences of rapid economic and security evolution in the Asia-Pacific has only increased over time. Despite the continued turmoil in the Middle East, the United States has resolved to "rebalance" its security, diplomatic and trade, and investment attentions towards the Asia-Pacific, just as it chose to concentrate on the Atlantic after the Second World War (Clinton, 2011). The stage seems to be set for yet another wave of research into Asia-Pacific states and societies, this time pondering their likely trajectories as newly empowered security actors.

Looking back at the centuries-long trajectories of humanities and social sciences research into the societies of Asia and the Pacific is humbling. From the stunning insights of classical philological research to the remarkable participatory field research on communities in conflict in the current day (see Jacob, this volume), one is struck by the complex facets of Asia-Pacific societies, and how much they offer us, not only on their own terms, but also in terms of the human condition generally. Occasionally, the general public catches a glimpse of the richness of research into Asia-Pacific societies (Jared Diamond's hugely popular *Guns, Germs, and Steel* is perhaps the best example), but more often than not Asia-Pacific research is consumed by Asia-Pacific specialists. It is remarkable that a region that contains nearly two-thirds of the world's population, and is soon to contribute a similar proportion of global productivity, with a majority of the world's classical civilizations and responsible for most of the world's dominant religions, is so little heeded beyond its specialists. It is perhaps a testament to the continuing ethnocentrism of Western academic and policy communities that someone who spends his or her life working on European or American affairs is regarded as a generalist, while an "Asia specialist" or an even rarer "Pacific specialist" is regarded as a niche career trajectory.

As a consequence, the humanities and social sciences study of Asia-Pacific societies has been remarkably non self-reflective. Certainly, for generations, scholars have responded to the work of others, either following their lead or reacting in objection to what other scholars have produced. And controversies over research methods and approaches that have erupted in the broader disciplines of the humanities and social sciences have made their way to Asia and Pacific studies. But few major methodological or conceptual debates have originated from within the study of Asian and Pacific societies, and it is very hard to find extended discussions of methods from within Asian and Pacific studies (major exceptions being subaltern studies and the impact of rising powers). This is most certainly not because Asian and Pacific research is conceptually unsophisticated; quite the opposite. It is more likely attributable to the enormous range, scope, and dynamism of the Asia-Pacific as a field of study, the additional time and effort to acquire vernacular proficiency required of its researchers, and the deep and complex history and contexts of Asian and Pacific societies. Who has time to engage in extended conceptual or methodological exegesis when there is so much of deep and pressing interest to be investigated and understood on the ground?

Muddy Boots and Smart Suits is an attempt by a contemporary community of researchers clustered around the Coral Bell School of Asia Pacific Affairs at the Australian National University (ANU) to reflect on the process of researching Asian and Pacific societies, politics, and security. The tradition of humanities and social sciences research into Asian and Pacific societies at the ANU is one of the oldest continuous traditions in the world, counting among its grandees C.P. Fitzgerald, A.L. Basham, O.H.K. Spate, Pierre Ryckmans, Wang Gungwu, and J.A.C. Mackie. Beyond this has been the ANU's ability to use this deep country expertise to inform its research into the international relations, strategic dynamics, and economics of the region, and the extensive networks of collaboration developed with other centres of world expertise in Asia and the Pacific, Europe, and North America. This volume is an attempt to write on the controversies, approaches, and dilemmas of researching the societies and politics of Asia and the Pacific, and to point to promising new avenues for research in the field.

This volume arose as the counterpart to a project on "deep security" (see Wesley, this volume). In preparing a special issue of the journal, *Asia Pacific Policy Studies*, teams of researchers at the Bell School selected four countries in the Asia-Pacific to subject to the deep security approach: Solomon Islands, Indonesia, Myanmar, and China. Three interlinked essays were written for each of these countries: one on the domestic sources and dynamics of security and insecurity; one on how state responses to these domestic security dilemmas impacted on regional relations; and one on the cumulative effect on global security relations. All twelve papers were workshopped extensively, including with policy specialists from government agencies; teams working on each of the levels interrogated and debated conclusions reached in the other papers. And out of this ferment and mutual learning emerged repeated reflections and observations on concepts and methods of Asia-Pacific studies by authors, commentators, and participants. Formalized, discussed, and debated, these reflections and observations comprise the chapters of this volume.

The "deep security" project has itself been inspired by path-breaking work on the complex relationship between academic research and policy in the security field (see George 1993) and applied to the Asia-Pacific region (see Taylor, Milner, and Ball 2006). The project is particularly sensitive to the question of how knowledge about security in the Asia-Pacific is produced and defended, and for whom (Evans 1994; Wilson and Dirlik 1995; Tan 2013). It also draws on studies that have applied international relations theory to the specific dynamics of the Asia-Pacific (Alagappa 1998; Ikenberry and Mastanduno 2003; Kang 2003; Suh, Katzenstein, and Carlson 2004; Acharya 2004; Goh 2007/08; Acharya 2013; Goh 2013).

The essays in *Muddy Boots and Smart Suits* are collected into five sections. The first is devoted to fieldwork: the advantages, approaches, and dilemmas of detailed research of politics and security affairs on the ground in Pacific and Asian societies. It begins with Julien Barbara's reflections on research into the Solomon Islands during the period when that state had been subject to one of the longest running and most comprehensive state-building interventions yet seen: the Regional Assistance Mission to Solomon Islands (RAMSI). Barbara distinguishes between research *of* policy — in which scholars have conducted detailed and objective studies of the progress of the intervention, thereby contributing to the growing corpus of critical literature on the state-building enterprise in general and the RAMSI mission in particular — and research *for* policy — where researchers are commissioned by governments to investigate aspects of Solomon Islands society deemed relevant to the state-building enterprise. Critical to both approaches has been deep country knowledge and a commitment to spending long periods of time in the society under study, understanding the complex political and social dynamics of a society responding to a state-building intervention.

Nicholas Farrelly turns his attention to the study of political culture within the tradition of political anthropology. He begins with the foundational argument that thought and action within Asian and Pacific societies must be understood on their own terms, and goes on to argue that so much of the understanding that can be achieved on Asia and the Pacific must come from an attentiveness to the differences among how societies, and subgroups in states, view the workings of politics and history. Farrelly returns to the "clash of civilizations" debate to rescue one of its forgotten insights — that the twenty-first century will see an empowerment of non-Western societies, making the ethnocentric assumptions of so much research and statecraft redundant, and making the variations in political cultures of critical relevance to world affairs. He concludes by looking ahead at the intriguing intersection of variations in political cultures and the different spatial arenas created by quickening globalization and the communications revolution.

Cecilia Jacob's essay concludes the first section. It is a fascinating reflection on the study of conflict that contrasts the macro approach — focusing on conflict as something states engage in and therefore, the province of grand anarchic forces — with the micro approach — in which conflict is something that happens to and is perpetrated by individuals and communities. She argues that there is much to be gained by bringing together the macro and micro approaches, for both research on and policy responses to persistent conflict. Jacob discusses at length the possibilities presented to the study of conflict by the "practice turn" in social science research; in particular to the rich understanding provided of conflict drivers and dynamics, by focusing on the interface between the dispositions of those involved and the position created by the conflictual context. As with so many of the essays in this volume, she points ahead to rich possibilities for further research.

The second section takes a closer look at research methods in the social sciences. Paul Kenny issues an invitation for researchers of Asian and Pacific societies to embrace the design-based revolution in the social sciences. He delves into the complexity of explanation and warns against the problem of confounding factors in what are often taken to be authoritative explanations of certain states of affairs in the Asia-Pacific. Kenny's call is for greater caution in our conclusions on Asia-Pacific affairs, thinking hard about what other explanations might account for what we are studying. He very usefully provides a half-dozen methods for guarding against confounding factors, pointing to the much deeper and more powerful insights to be gained from carefully designed and executed research methods.

Charles Miller's essay provides a counterpart to Kenny's invitation to qualitative research rigour by providing a strong case for the utility of quantitative research into Asian and Pacific affairs. Speaking across the qualitative-quantitative divide, he argues that many of the charges used by qualitative researchers to dismiss quantitative approaches are ill-founded and inaccurate. Urging us to take a new look at game theory, he argues that such approaches do not rely on an assumption that human beings are rational, but on the assumption that human beings are inherently *strategic*. Importantly, Miller draws our attention to the new frontiers of quantitative analysis in examining the role of ideas, culture, and history on contemporary situations in Asian and Pacific societies. Ultimately, argues Miller, the qualitative-quantitative divide is unhelpful and restricting. While "quants" invest heavily in their statistical training, they still rely heavily on the vernacular capacities and detailed country knowledge of their qualitative colleagues; in return, qualitative scholars should be open to the insights and advantages offered by quantitative approaches.

Section three is devoted to big-picture approaches to understanding the Asia-Pacific as a region. Joan Beaumont examines the role of war memory in the construction of and relations between Asia-Pacific states. She points to a "memory boom" across the world, and observes that this has great implications for the Asia-Pacific. War and its memories have played a powerful role in how nations have been imagined and constructed in the region, and there is much to be gained in understanding the constitution of its societies by examining the intriguing variations in how war is remembered. Memories of war are also becoming much more important in how Asia-Pacific states relate to each other. Memorials, parades, and other markings of war memories are increasingly infused with political and even strategic importance in the Asia-Pacific; whereas war memory has been an important facet of reconciliation and accommodation in Europe, in the Asia-Pacific, they are becoming an important ingredient in rivalry and contestation. Beaumont concludes by pointing the way forward for further research on the contemporary roles of war memory in the Asia-Pacific.

Evi Fitriani focuses on regionalism as a key element in the Asia-Pacific order, now and into the future. She provides a detailed history of the evolution of regionalism in Southeast Asia and the broader region, noting the consistency of the drivers of accommodation among such a heterogeneous collection of states. Looking back as well as ahead, Fitriani argues that the great powers, which she defines as the United States, China, and Russia, are locked in a mutually-consequential embrace with Asia-Pacific regionalism. Regional institutions are heavily affected in what they are motivated to do and prevented from doing by the preferences of the great powers. At the same time, the great powers are strongly constrained by the power of regionalism in what they are able to achieve in the Asia-Pacific.

Section four considers how studies of conflict and order have been approached in the Asia-Pacific context. Hugh White opens this section by examining the largely-forgotten relationship between war and international order. Diagnosing our inattention to this connection to the long period of U.S. primacy following the Second World War, he argues that the period ahead, marked by the recession of this primacy and the growing potency and assertiveness of Asia's largest societies, will sketch much more starkly the relationship between war and order. In typically clear prose, White argues that the boundaries of international order are drawn by what the great powers are and are not willing to go to war over. This draws our attention to a great range of insights that the study of conflict and bargaining in the Asia-Pacific can yield — security scholars can offer us much more than simply observations about war, particularly at a time when there is so much uncertainty about how global power shifts will affect the future of global order.

Nick Bisley turns our attention to the often-assumed but ultimately murky connections between economic capacity and international influence. How and when does wealth translate to power, and are there trade-offs made during that translation? Bisley shows that these questions are of more than passing concern in the contemporary Asia-Pacific, but are deeply relevant to the evolving rivalries and order that will result. He then turns to the even more difficult question of the impact of nationalism, ambition, and prestige considerations on the interests and perceptions of rising states. Out of this rich and complex mixture, Bisley sketches four possible futures for the Asia-Pacific: "muddling through" as the region's states pragmatically manage their interdependence and rivalries; collaboration to bring about a stable order based on explicit order agreements; contestation, in which rivalries become the driving factor in regional affairs; and transformation, in which interdependence and rivalry drive the formulation of a new corpus of rules and norms in the Asia-Pacific.

Peter Dean and Greg Raymond round out section four by presenting strategic culture as an approach that offers great advantages in understanding the deepening rivalries in the Asia-Pacific. They show strategic culture as a rich but highly contested field, often prone to fervent and ultimately unresolvable debates over what is to be explained and what does the explaining. Dean and Raymond provide a comprehensive introduction to the literature on strategic culture, as the evolution of four consecutive "phases" of scholarship, and discuss the extent and limitations of strategic culture scholarship in Asia and the Pacific. They conclude by pointing to new avenues for future research, ultimately observing that an era of rising non-Western societies will need to be understood in terms of the distinctive ways these societies conceptualize and act on their own security imperatives.

The fifth section examines the interface between research and policy in Asia-Pacific affairs. Michael Wesley's essay begins by observing the very different nature of the research-policy nexus in economics from that in the security realm. The result of the particular context and subject of security studies, he argues, creates the real peril of an "academic-policy complex" as pervasive as the military-industrial complex. Wesley sketches out an "independence-compliance" dilemma at the heart of the research-policy relationship in security studies: the more independent and critical a security scholar is, the less likely she or he is to be influential on policy; whereas the more willing she or he is to observe the conventions and even imperatives of the policy community in the interests of building and preserving influence, the more she or he sacrifices her or his independence. Wesley concludes by suggesting a different approach — that of "deep security" — which offers both researchers and policy officials the richness of detailed country-based knowledge with clear security analysis, as a clear differentiation in expertise and contribution between the scholarly and policy communities in the field of security.

In the volume's final chapter, Amy King and Nicholas Farrelly reflect on the traditions and approaches to Asia-Pacific research and look forward to its evolving dilemmas. They begin by exploring the richness offered by the marriage between disciplinary and Area Studies expertise, and by the interface between research and policy practice. They caution, however, that both of these interactions have their own challenges. The paucity of Asia-Pacific scholarship in leading academic journals is a persisting anomaly, while policy-facing academics face an ongoing dilemma between measuring policy "impact" and racking up academic citations. King and Farrelly then turn their attention to the challenges facing scholars of Asia-Pacific affairs into the future. They point to five in particular: the problem of access to states that are sensitive to what they perceive as external criticism of their domestic affairs; the deluge of "hyperinformation" where researchers now are confronted with a bewildering array of sources, including those on the Internet; the challenge of maintaining language skills; the physical dangers in researching conflict zones; and the patient work of building research collaborations.

Muddy Boots and Smart Suits is not the last word on the techniques and dilemmas of studying Asia-Pacific affairs; nor is it the first. It is a series of reflections by one community of scholars about what they do, and it is intended to begin a conversation along these lines among the broader — and global — community of Asia-Pacific scholars. For all of the difficulties and dilemmas they face, scholars of Asia and the Pacific are united by one thing — the conviction that the region and societies they study are endlessly fascinating and rewarding — and that scholarship and understanding of these societies will be increasingly consequential for understanding how the world works. It is an exciting time to be a scholar of Asian and Pacific affairs.

SECTION I
In the Field

2

STUDYING POLICY FROM THE GROUND UP: THE SOLOMON ISLANDS CASE

Julien Barbara

INTRODUCTION

This chapter considers the relationship between country-level or ground-up research, policy, and policymaking. It focuses on the interface between research and policy issues — that is to say, how policy can be the subject of research and the role research can play in informing policy — using the experience of the Regional Assistance Mission to Solomon Islands (RAMSI) as a case study. RAMSI is a regionally mandated but Australian-led state-building mission developed in response to civil conflict in the Solomon Islands (Braithwaite et al. 2010). Arriving in Solomon Islands in 2003, RAMSI involved a large-scale policing component and an ambitious development programme focused on rebuilding the post-conflict Solomon Islands state. Conceived in a global "state-building moment" (Allen and Dinnen 2016), when international enthusiasm for external intervention was at its fullest flush, RAMSI was a major Australian security and development policy initiative with regional and international significance (Fry and Kabutaulaka 2008). Today, overt references to state-building have receded from Australia's policy lexicon but state-building remains central to its regional security and development policy including as an implicit part of good governance and institutional strengthening programmes across the Asia-Pacific region. With a reputation as one of the most successful state-building interventions from the period (Fullilove 2006), RAMSI has been the object of significant research interest amongst transnational research and policy communities. At the same time, as a complex and long-term mission, RAMSI has had to evolve and adapt, responding to a range of policy challenges over time. This has created demand amongst policymakers for policy-focused research to help explain and resolve policy problems and to identify new policy solutions.

Recognizing RAMSI as the focus of extensive country-level research, this chapter will explore how researchers have responded to and engaged with policy issues from two different perspectives. The first involves RAMSI as the object of research, with the intervention providing an example of *research of policy*. From this perspective, the chapter will consider how country-level research of RAMSI has contributed to broader scholarly debates on state-building and intervention, which has been a major debate in world politics and international relations in the twenty-first century. The second involves RAMSI as a complex policy initiative that has generated demands amongst policymakers for research to inform decision-making, both in providing an evidence base and in identifying policy options. This perspective engages with RAMSI as a focus of *research for policy*. It will be seen that from this perspective, critical country-level research has been important in challenging established policy approaches and identifying alternative policy approaches. The nature of RAMSI, as a significant policy venture which has been the focus and demander of research, provides an interesting case study from which to consider broader issues regarding what has been called the research-policy divide (Edwards 2005; Nutley 2003) and the challenges of studying policy from the ground up.

The chapter does not approach the issue of the policy-research interface from a particular methodological or disciplinary perspective, given the diversity of approaches scholars have brought to bear on the issue. It should be noted, however, that state-building and external intervention as a policy response to state fragility had its origins in new institutionalism and neoclassical economics (Hameiri 2013). This meant that much early thinking on state-building was characterized by a universalized, abstract, and technical understanding of the state and the challenge of state-building (Chandler 2006). As a basis for policy, such a perspective has not translated well in highly diverse and complex local environments. This is most clearly evidenced by the policy disasters ensuing from interventions in Iraq and Afghanistan. One of the most important research contributions made by country-level studies to state-building has been to challenge ambitious and, oftentimes, naïve policy assumptions that "states" are amenable to external reconstruction, and to call for more nuanced and locally-responsive forms of policy engagement. This chapter considers the ways in which country-level research on the broad range of security and development policy issues arising from RAMSI has made an important contribution as a corrective to sometimes misguided policy approaches.

STATE-BUILDING, RAMSI, AND THE POLICY LEGACIES OF INTERVENTION

In the late twentieth century through to the first decade of the twenty-first, Australia found itself in what Allen and Dinnen (2016) have described as a "state-building moment". Australia's regional security and development policy was heavily influenced by the globally influential idea of state-building and intervention as an antidote to state instability and political disorder within the Asia-Pacific region (Fry and Kabutaulaka 2008). Australia was already a leading participant in the United Nations-mandated trusteeship in Timor Leste (Leach and Kingsbury 2012). Its state-building impulse reached its apogee in the Solomon Islands, where, as the principal architect and resourcer of a regionally-mandated intervention, it enjoyed significant latitude to shape the mission. As a policy rationale, state-building saw Australia deeply implicated in the long-term processes of security stabilization, institutional reconstruction, and development in its near region. Such obligations have persisted long after formal interventions have been drawn down, embodied in large, long-term development and security programmes.

RAMSI was in many ways a textbook example of neo-liberal state-building (Barbara 2008; Hameiri 2013, p. 55), focused on strengthening market democracy through a state-building programme focused on three pillars — economic governance, machinery of government, and law and justice. RAMSI's ambitious development programme aimed to fortify the central institutions of state and restore key democratic institutions. This approach was based on a policy rationale that sought to create an enabling security and governance environment conducive to economic growth and peaceful political development that would provide a peace dividend and local resources from which to strengthen the post-conflict state in a virtuous cycle of post-conflict consolidation and development.

As an ambitious state-building programme, Australia's decision to intervene in the Solomon Islands has had long-term policy consequences. RAMSI successfully restored security but has struggled to lay the foundations for a sustainable state and long-term economic development (Braithwaite et al. 2010). The country's state institutions remain fragile and dependent on donor support, with the Solomon Islands being one of the world's most aid-dependent countries. RAMSI was also a very costly mission, costing an estimated $2.6 billion over ten years (Heyward-Jones 2014), for a country of less than 500,000 people at the time of the intervention. Importantly, while RAMSI helped strengthen key institutions and consolidate democracy — reflected in the conduct of "free and fair" elections and relatively peaceful government transitions (Barbara 2014) — democratic state-building has not enabled a more productive national politics focused on the resolution of deep political tensions through collective responses to critical development challenges. This is a significant issue given that an implicit logic of RAMSI was to create space for political elites to address the root causes of the tensions as a basis for long-term peace and development. Instead, the large-scale intervention appears to have created moral hazards reducing pressure on elites to agree on a more inclusive political settlement (Barbara 2014). With the state-building mission unfinished, RAMSI has created long-term obligations for Australia in the form of security and basic governance obligations. It has also raised significant policy challenges in terms of how to preserve security and development gains made under RAMSI while reducing the moral hazards of high aid subsidization to enable the country to move "beyond life support" (Allen and Dinnen 2016). Efforts to reconcile these challenges was an important factor leading to RAMSI "transition" and the gradual draw down of the mission (RAMSI's development programmes were rationalized and transferred to bilateral and multilateral donors in 2013 and the police mission is slated to end in 2017) in a bid to strengthen Solomon Islands' ownership of development issues (Barbara 2014).

It should be noted that RAMSI was not a static mission. It evolved over time as the situation on the ground changed, moving from a mission focused on stabilization to one focused on sustainable institution building. This was paralleled in changing working level approaches, as RAMSI moved from an early reliance on heavy capacity substitution and supplementation by external advisers to fill significant gaps in state capacity (Baser 2007), to a form of policy engagement focused on long-term development partnership and local capacity building (Barbara 2014). In its later years, RAMSI's development and security programmes were influenced by international thinking on development effectiveness and the need for aid to be locally driven (OECD 2008). This resulted in a strengthening of partnership arrangements designed to strengthen the Solomon Islands' ownership of RAMSI's development programme, in line with the Solomon Islands government's priorities.

The continued security and development policy challenges facing the Solomon Islands point to the significant tensions between theory and practice. RAMSI's perceived "success" as one of the few effective large-scale interventions makes it of continuing interest to policy communities. Conversely, the continued challenges arising from RAMSI's intervention make it of ongoing interest in understanding complex processes of state formation and political development, and the role of development assistance. RAMSI's qualified success in "fixing" the Solomon Islands state points to fundamental problems with state-building as a policy aspiration and the evident need for different policy approaches to conflict and state fragility. Given the consequences of misguided state-building across the globe, exploring and responding to the tensions between state-building in theory and practice remains an urgent research priority. RAMSI, therefore, provides an excellent case study to examine the interface of research and policy.

RESEARCHING STATE-BUILDING THROUGH RAMSI

The policy case for intervention in the Solomon Islands was legitimized in part by a broader transnational policy and research debate on state-building as a response to state fragility and localized conflict. While Australia's decision to support RAMSI as a response to prolonged conflict in the Solomon Islands arose from a careful assessment of its own national interests in the Pacific region (Barbara 2008), changing global norms about intervention as an acceptable policy response to complex security and development challenges was important in putting the idea on the policy table as an acceptable option. Australia was initially reluctant to countenance intervention as a response to the conflict in the Solomon Islands, given, amongst other things, the region's recent colonial past and Australia's position as a predominant metropolitan power. Concerns that any Australian-led intervention would be labelled neocolonial saw Australia initially rebuff calls to intervene, with then Australian foreign minister,

Alexander Downer, describing such demands as "folly in the extreme" (Downer 2003). But sustained policy debate about the merits of intervention as a response to regional state failure was important in legitimizing Australia's eventual decision to support a large-scale mission. The Australian rendition of the failed states debate drew heavily on international concepts and perspectives and represents a good example of global policy transfer. This process reached its clearest expression in the influential ASPI report *Our Failing Neighbour* (ASPI 2003), which linked the conflict in the Solomon Islands to a globalized state failure discourse and made a high profile policy case for robust intervention to prevent imminent state collapse on Australia's very doorstep.

As a self-consciously described state-building mission operationalized at the height of the state-building moment, RAMSI inevitably found itself the object of significant scholarly research. RAMSI was interesting in terms of comparative state-building because of its novel geographical location, "interventionary" structure as a police-led regional mission (Fullilove 2006), its early success in restoring security, and its ability to sustain public support. It thus stood in contrast to more high profile interventions in Afghanistan and Iraq which rapidly became messy amidst a litany of security and development failures.

Country-level research on RAMSI as part of a broader state-building moment has made important contributions to broader scholarly and policy debates on a number of levels. Some of the best work has engaged with fundamental conceptual questions about the nature of contemporary statehood, and, in this light, the capacity of external interveners to rebuild "failed" or "failing" states. Hameiri (2013) has observed that despite a professed focus on state formation and how to build strong states, much of the early state-building literature was based on a "disembodied, normatively conceived, notion of state capacity" with little recognition of the state as an expression of "the distribution, production, and reproduction of political power in the intervened states, as well as in the intervening states" (p. 53). One of the most peculiar aspects of the "voluminous" state-building literature has been the "very little interest in understanding the 'state', despite its apparent place at the centre of the research agenda" (Hameiri 2013, 52). Hameiri's (2010, 2012, 2013) own research on regulatory state-building has used the experience of RAMSI to challenge ideas of state-building as a simple process of Weberian institutional transfer. He argues that contemporary efforts to construct viable states, exemplified in Australia's support for RAMSI, have had the result of integrating rebuilt states into regimes of transnational regulation and control which often favour international interests at the expense of domestic polities.

An important contribution made by ANU scholars has been to set efforts to rebuild the Solomon Islands state by RAMSI in a broader historical context. This work has been an important corrective to universalized policy approaches that have treated the Solomon Islands as a *tabula rasa* (Dinnen 2007). Notable here have been important contributions by Dinnen (2008, 2007), Allen and Dinnen (2016, 2010), and Braithwaite et al. (2010) that have examined the origins of the conflict and the fragilities of the postcolonial state which predate the "tensions". For example, Dinnen's (2007) research has responded to the significant "analytical separation between academics and practitioners on state-building", whereby the former's apolitical and ahistorical understanding of the Solomon Islands state gave rise to ambitious and unwarranted assumptions that the Solomon Islands state could be rebuilt through external intervention and a conception of state-building "primarily ... [as] a technical and problem-solving exercise" (p. 259).

More recently, scholars have begun to use the experience of RAMSI in the Solomon Islands as a case study to test and explore the concept of political settlements. While a contested and conceptually and analytically vague concept (see Dressel and Dinnen 2014 for a good critique), scholars have become increasingly interested in using the concept of political settlements as a heuristic tool to explain the challenges of institutional development and political stabilization. The central idea behind political settlements centres on how institutional structures — formal and informal — both reflect and shape the distribution of power in societies, and the implications of such settlements on processes of economic and political development (Goodfellow 2014, p. 313). For political settlements to be sustainable (that is, supportive of political order), they must reflect and underwrite some form of sustainable political accommodation between powerful groups. The experience of RAMSI in the Solomon Islands has provided a fruitful case study to ground empirically the concept of political settlements. This may be because the scale of the intervention relative to the small island state, and its explicit focus on institutional development, lays bare important questions about institutional formation and state-society relations. One of the best studies in this regard is Craig and Porter's (2014), which uses a political settlement frame to describe and explain the complex nature of the political order following RAMSI in the wake of violent conflict. This order requires high donor subsidization to support a state apparatus which can provide basic security and governance in the Solomon Islands, while leaving political elites space to extract sufficient economic rents to buy their support for the status quo. One of the main ways this is being done is through the increased use of discretionary funds which channel state resources directly to parliamentarians to manage development, bypassing orthodox state channels and thus weakening the state. The situation is conducive to peace, but not development, with high aid flows compensating for the unproductive nature of an economic system predicated on intensive resource extraction.

RAMSI has provided scholars with a rich country case study with which to engage in and contribute to significant global policy and scholarly debates. This research has, amongst other things, contributed to more sophisticated and critical understanding of the role of the state and the wisdom of external intervention as a policy aspiration. While it is difficult to attribute direct policy impact arising from such debates, it is reasonable to say they have been important in changing the conceptual context within which policy debates have been conducted. They have thus tempered general enthusiasm for intervention and acted as a corrective to misplaced policy ambition. The following section considers some of the specific ways in which research has been used directly *for* policy in Solomon Islands.

POLICY RESEARCH FOR RAMSI

A recent study by Waldman (2014) on the use of state-building research by the United Kingdom policy community, including policymakers within the Foreign and Commonwealth Office, Department for International Development (DFID) and Defence, found that a broad range of demand and supply factors influenced how and why policymakers engaged with research. DFID, in particular, has invested significantly in state-building research to inform policy development, and has also sought to foster an internal organizational culture that values and engages actively with the research community. Waldman's study found that research had influenced DFID's state-building policies, both directly and indirectly. Policymakers used research as an evidence base to inform programming decisions, to provide operational answers to specific governance problems policymakers are grappling with, and as justificatory ammunition to argue for particular policy directions within the development community. Research has also been indirectly influential in framing the way policy issues are understood, influencing what policy communities understand to constitute legitimate policy responses and "acceptable" policy options to resolve problems (Paris 2011). In this sense, research has played an important role in setting the tone of a broader policy ecology within which policymakers work.

A variety of factors have been found to influence research uptake by policymakers. Particularly important is the issue of translation: "[t]his essentially refers to the difficulty of boiling down, synthesising or condensing often complex research into practically relevant and operationally useful findings, recommendations or conclusions" (Waldman 2014, p. 164). The way in which research responds to the policy cycle is also important. For example, the aid policy cycle is a staged cycle starting with a period of programme design, leading to a process of implementation and review. Each of these stages requires different types of research to justify aid investments, support programme implementation and adaptation, and to assess programme effectiveness. The broader policy environment and the general receptiveness of policymakers to research has much to do with organizational cultures and the degree to which research is valued as a necessary input (Waldman 2014, pp. 157–63). Organizational resourcing (declining staff numbers, increasing workloads, and turnover mean staff have less time to engage with research) and risk aversion (ignoring critical policy research that challenges fundamental policy positions) can be particularly important factors influencing research uptake.

One of the most important factors influencing research uptake by policymakers is the nature of personal relationships between policymakers and the academic community. Waldman (2014, p. 164) emphasizes the importance of robust linkages between researchers and policymakers if the research-policy divide is to be bridged. Effective translation of policy research into policy actions has been found to depend on the quality of networks (formal and informal) between researchers and policymakers, the role played by intermediaries inside and out of government to bridge academic-policy divides, and the degree of active policymaker involvement in research activities. Research has been found to be particularly influential in changing head-office thinking about policy issues such as state-building, which then permeates an organization through its strategic and operational policies and protocols.

Waldman's findings are of interest in the Australian context where policymakers have begun to invest heavily in research to inform policy development. For example, in the late 2000s, Australian Aid (AusAID) consciously scaled up its investment in policy-focused research to parallel the large scale-up of the aid programme itself, with research investments growing from $19 million in 2005–6 to $181 million in 2012–13 (ODE 2015, p. 1). AusAID's research strategy for the period 2012–16 highlights the importance of research for improving programme effectiveness and ensuring value for money. It states that the main reason for supporting research is "to improve the quality and effectiveness of Australian aid in developing countries ... [with] practical research ... [to] help inform where and how our own and our partners' resources can most efficiently and effectively be deployed" (ODE 2015, p. 8). The strategy lists specific priorities including: finding solutions to global development problems; predicting and responding to development challenges and opportunities of specific interest to the Australian aid programme; informing country programme decision making; and improving partner country capacity to use and undertake research (ODE 2015, p. 9). It is not possible to disaggregate Department of Foreign Affairs and Trade (DFAT) research funding on a regional or country level. However, a significant part of this funding has gone to Australian research institutions including academic centres such as ANU's State, Society and Governance in Melanesia (SSGM) programme and the Centre for Democratic Institutions (CDI) to focus on Pacific policy issues.

In the case of RAMSI, there are a variety of ways in which research has influenced policy development. At the country level, research has long been recognized by policymakers as important in deepening policymaker understanding of country context. More recently, the "political turn"[1] (Booth and Unsworth 2014) in international development thinking has resulted in a much greater emphasis on political economy and deep country analysis as a starting point for policy engagement, particularly aid policy. Such analysis is recognized as important not only in providing policymakers with a more realistic understanding of how the countries in which they work operate, but also in informing "theories of change" and assessments of how particular policy interventions will translate in specific contexts. Extensive research on the Solomon Islands, and RAMSI specifically, means policymakers now have a significant body of research to draw on to inform how they understand the country context in which they work. For example, Braithwaite et al.'s (2010) detailed analysis of the Solomon Islands conflict and state-building response has been influential amongst policymakers as a key background document. DFAT's considerable investments in sustaining a Pacific research community, including its support for SSGM, helps maintain an important general policy resource to inform policymakers of changing country context.

At the sectoral level, more granulated issues-based research has become increasingly important in providing a specific evidence base for aid programming. For example, research on Solomon Islands' politics and elections has been important in informing donor support for elections and democratic governance — a key focus of RAMSI's Machinery of Government programme. Such research has led to more sober donor assessments of how politics works and the limited ability of donor-supported electoral reforms to re-engineer politics so it is more orderly and productive. For example, research by ANU's Terrence Wood (2014) has illustrated the highly localized and personalized voting incentives of Solomon Islanders. This means electoral politics is played out at a very localized scale, with any performative element of the Solomon Islands politics based on the capacity of individual Members of Parliament (MPs) to deliver valued goods to local communities. This political dynamic is confounding for donors who assume — indeed require — strong national ownership of development agendas and provide governance support on the assumption that citizens agree on some idea of the common good, and will judge their political representatives accordingly (Barbara 2014). These assumptions have in the past seen significant aid devoted to civil society strengthening to improve electoral accountability and voice, on the assumption voters will elect better governments if they understand better the importance of good governance. But such support has proven largely ineffective in changing the quality of the Solomon Islands' politics.

One consequence of recent research has been a recalibration of donor expectations of the capacity of democracy aid to "fix" politics, leading to a refocus of support on basic institutional strengthening to support election delivery, and different forms of support for political participation at the local level. This is particularly so in the area of electoral and broader political reform, where the prospect of engineering greater political stability has been attractive to local political elites and donors alike — albeit for different reasons (the former seeking to strengthen political power bases, the latter seeking to stabilize parliamentary politics as a basis for better governance). In the Solomon Islands, such interests inevitably turn to Papua New Guinea (PNG) which has been particularly experimental in its institutional arrangements, such as with the introduction of limited preferential voting, and which, because of the similarities between the two countries, policymakers often see as a template for similar reforms. Scholarly research, much of it coming from ANU, has been important in challenging assumptions about the transferability of policy to a Solomon

Islands context. For example, research on PNG's experience with efforts to strengthen political parties through explicit laws has arguably helped temper donor interest in supporting ambitious electoral reform programmes in the Solomon Islands (Fraenkel, Regan, and Hegarty 2008) (noting that the Solomon Islands introduced party strengthening reforms based on the PNG model in 2014). DFAT is continuing to make investments in electoral research to inform programming. For example, it supported a large and long-term election observation mission of the 2014 national elections in the Solomon Islands, led by CDI and SSGM. This will provide a wealth of policy-relevant data which will be of direct benefit for policymakers, including how to provide support for electoral institutions in ways that will strengthen electoral integrity and how to support positive forms of collective political participation in a democratic environment where political parties are weak (Haley et al. 2015).

Research has also helped support, albeit modestly and often indirectly, policy innovation and the identification of new policy solutions. In a country where policy processes are weak, scholarly research has been important in filling policy voids and expanding the policy repertoire of those charged with progressing reform programmes, both amongst donors and local stakeholders. Some major research reports have been commissioned by donors explicitly to fill this void and will play an important role in framing future policy directions. For example, the World Bank's *Justice Delivered Locally* report (Allen et al. 2013), included a group of ANU scholars and funded by AusAID including RAMSI's Law and Justice Program, was the result of a long-term qualitative research programme, involving extensive field work. It provided comprehensive analysis of the nature of disputation and grievance in Solomon Islands, the challenges Solomon Islanders have in accessing justice systems locally, and the pressure justice institutions face in delivering services. In providing a deep analysis of how local justice systems work, the research provides policymakers with a better sense of how to work at the local level.

Research has also been important in assisting policymakers to assess programme effectiveness. The issue of programme effectiveness — the degree to which aid is helping improve development outcomes efficiently and cost-effectively — places a particular emphasis on evidence-based programming (OECD 2008). In Australia, increasing the evidence base through better use of research was a key part of the scale-up of the aid programme, to ensure aid spending was well targeted and cost-effective (Commonwealth of

Australia 2012). Over time, programme effectiveness became an important preoccupation for RAMSI, particularly as it sought to assess whether the basis for RAMSI's own draw down was in place. The SIG-RAMSI (Solomon Island Government-RAMSI) Partnership Agreement, finalized in 2007, established specific performance baselines and an annual performance review mechanism to assess the effectiveness of RAMSI's development programmes. Scholars have contributed to the assessment process, alongside a broader group of technical experts and aid consultants (see Emmott, Barcham, and Kabutaulaka 2011 for an example of a performance report). Scholarly researchers have also played a key role in helping gather core data. For example, the ANU played a central role in designing and managing RAMSI's annual People's Survey, an independent annual survey that sought to gauge public opinion on a broad range of issues, including law and order, service delivery and accountability, and the role of RAMSI itself. Conducted from 2007 to 2013, the surveys were an important source of objective data that could measure RAMSI's development effectiveness and remain an important public resource (see RAMSI 2007–13).

CONCLUSION ON THE CHALLENGES OF POLICY RESEARCH

This chapter has considered the ways in which scholars have used RAMSI as a case study of policy, and also how RAMSI, as a major regional policy initiative, has itself demanded policy-relevant research from the scholarly community. Research *of* RAMSI has been used to contribute to significant scholarly debates on fundamental issues such as the changing nature of the state and international intervention. Research *for* RAMSI has been used to support policy innovation and the provision of more effective donor support.

While RAMSI has provided a rich vein for scholarship and a fruitful basis for research-policy collaboration, it has also highlighted the challenges involved in bridging the research-policy divide. The biggest challenge arguably lies in the degree to which research is useful for policymakers. While research has helped challenge the way policymakers think conceptually about issues of intervention and state-building, it has not always equipped them with practical tools to respond to such analysis. This is partly the consequence of what Edwards (2005, p. 68) has described as "quite different frames of reference", reflecting historic tensions between social scientists and policymakers over the purpose and use of research:

> There is often an uneasy relationship between researchers and policy practitioners. Each looks at the world through different perspectives on what the problem is, and the unrealistic expectations of each other. This dynamic reflects the complexity of interacting factors, and can impede a good relationship between policy practitioners and researchers.

Whereas researchers have an interest in challenging the way in which we understand real world phenomena — in many respects making issues more complex and open-ended — policymakers have a more instrumental objective, finding solutions and "resolving" problems by narrowing debate parameters.

Related to this issue is how best to structure research-policy relationships so research can be policy-relevant while preserving space for broader scholarly enquiry. Edwards (2005, pp. 71–2) identifies a number of things policymakers can do to strengthen the role of research in policy, including providing institutional space for research within public agencies, seconding researchers into government, and investing in research communities. But while researchers have much to gain from deeper policy engagement, including gaining access to new data and improving the relevance of research, they have also been cautious about deepening policy relationships. Researchers have legitimate concerns about the maintenance of academic integrity, the risk of intellectual compromise, and the instrumentalization of research. Such risks become more concerning as research funding sources come under increasing strain and dependence on government resourcing becomes more important.

Managing these challenges will be difficult, but can be done. Perhaps the best way to reconcile these pressures is by thinking about policy-focused research as a partnership between researchers and policymakers. Strong partnerships between researchers and policymakers must be cultivated, but provide the best basis for mutually beneficial collaboration. Partnerships represent one way that researchers might deepen their understanding of the challenges policymakers face on the ground as they seek to implement a development programme. Partnerships also represent one of the best ways to educate policymakers of the concerns held by researchers in collaborating with them and agreeing to honest protocols regarding the limits of collaboration.

Building productive relationships between scholars and policymakers necessary for the translation of research into useful policy is not without its challenges. On balance, however, management of these challenges is, in my view, worth it. Productive relationships between policymakers and researchers provide scholars with unprecedented opportunities to engage with meaningful policy issues and to potentially influence policy directions, making research relevant. But navigating these risks will remain a long-term challenge.

Note

1. The idea of the "political turn" recognizes that effective aid policy must move beyond a focus on technical issues to consider how local political economies impact upon reform processes. This requires policymakers to understand the nature and interests of political elites, how political settlements are constituted, the basis of power, and the incentive structures within which political actors operate. Effective aid must consciously situate itself within this environment and be provided in ways that are responsive to local political economies.

3

REFLECTIONS ON POLITICAL CULTURES IN THOUGHT AND ACTION

Nicholas Farrelly

INTRODUCING RESEARCH PRACTICE

In 2015, the Australian National University relaunched its famous School devoted to the study of regional politics, strategy, international affairs, and diplomacy. It had previously been known by a generic name. It was reincarnated as the Coral Bell School of Asia Pacific Affairs. At the time, some effort was put into finding quotable lines from the School's namesake, who was, for five decades, a leading figure in Australia's official and academic engagement with the Asia-Pacific region. Among her many sharp observations, one that caught my fancy was on the topic of nationalism. Bell once wrote, "Nationalism, like some wines, doesn't travel well". This piercing thought, wrought with abruptness, reminds us that scholarly communication is, at its essence, about explanation. Making sense of the world around us, putting ideas and issues in their rightful contexts, comparing conditions across time and space, and developing models that can integrate all the different aspects of multifaceted human experiences (and dilemmas), requires a deep appreciation that, by definition, should grow over time. The cultivation of such awareness about the places that we research eventually needs to be harnessed to clear and effective language that allows other people to understand such hard-won insights. A specific mix of academic skills and other less easily quantifiable attributes seems to support the best research on politics and political cultures. Where researchers need to step outside of their own frames of cultural and political reference, the task is naturally made more difficult.

Such scholarly engagement remains the perpetual challenge of studying politics in the Asia-Pacific region, especially when we take seriously the requirement that thought and action must be understood on their own terms. The foundation for such research is a solid grounding in history, language, politics, and culture. Perhaps the best way to begin the journey of understanding a place and its people is to spend a sufficient period of time there. It is no surprise that doctoral candidates focused on political change and social upheavals are commonly advised to immerse themselves in their field research for as long as possible. This helps, naturally, with the development of language skills, but also with the expansion of social networks, the consolidation of goodwill, and the broadening of experiences, to include those that could never have been anticipated. Much research insight relies on the erratic, uneven, and haphazard interactions that are only possible when time is allowed for events to run their course and for gentle evolutions in understanding to occur. Whether the topic is nationalism (Reid 2010), rural society (Unger 2002; Walker 2012), military reform (Mietzner 2006), elections (Aspinall 2005; Farrelly 2015a), spaces of contention (Walker 1999; Farrelly 2013), or peace and order (Dinnen 2001), the principles for grounding effective research practice are much the same. It takes patience, a breadth of exposure, and a finely calibrated sense of what might prove to be most important for the future.

To illuminate these opportunities, this chapter introduces some of the ways that research on political cultures can draw strength from across the disciplinary spectrum. It requires a foundation in history, anthropology, and linguistics that helps to build the type of knowledge of most relevance to the study of development, politics, and, even, strategy and security. This chapter begins by explaining why and how political culture is a meaningful concept for understanding complex social dynamics. My approach to these issues is inspired by Benedict Anderson's (1990, p. 20) interpretation of "political cultures" in the development of the Indonesian nation state, and also by Anthony Milner's (1982) appraisal of Malay "political culture" on the eve of British colonial rule. Anderson, for his part, argues that through close examination of particular "political cultures", we can understand "contrasting views of the workings of politics and history". In this chapter, the general appreciation of this scholarly approach is followed by more specific discussions of: (1) ideology, (2) institutions, and (3) spaces. Each emphasizes a different mode of academic engagement, from the conceptual, to the structural, and then to the ethnographic. The final section ties these modes together with a brief consideration of the role of the Internet in how we might understand political cultures from a grounded perspective as the technologies of politics continue to change.

RESEARCHING POLITICAL CULTURES

With the right tools, the study of politics and culture can fuse two of the most significant aspects of the human experience. Politics is widely associated with the professional political classes, yet there is much more to it than that. Politics is how we organize ourselves. Taken in this broad sense, the academic study of politics is the critical exploration of power. Such critique, whatever form it takes, usually needs some foundation in culture. Our own academic cultures merit scrutiny in this regard. We tend towards an incrementalist mindset, where knowledge builds over time. The study of political cultures makes sense when it can take advantage of the grand traditions and recent refinements of ethnographic method that allow researchers to get close to the alternative visions of the world that form the core of anthropology (see Dutton 1998). The careful study of different systems of thought, meaning, purpose, and response are all part of what makes a treatment of political culture so profound. In a classic statement on the topic, David Kertzer argued that "[t]he political elite employ ritual to legitimate their authority, but rebels battle back with rites of delegitimation" (1988, p. 2). To understand this interplay, at both symbolic and physical levels, is to appreciate the ways that conflicts draw on deep reservoirs of cultural context.

My own research on political culture and ethnic conflict in Myanmar has sought to weld adjacent disciplinary perspectives together. It all starts with the historical context. This means serious and regular engagement with the work of historians, especially those who are presenting new theoretical or thematic arguments. In my own areas of attention, a debate has emerged over the past fifteen years about the character of political spaces in highland and lowland areas of mainland Southeast Asia. It is helpful that Willem van Schendel's (2002) "Zomian" contribution playfully undermined any lingering certainty about the character and coherence of geography across Asia. From his vantage as an historian of the Bengal borderlands, van Schendel was motivated to take aim at the prevailing conceptualizations of space, especially as reflected in Area Studies blocks, but also in the predominance of attention granted to prestige cultures in the lowlands (see van Schendel 2004). It was, in this imagining, the valleys of South Asia, East Asia, and Southeast Asia that have drawn the bulk of attention and resources, from both political elites and also from academic analysts. The major cities and civilizational hubs of these lowlands — places like Bangkok and Mandalay — made it seem obvious that space and power align with culture. Van Schendel's "Zomian" rebuttal insists on a careful treatment of other forms of connection and the need to take seriously the historical discontinuities that borderlands and frontiers enforce. It was through James C. Scott's expansion of the original Zomia argument, most notably in 2009's *The Art of Not Being Governed*, that these ideas gained widespread attention. Since then, appraisals of Zomia have lurched in critical directions with scholars enthusiastic to undermine the empirical foundations on which these new arguments have been made. It is an eternal process of push-and-shove. The most effective of these critiques of Zomia have been an anthropology written by a historian, Mandy Sadan (2013), and a historical argument put forward by an anthropologist, Hjorleifer Jonsson (2010). Their combined efforts have marked out a new path for those seeking to understand the long-term role of Southeast Asia as an interstitial and transaction-laden space.

Such historical reflection is the foundation for political, social, and economic analysis that looks at the challenges of the present-day, and makes them relevant to the long-term development of human societies. Armed with the insights that can be offered by scholars who look closely at trends over the very long-term (see Milner 1982; also Milner 2008), we are much better prepared to conceive of the world in all its richness and variety. This is an especially important principle when we turn to the study of the Asia-Pacific region. Bell's suggestion that "nationalism…doesn't travel well" is a reminder that what makes sense, and is accepted, in certain places may not be applicable in others. These layers of contradiction, even repudiation, make up the ongoing contest of ideas and practices. It is such thoughts and actions that, taken together, provide the empirical material that can support our analysis in comparative and critical modes. Such material can be drawn from field surveys, interviews, participant observation, laboratory experiments, and all manner of other data gathering activities.

These activities are all subjected to continued academic criticism. Part of the reason there is so much effort to consider the value of different approaches is that our understanding of the world, whatever tools we use, still usually feels inadequate. Other contributions in this volume have considered how fragmented understanding can become. One approach to this problem is to ever more aggressively narrow the terms of scholarly debate. This has certain advantages, particularly where it gives specialists a chance to fully engage with different contributions to knowledge. A special form of collegiality tends to form among those who work on such topics. From a different angle, the conundrum of generalizability has increasingly been approached through quantification (see Kenny, this volume). This requires the skilled manipulation of data to keep some variables from interfering unduly with the analytical conclusions. These statistics can generate useful appreciations of many different social and political phenomena, including some of the most complex. It makes sense that such approaches are applied to the study of culture and politics, with varied degrees of success. The problem, ultimately, is that where data quality is poor, or where there are other systemic complications, the quantitative method can prove frustrating, offering only temporary respite in a world of seemingly endless potential for confusion.

For this reason, it is unclear how well such statistical methods can explain the political cultures that will remain important to our understanding of social experiences and problems. By their definition, these cultures are constantly in flux, bombarded by technological and economic trends, and in permanent conversation with their immediate environments, and the wider world. To appreciate an approach to studying politics that draws on what we can learn from culture, the next sections of this chapter will turn to: (1) ideas, (2) institutions, and (3) spaces in the hope of more fully explaining academic analysis that falls, inelegantly, between the concerns of political scientists and those who are more ethnographically-minded. It gives us the chance to build typologies that can help explain the world.

Ideology in Thought

Samuel P. Huntington, in an essay published in *Foreign Affairs* (1993), introduced perhaps the most famous and controversial of these typologies. Titled "The Clash of Civilizations", his essay argued that after the demise of the Soviet Union, the fault lines in the international arena would be defined by cultural units rather than by political ideologies. It was a provocative argument that elicited much debate in journals, magazines, and newspapers around the world. Huntington later expanded and refined his points in a book, *The Clash of Civilizations and the Remaking of World Order* (1997). On the 20th anniversary of the original publication in 2013, *Foreign Affairs* published a follow-up on "the debate". Huntington is a useful starting point if we are serious about understanding how political cultures envelope our understanding of both politics and culture.

What is often overlooked is that Huntington makes it clear that he did not set out to provide an argument that is supported by the deployment of social scientific research methodologies like those explored in this volume. In fact, Huntington (1997, p. 13) explains that:

> This book is not intended to be a work of social science. It is instead meant to be an interpretation of the evolution of global politics after the Cold War. It aspires to present a framework, a paradigm, for viewing global politics that will be meaningful to scholars and useful to policymakers.

He justifies this framework by writing that "simplified paradigms or maps are indispensable for human thought and action" (Huntington 1997, p. 30). To provide the foundations of his paradigm, Huntington actually relies on one map in particular. In that scheme, he divides the world into Western, Latin American, African, Islamic, Sinic, Hindu, Orthodox, Buddhist, and Japanese "civilizations". This remains a contentious model, one that is open to sustained and often withering criticism from those who resent such "simplified" models of civilizational, or ideational, affiliation.

To answer some of his critics, what does Huntington mean by civilization? He writes (1997, p. 41) that "civilization and culture both refer to the overall way of life of a people, and a civilization is a culture writ large". This conceptualization of large cultural units is based on a belief that these abstractions are at the level where competition for resources and the maintenance of misgivings about the priorities of *other* groups is most telling. Some further reflections clarify this provocative point. As Wilson (1997, p. 461) reminds us, "Lucian Pye, the MIT sociologist, used to describe China as a civilisation trying to be a state. This double identity makes China difficult to analyse". Drawing on this logic, and using it to help explore political and other conflicts, Huntington (1997, p. 218) explains that, "[e]conomic exchange brings people into contact; it does not bring them into agreement... If past experience holds, the Asia of economic sunshine will generate an Asia of political shadows, an Asia of instability and conflict". We would often be content to accept that such arguments are based, in their key characteristics, on political models. But where politics and culture blur together any reconciliation requires careful consideration of what happens at the local level.

It is at these subsidiary levels of social and political organization that considerable scholarly attention has also been devoted since the end of the Cold War. As one example, Crawford Young, a political scientist from the University of Wisconsin, provided a seminal argument on the structure of nations and states. Young (1993, p. 3) suggested that:

> [b]y the 1990s... [g]one with the cold war were the comfortable certainties concerning the nation-state. Both 'nation' and 'state' were now subject to relentless interrogation: the former by deepening cultural cleavages in many lands, the latter by currents of economic and political liberalization now girdling the globe. The potent force of politicized and mobilized cultural pluralism is now universally conceded.

According to this line of reasoning, the years immediately after the Second World War saw "the apotheosis of the nation-state... [w]ith the idea of progress still robust, those polities were perceived as leading humanity's march to a better future had singular power as authoritative models" (Young 1993, p. 7). Young goes on to explain how this led to unhelpful dichotomies within the vocabulary of social science. In his words, it became "saturated with such imagery: 'modernity' versus 'traditionality'; 'developed' versus 'underdeveloped' (or 'developing'); 'advanced' versus 'backwards'". The idea of "progress" that was captured by this vocabulary was wedded to a certain conception of political organization where nation-states, mandated usually by some civilizational claim, took control of defined spaces.

Defining those spaces has meant that, at least from a distance, the borders of the global map mark substantive, and even "natural", differences between nation-states. These may also be open to some significant contestation. The "geo-body" introduced by Thongchai Winichakul (1994) implies territorial delineations and distinctions that are defended by governments concerned by their mastery of every last part of national terrain and, it follows, national sovereignty. Winichakul's description of the links between the nation and its territory clarify that even though there is blurring at the edges, there are certain contexts and places where governments are prepared to fully defend their perception of national interests. For his part, Huntington acknowledges that in his civilizational model, there *is* blurring and interaction at the borders that can lessen the impact of political demarcations. This is a process that Sturgeon, for the mainland Southeast Asian example, calls "landscape plasticity" (2005, p. 10). Similar ideas have been put forward for other cases. Awareness of the ways that geo-bodies merge, and for how borders are blurred, is appropriate. It is one of the ways that any appreciation of how politics interacts with culture can make sense of the rigid institutions that human societies create.

Institutions Take Exception

The study of political institutions has drawn attention for generations. In recent times, scholars seeking to understand the limitations of political systems, and strategies of government control, have held to the idea that the "exception" has special significance. This emerges from Giorgio Agamben's notion of a "state of exception" and, in the context of political culture, perhaps its most relevant application is in the work of Aihwa Ong (2006). She is the key proponent of the idea in Asia and deploys the "exception" as a way of conceiving different types of political space. The major thrust of her argument is that neo-liberal projects in East Asia provide exceptions to standard methods of government management and control. Her specific concern is how "neo-liberal" interventions seek to articulate types of citizenship and belonging "in political spaces that may be less than the national territory in some cases, or exceed national borders in others" (Ong 2006, p. 6). Ong targets the "selective development" of these neo-liberal exceptions with reference to spatialization in East Asia (2006, p. 18). Preoccupied with special economic zones, free trade areas, and other "neo-liberal exceptions", she looks to the ways that governments can disregard their own ideological and political commitments if the contradictions prove effective. Contradictions of these sorts sometimes also justify "exceptions to neo-liberalism" (that is, through authoritarian impositions) which ensure that the governments respond forcefully to any perceived weaknesses. She argues that in these environments "the state tends to be robust and centralized".

Such exceptions are often discussed in relation to capitalism, particularly when it is partnered with ideas about democratization. As one example, Holm and Sorensen (1995, p. 17) make the point that "the dominant notion of global liberal democracy sustained by an economy controlled by market forces" can ultimately "create... severe problems in several parts of the periphery when translated into concrete measures of rollback of the state". Special economic zones in China, Myanmar, and Sri Lanka, not to mention autonomous zones and other spatial exceptions, demonstrate that not all territory needs to be controlled to the same rigorous extent. Anna Tsing has pursued this logic in the context of Southeast Asian borderland spaces, some of the same places that received attention under the terms of the "Zomian" debate. Her conclusion is that "[f]rontiers are deregulated because they arise in interstitial spaces made by collaborations among legitimate and illegitimate partners: armies and bandits; gangsters and corporations; builders and despoilers" (2005, p. 27). The resulting "confusions" lead to what Tsing calls "extravagant new economies of profit—as well as loss" (2005, p. 28). As Tsing demonstrates, there may be good commercial or political reasons for allowing portions of the nation-state's territory, its "geo-body", to be left with an exceptional, and therefore contradictory, system of control.

When it comes to understanding institutions, even those as abstract as borders and spaces, there is a need to look beyond their superficial characteristics. This is how an approach to politics that brings culture into the discussion can provide a helpful alternative to studies where structure takes the place of day-to-day substance. This position on the study of political cultures is particularly important to our understanding of the rapidly evolving online spaces, and digital institutions, that cannot conform to the expectations of centuries past. The exceptions to ordinary practice now come thicker and faster than before. Nowadays, the term "disruption" is applied in wildly different situations to help explain how our societies, cultures, politics, and economies are being upended by a new set of expectations. Old industries are dying. This pattern is particularly apparent across the Asia-Pacific region where there is little certainty about the next steps for a continent poignantly described as "restless" (Wesley 2015). Appreciating political cultures is a process that needs careful attention to what has changed and what has stayed the same.

Spaces and the Online Realm

The Internet has changed most aspects of human experience, including how we understand the spaces where we live. Political cultures, and the study of political cultures, have not been immune. When I first started doing serious field research in northern Myanmar more than a decade ago, it was almost impossible to keep in touch online. The town where I devoted much of my attention had no Internet connectivity. The best global link I ever managed was when a businessman handed me a satellite phone on the off-chance that I wanted to call my parents. I did, and woke my dad in the middle of the night from the back seat of a four-wheel drive bouncing along a mountain road. He was shocked, to say the least, such was the non-communicative haze that descended over my movements in those early efforts to understand northern Myanmar. It was not until I returned in 2008 that a slightly greater level of connection was apparent.

Internet cafes, of the likes that had emerged in Thailand a decade earlier, were, by then, making their mark. But most of the young men who spent their 200 kyat an hour (around US$0.15) gravitated to the shoot-'em-up games. Multiplayer, first-person, guts and glory, grief and gore: such experiences certainly do chew through the hours after school or work. Back then, Internet speeds were so slow that it was almost impossible to download emails, let alone send them. Yet a few years later, in 2011, when I returned for a further tranche of field work in northern Myanmar, the Internet connections were starting to get much faster. The Myanmar Internet remained censored, and the Facebook boom had yet to really take off in its vernacular format, and yet, many more people were using Internet terminals to send emails, or even make international phone calls. One day, sitting alone in a restaurant, I found some young guys playing with a Chinese-made tablet computer. I knew, from then on, that nothing would ever be the same.

On my most recent visit to that part of northern Myanmar, it was clear the transformation of local life in the Internet spaces has been extreme. Internet cafes now struggle for business, mostly because hotels, offices, and many homes have their own link-ups, with wireless access becoming run-of-the-mill. People also own devices of a bewildering diversity, but smartphones tend to be the tool of choice. These are cheap and accessible, a technological change made possible through major investments by European and Middle Eastern telecommunications companies. In less than a decade, that distant corner of Myanmar, often considered out of touch with the rest of the world, is being fully captured by the technologies that will, perhaps more than anything else, reshape the ways that connections are maintained within villages, towns, and cities, but more broadly to other regions, other countries, and the rest of the world. The fact that the Internet increasingly includes everyone, even the very poorest people, gives us reason to think seriously about the implications of full global enmeshment.

Huntington speculated that "the Asia of economic sunshine will generate an Asia of political shadows, an Asia of instability and conflict" (1997, p. 218). He could not foresee that less than two decades later, any of those difficult and historically dangerous corners of Asia would be so well connected. In those especially lonely corners of Asia that have been long "disconnected" because of some mix of terrain, weather, and poverty, there is a new set of opportunities emerging. What this means remains uncertain, precisely because a world where everyone can speak to each other, when ideas can circulate within minutes, and it can all happen simultaneously, without any centralizing controller, is a world without precedent. It also changes what spaces mean in the context of political cultures. When the dust eventually settles, this may make the transformations of earlier centuries look mild by comparison. The serious academic study of these issues is only just beginning. It is the universal participation that emerging Internet technologies make possible that has the greatest transformational potential.

In some parts of the Asia-Pacific, we can already see what this looks like in practice. Malaysia's 2013 General Election was its first full-blown contest in the Internet landscape. Malaysians, voracious for information, especially about the opposition, took to the rebellious spaces of the web with vigour. They tweeted, searched, and Facebooked up a storm. The website on Southeast Asia that I run, the New Mandala, could not handle the load and toppled offline, only to be salvaged by savvy technicians and the cloud computing horsepower of Amazon.com. When everyone in Malaysia is looking for up-to-date information, the surge in traffic was, we later realized, simply overwhelming. But it is not just Malaysia that now faces such challenges. The experience in Myanmar for the November 2015 general election shows just how far the Internet is reshaping political communication and therefore what we can understand of political cultures. There is no corner of the Asia-Pacific that will escape these changes or their ramifications for scholarly research practice.

CONCLUSIONS ON THE POLITICS OF
INTERNET HYPERREALITY

Earlier generations of scholars grappled with the ideas of political cultures during different moments of technological development. Famous conceptualizations of nationalism, including Benedict Anderson's regularly rehearsed notion of "imagined communities" (1991), have roots in the media and printing industries of an earlier age. A specific confluence of power, wealth, and distribution framed Anderson's argument. The challenge, under current circumstances, is to adjust our analysis to meet what Edward Aspinall (2016) has called "the hyperreality of the Internet age". This is a new problem for the analysis of ideology, institutions, and spaces, none of which can be expected to change in the same ways given the immediacy, vibrancy, and potency of Internet cultures. Perhaps we do not yet really know, or have a way of knowing, what this means for the political cultures that will swirl around us.

It makes sense that we may not yet have adequate tools and techniques for such study but given the importance of the subject matter, and its clear relevance to the serious analysis of the Asia-Pacific region, it might be one area where a major effort could be undertaken right now. A basic challenge of Internet hyperreality is that we are yet to adequately explain precisely how, when, and why it connects to the flesh-and-bone world that we inhabit. Explaining issues of causality and continuity is difficult enough without having to consider what has, for some, become a new plane of existence: the digitized self. Where politics meets the Internet, we all still have much to learn. Coral Bell warned of the dangers posed by nationalism on the move. She made us listen by giving us reason to remember her elegant phrase. For those of us looking to keep the study of the Asia-Pacific region fresh and relevant, the extra complexity of the Internet age will only multiply the opportunities as we retool for a new era of social scientific enquiry. Our words and ideas will need to explain the big trends in ways that matter for a world in flux.

4

HUMAN CONSIDERATIONS IN CONFLICTED SOCIETIES

Cecilia Jacob

INTRODUCTION

War is a complex and deeply social process that reaches lives far beyond soldiers on the battlefield. The first department of international relations was founded in Aberystwyth in 1919 following the horrors of the First World War, and as a discipline, it has always been captivated by the central problem of preventing the devastation of war on human populations, even if scholars disagree on how this can be achieved. Although war is an enduring feature of global politics, the character of war itself has changed significantly over the past century (Strachan and Scheipers 2011). We are fortunate not to have experienced another major world war despite the creation of 142 new nation states since 1945, yet war itself has become much more fragmented and internalized within this period. The rapid changes in the mode and characteristics of today's conflicts challenge the way that scholars consider their methodological approaches to studying the impact of armed conflict on societies.

This chapter focuses on methodological considerations for researching populations impacted by armed conflict in the Asia-Pacific, a region that experienced major conflicts in the Cold War period, has the potential for major interstate conflicts, and continues to be confronted by a range of diverse internal conflicts that threaten the security of domestic populations. The starting point for thinking about methodological approaches here is to consider the nature of the field that is being researched — what are the historical, social, and political characteristics of the conflict settings? How are conflict-affected populations situated within this overarching field? What are the implications of the way that the field is conceptualized for advocating for the agency, protection, and human rights of the affected populations?

This chapter is therefore concerned with two sets of developments in international politics and academic practice that are important for considering approaches to research on the humanitarian impact of armed conflict. The first set of developments is in global politics where we find, on the one hand, the strengthening of international norms and rules to regulate armed conflict that are increasingly geared towards the protection of individuals in war. On the other hand, the fragmentation and internalization of armed violence within the state creates ambiguity in the international legal and regulatory space, and challenges international efforts to protect populations affected by conflict. The international politics of protection is therefore contested in a domain that is far removed from local experiences and strategies of participation, protection, and survival.

The second set of developments is found in the divergent approaches to the study of armed conflict in international relations and political science. Alongside the long-standing research focus on systemic and state-level understandings of the nature and causes of war in international relations, there is a growing scholarly interest in the micro-sociological dynamics of armed conflict that incorporates individual and group level perspectives more commonly associated with the traditional peace research agenda. I argue that, rather than seeing these developments as distinct research agendas, it is the interaction between the micro- and macrodynamics of armed conflict that is of significance for understanding the nature of armed conflict today, and for carving out a research agenda to advocate improvements in both international and state level protection of conflict-affected populations that is attuned to these internal dynamics.

This chapter then sets out a case for a conceptual reorientation to the field to account for these overarching developments by employing a relational ontology. The chapter engages with the "practice turn" in international relations, arguing that a relational ontology makes sense of the complex dynamics and range of actors shaping contemporary armed conflicts, and contributes significantly to the way that we see civilians in conflict zones by situating them in the broader social context of conflict analysis. I draw briefly on my own work in the region to demonstrate the potential of this approach for expanding the conceptualization of concepts such as civilian protection, and to consider tangible sites for promoting international norms of protection in social contexts of armed conflict. The chapter concludes with some reflections on the ethical considerations of a sociological approach to researching the humanitarian impact of conflict in the Asia-Pacific.

THE INTERNATIONAL POLITICS OF PROTECTION

A number of significant trends have occurred in international politics following the end of the Cold War that have generated momentum for the creation of more robust international norms and laws to protect individuals affected by armed conflict. At the normative level, as well as the strategic level, the post-Cold War period has been marked by the willingness of the international community to reconsider their national security imperatives and responsibilities in relation to the internal mass atrocities taking place in parts of the world that had experienced decades of civil war. Despite significant mass atrocities that took place during the Cold War period, such as in Bangladesh, Cambodia, Ethiopia, and Nigeria, it was only in the early 1990s that failures by United Nations (UN) peacekeepers in Somalia, Rwanda, and Bosnia-Herzegovina catalysed significant international legal and institutional reforms to protect civilians.

The emergence of critical theoretical approaches to security and the language of Human Security (UNDP 1994) assisted to a large extent in influencing international debates about who the referent of security should be — states or people — and how policy agendas in the areas of security and development could be increasingly coordinated to achieve the goals of "freedom from fear" and "freedom from want" through a security-development nexus (Stern and Öjendal 2010). The tendency by scholars to pit human security in opposition to state security has diminished many of the possibilities of employing a human security lens to improve the protection of populations within conflict-affected states through the contestation of state security practices detrimental to domestic populations (Jacob 2014b). Nonetheless, the idea that sovereignty entails responsibility by states towards populations within their borders (Annan 1999; Deng et al. 1996; ICISS 2001) built on this conceptual reorientation in security debates, and has had a significant impact on the development of international norms and institutional arrangements for the protection of civilians.

Some of the trends that point towards the "individualization" of armed conflict (Welsh 2014) today include the extensive development of the international refugee protection regime and the creation of international guidelines on the protection of internally displaced persons (IDPs) (Betts 2010; Milner 2014). During the mid-1990s there was also an increased focus in the UN on issues such as children affected by armed conflict, women, peace, and security, and the protection of civilians that expanded traditional conceptions of civilian protection embedded in international humanitarian law. Each of these are now thematic issues that are debated annually in the UN Security Council (UNSC), and the subject of numerous UN Security Council Resolutions. There are now also special representatives of the UN Secretary-General (UNSG) on children and armed conflict, sexual violence in conflict, the human rights of IDPs, the prevention of genocide, and the responsibility to protect. The mandate of these offices is to promote these human protection agendas within the UN and across member states, and has brought many states and non-state actors into formal agreements on issues such as the demobilization of child soldiers in conflict zones, and the creation of institutional protection mechanisms for particularly vulnerable populations.

Other areas of international normative progress on human protection issues include the Responsibility to Protect (R2P) doctrine, on which there is now wide international consensus. R2P is the clearest articulation of the principle of "sovereign responsibility" that emerged out of the conceptual debates of the 1990s. At their heart, these debates grappled with the tension between state sovereignty (the right of states to non-interference in domestic affairs) and the protection of human rights. The failure of the international community to protect hundreds of thousands of civilians in Somalia, Rwanda, and Bosnia-Herzegovina, and the controversial use of air strikes by the North Atlantic Treaty Organization (NATO) without UNSC approval in Kosovo were significant events in the 1990s that compelled the Canadian government to establish the International Commission on Intervention and State Sovereignty (ICISS) to consider the ethics and legality of humanitarian intervention in such urgent circumstances. R2P, originally introduced at length in the report by ICISS (2001), argued that the international community had an imperative to intervene to protect populations from mass atrocity crimes when states proved unwilling, or unable, to do so themselves, and set the parameters for the circumstances in which such interventions would be warranted.

R2P was endorsed unanimously by the 150 heads of state that attended the 2005 UN World Summit in a condensed version from the original report (paragraphs 38–39 of the World Summit Outcome Document). R2P is not legally binding on states (Welsh and Banda 2010; Rosenberg 2009; Stahn 2007; Strauss 2009), rather it brings together the range of obligations on states that exist in international law, including international humanitarian law, international human rights law, international criminal law, and international refugee law into a coherent framework for the prevention and protection of populations from mass atrocity crimes (Welsh and Banda 2010). In terms of normative developments, Pillars One and Two of R2P (UN 2009) that pertain to state responsibility towards their own populations have received the most attention in UN debates in recent years, promoting prevention and international cooperation with states on institutional, legal, security sector, and social justice reform (UN 2013; UN 2014). Pillar Three of R2P on international intervention, including military intervention as a last resort, has been highly contentious among many states that are wary of international intervention into their internal security issues. However, there is much more consensus among states on the elements of R2P that promote state sovereign responsibility to prevent and protect populations from atrocity crimes within their own jurisdiction, reflecting a high level of normative commitment within foreign policy circles on the core tenets of R2P as a preventative doctrine. This normative consensus therefore creates space for leveraging prevention efforts geared towards the enhanced protection populations from internal conflict and political violence that create a high level of risk for atrocity crimes (Jacob 2015a; 2015c).

Alongside increased international protections for individuals that have been made over the past two decades is the increased accountability of individuals for the commissions of genocide, war crimes, and crimes against humanity through the International Criminal Court (ICC) that came into force in 2002. The role of the ICC is to deter individuals at the highest levels of responsibility from committing mass atrocity crimes, whether they be conducted in peacetime or wartime. It has also served to expand the scope of human protection issues that can be classified as a war crime, with the use of widespread sexual violence one notable area where international protection efforts have been directed in recent years. The articulation and classification of the protection needs of particularly vulnerable groups —

such as children, women and the elderly — in conflict settings within both the UNSC and ICC has created legitimacy around these groups and spurned greater international advocacy, research, and protection programmes directed towards their needs that is further evidence of the extent to which international norms have evolved.

Finally, efforts are underway within the UN to streamline human rights accountability in all of its operations through the "Rights Up Front" initiative launched by UN Secretary-General Ban Ki-moon in 2013. The purpose of the initiative is to ensure that the UN operates as a robust organization for meeting human protection needs. It calls for a deep cultural change across the entire UN system, to be able to effectively respond to early warning signs of conflict, to prevent mass atrocities and protect populations affected by armed conflict, correcting its "systematic failure" as an organization to prevent human suffering (Ban 2013).

The normative developments at the international level are therefore unprecedented, and have been matched by the creation of new principles, laws, and institutional reform that were not conceivable during the Cold War period. The international context is therefore a crucial starting point for considering approaches to researching questions related to human protection in areas affected by armed conflict. It provides the normative, legal, and institutional backdrop for considering the extent to which state and non-state actors responsible for widespread human rights violations can and should be regulated, and for considering the points at which international intervention into the domestic affairs of states for the purpose of human protection is now conceivable and legitimate.

SITUATING HUMAN PROTECTION IN ACCOUNTS OF ARMED CONFLICT

The previous section emphasized the rapid progress towards international consensus on norms of human protection. Yet, despite this emergent consensus, internal armed conflicts proliferate across the world, including those that have been internationalized. The numbers of people being displaced by armed violence today is unprecedented, and internal conflicts themselves are increasingly fragmented, with multiple conflict dyads present in most of today's internal conflicts (Pettersson and Wallensteen 2015). According to 2014 data from the Uppsala Conflict Database, thirty-nine of the forty armed conflicts currently active around the world are internal, thirteen of these are internationalized (such as those in Syria, Iraq, Ukraine, and Yemen) and the only international conflict is the low-intensity conflict (less than fifty deaths per year) between India and Pakistan over its disputed territories.

There are also still many gaps and inconsistencies in the definition, classification, and application of international law as it applies to contemporary internal conflicts (Wilmshurst 2012). These conflicts involve increasing numbers of non-state actors, often fall below — or evade — international legal thresholds for the definition of armed conflict in which international humanitarian law (IHL) applies (ICRC 2011; Mundy 2011) or lack sufficient momentum and strategic significance to garner international intervention (military or non-military) given the low-intensity and protracted nature of political violence that we find throughout the world, including the Asia-Pacific region (Jacob 2015*b*, 2015*c*).

As a result of the contemporary nature of political violence and armed conflict, the connection between international legal, normative, and institutional developments that promote improved protection for populations caught up in conflict are much more difficult to apply in practice. How international normative and regulatory developments pertain to state and sub-state actors largely outside the purview of international oversight, such as through peacekeeping operations, is a particularly challenging area given the resistance that states in Asia have to interference in their domestic affairs. Here, for example, we can think of protracted conflicts in Mindanao in the Philippines, ethnic minority states in Myanmar, insurgency in southern Thailand, the Chittagong Hill tracts in Bangladesh, the separatist movements in Jammu and Kashmir and Northeast India, and the Naxalite insurgency across India's central and eastern states, or the former civil war in Sri Lanka. Nonetheless, this is the area that has now gained the international community's attention in the re-conceptualized UN peacekeeping and peace-building efforts, and the women, peace, and security agenda in which the protection of civilians (POC) and R2P are increasingly integrated (see for example the report of the High-Level Independent Panel on Peace Operations 2015).

Explanations for the nature of armed conflict in the post-Cold War era diverge in a number of areas, yet do agree on many fundamental features of contemporary armed conflicts that are useful for considering developments in both warfare and international norms on civilian protection. Some scholars have argued that the 1990s ushered in a new paradigm of war, the so-called "New Wars" (Duffield 2001; Kaldor 2006; see also van Creveld 1991, 2008), defined by identity rather than ideology, and indeterminacy of military objectives due to sustained access to global black economies rather than being tempered by finite military objectives with limited resourcing. Yet the civil wars of the 1990s were more of a continuation of the post-colonial wars that had defined the post-World War Two era, and the "newness" of today's armed conflicts as a radical rupture from the past is a tenuous claim (Haines 2012; Malešević 2010; Melander, Öberg, and Hall et al. 2009; Newman 2004; Strachan and Scheipers 2011). Nonetheless, both the geostrategic changes at the systemic level and technological advances have undoubtedly transformed the character of war that we see today. Among these changes are a notable move away from conventional and irregular guerrilla warfare towards symmetric non-conventional warfare that engages state actors in more direct confrontation with non-state belligerents than the protracted guerrilla insurgencies of the Cold War period (Kalyvas 2012).

According to macro-accounts of armed conflict, war is shaped by the international system, and interactions between state units (Waltz 1979). The international legal and institutional developments discussed in the first half of this chapter reinforce the understanding that war, and the regulation of war, is a state affair. The international institutions that states have created to facilitate interstate cooperation and mitigate interstate conflicts work to maintain order and stability within this system and have been successful in their central purpose of preventing a major interstate war, and responding — with mixed success — to significant internal conflicts in which large numbers of civilians are killed, harmed, and displaced. Parallel to these systemic and macro-level explanations is a growing body of literature in political science and international relations that is concerned primarily with the micro-dynamics of armed conflict for understanding how to prevent and solve contemporary internal conflicts.

Micro-accounts include in-depth studies of the local social and political dynamics of armed conflicts, political violence, and mass atrocities. These include research on areas such as the divergent motives and cleavages among different actors using violence that shape civil conflict (Kalyvas 2003), the organizational dynamics (Christia 2012; Staniland 2014; Weinstein 2007) and ideology (Sanín and Wood 2014) of insurgent groups, and the local social and political dynamics of genocide (Lemarchand 2009; Straus 2008). These accounts are far removed from the systemic and macro levels of analysis in detailing the central workings of significant civil conflicts and mass atrocities that feature today, yet have profound insights for improving international efforts to enhance human protection through interventions in internal conflicts.

One of the seminal works in this field provides a devastating critique of the top-down nature of the UN peace-building intervention in the Congo, which was structured to address state and international level conflict (Autesserre 2010, pp. 120–25). By feeding into simplistic accounts of the situation that bypassed local sources of conflict, namely rivalries over land, access to resources and political power, UN peace-building activities in the Congo systematically failed to achieve their broader objectives related to human protection and conflict cessation. Nuanced accounts of the local dynamics of political violence and armed conflict in unstable regions strengthen understanding of the contexts to which broader trends being observed at the international level correspond, and pinpoints areas of fruitful engagement where the normative and regulatory developments at the international level need to be much more effectively and strategically interpreted into local practice.

One of these sites includes a re-conceptualization of state understandings of "sovereign responsibility" as articulated in the R2P doctrine. States have unanimously endorsed R2P in principle through the UN, and many have demonstrated a preference for the first Pillar of sovereign responsibility for population protection and prevention of atrocity crimes within state borders, over the third Pillar of international intervention for protection purposes when states fail in this responsibility.[1] As I have argued elsewhere, however, the repeated reference to genocides, such as those in Cambodia, Rwanda, and Bosnia-Herzegovina, have reinforced the misconception that the levels of political violence or low intensity conflicts within their own borders do not equate to the types of scenarios where R2P applies (Jacob 2015*b*). While genocides may be rare events, atrocity crimes are not (Karstedt 2013). Further, effective Pillar One responsibilities of states are much more ubiquitous than current UN prevention frameworks suggest, given that the effective protection of populations by states with high levels of existing risk of atrocity crimes corresponds with lengthy historical trajectories of violence, and often decades of military encounters with the civilian population (Jacob 2015*c*).

One of the implications of the research on the micro-dynamics of armed conflicts is that there is a pressing need to develop a stronger understanding of how international human protection norms, law, and institutions are mediated by state and sub-state level actors, and implemented on the ground. In the next section, I outline an approach to research in this area that emphasizes the importance of understanding historical trajectories of political violence and armed conflict, and identifying routine practices of key security and protection actors that have developed over time. It is argued that this broader sociological and historical context of contemporary conflict-affected societies give meaning to the contemporary practices of security actors within the research site, and situate international efforts to promote what are — in cases such as R2P, POC, Children and Armed Conflict, and Women, Peace, and Security, for example — quite recent norms and standards of human rights and protection.

INTERNATIONAL PRACTICES

The chapter so far has described the broad international context of contemporary armed conflicts, and situated populations affected by armed conflict at the intersection of international politics of protection and micro-sociological dynamics of armed conflict. This final section introduces the practice turn in international relations, arguing for a conceptual reorientation towards the field of armed conflicts in which populations are present. The practice turn in international relations is inspired by the work of Pierre Bourdieu,[2] and challenges conventional international relations theory by employing a relational ontology towards the field of research.

International relations theory has traditionally focused on the state, and relations between states, as its object of analysis to explain the causes and dynamics of armed conflict. The study of practice, however, includes an emphasis on the sites of *habitus* and *field* to explain social action and uncover relations of power (Pouliot and Mérand 2013) that is a pertinent framework for the analysis of political violence and armed conflict within, between, and across state borders. The notion of *habitus* in Bourdieu's work refers to the subjective disposition (*dispositif*) of actors that is constructed through a culmination and internalization of life experiences and reiterated patterns of behaviour; that is, "history turned into nature" (Bourdieu 1977, p. 78). *Habitus* inclines actors towards certain actions in relation to the *field*, with the unconscious, socialized *disposition* of individuals shaping their interactions within a given social context. In the context of international relations, scholars have been interested in the disposition and reiterated practices of actors such as diplomats (Pouliot 2010), security professionals and bureaucrats (Bigo 2006), and refugee activists (Nyers 2003); those actors whose daily actions constitute the substance of international politics. Given that significant actors in today's conflict include not just soldiers in uniform, but non-state (or pro-state) militia, terrorists, insurgents — some of whom may be children, female, local supporters, resistors, and so on — analyses of armed conflict that take the disposition of these actors into account provide a more nuanced account of the dynamics of conflict processes taking place within (or across) the state border.

Actors are positioned within a *field*, that is "a social space structured along three principal dimensions: power relations, objects of struggle, and rules taken for granted within the field" (Pouliot and Mérand 2013, p. 30). A field is shaped around a specific site of struggle, where certain rules of the "game" (Bourdieu 1977, p. 40) operate and are known by social actors, and power is unequal. Operating in the field requires a certain tacit, practical knowledge that is acquired through being situated within a given social context. Bourdieu's relational ontology asserts that the interface between habitus and field — or disposition and position — is the site of social practice and action, a conclusion that offers practical implications for research methodology and analysis of security in international relations (Côte-Boucher, Infantino, and Salter 2014; Salter 2013, pp. 85–90). More precisely, the interface between social disposition and position is an important site for understanding political violence contextually (Bakonyi and De Guevara 2009) and is therefore of crucial importance for formulating successful protection efforts.

In international relations specifically, a field can be understood as a globalized space as long as the same sociological principles defined above are operating (Pouliot and Mérand 2013, p. 32). This approach has enabled international relations scholars to go beyond levels-of-analysis visions of the international system in the identification of specific fields of politics that transcend state-international distinctions (Bigo 2011, p. 226), ask new questions related to international politics, and offer original analyses through empirically rigorous and sociological grounded methodologies (noteworthy examples being Bigo 2006 and Pouliot 2010). Importantly, taking a particular field, or site of struggle, as an alternative starting point for theory (Adler-Nissen 2013, pp. 1–2), facilitates analysis of the social space surrounding a specific issue in international relations as opposed to a pregiven and bounded subject, such as the state.

A relational ontology is important, given that analyses of human protection within security studies have, for far too long, been hindered by the debate between "state-centric" and "human-centric" definitions of security, rather than concerned with the overarching objective of transforming the security politics in which civilians are rendered insecure (Jacob 2014*b*). Debates over "centricity" are also redundant; theoretically speaking, it does not make sense to try to replace one central referent of security analysis with another as this approach merely serves to reify an alternative (arbitrary) threat construction rather than change the ontological underpinning of the approach to security on which methodological choices are built (Jacob 2015*a*). Rather, by focusing on the politics of security and protection, the state comes into full purview given its relations with societies, and a deeper understanding of the extent to which the state exercises both sovereign authority and legitimacy within its territory, and to which competing claims for jurisdiction and the monopoly of violence are made.

Given the emphasis in practice theory on the actors that operate within a given field and identifying the patterned logics that shape their interactions, a practice approach to the study of populations in armed conflicts must start with an empirical investigation of the field in which one is researching. My own research on the protection of children affected by armed conflict in Southeast Asia,[3] for example, took me to the field in 2008–9, where I conducted interviews with a range of professionals whose work constituted the field of protection for the children affected by violence that were identified in the research. The fieldwork included workshops with over seventy children affected by armed conflict, displacement, trafficking, or exploitation for hazardous labour.

The methodology for this research was shaped by an interest in a particular site of struggle — that of routine violations of rights of children impacted by armed conflict in the region. The two research groups I selected were children living within the remaining conflict zones in the ethnic minority states in Myanmar, zones renowned for the widespread use of child soldiers and conflict-induced displacement, and children exposed to trafficking and sexual exploitation in post-conflict Cambodia. By honing in on a specific protection issue, it was possible to identify the wide range of actors whose work was associated with the increased protection of this particular population group. These actors included UN agencies (such as the United Nations Children's Fund or UNICEF, the International Labour Organization or ILO, the United Nations Inter-Agency Project on Human Trafficking or UNIAP, and the United Nations Development Programme or UNDP), government ministries with delegated responsibilities for child protection (such as ministries of interior, social affairs, and women's affairs), international non-government organizations (NGOs) and local NGOs, and the child protection workers themselves in IDP camps and safe houses.

In taking this approach I was able to map out the "field" of protection that spanned from Myanmar's capital city, Yangon, to an IDP camp in Karen state on the Myanmar border, UN agency headquarters in Bangkok, and Cambodia's capital Phnom Penh. The picture that emerged was a complex array of definitions, practices, and legal, institutional, and political approaches around the issue of child protection in conflict-affected societies. The politics that shaped this field included UN-government relations, donor-government relations, hierarchical relations between government ministries themselves (the military and home affairs sectors, for example, were significantly privileged over social welfare and justice ministries in both states), patronage relations between government elites and lower-level officials, and contending visions of rights and protection between NGOs operating in the field. Each of these relations came with their own power relations and hierarchies, and perpetuated differentiated visions of "protection", such as those between the security sector and social welfare and development oriented agencies. Actors pursued different logics and outcomes in their work, outcomes that in some instances created an evident "protection gap" for the most vulnerable children in these countries.

It was also clear that significant change in the understanding, priorities, and response of domestic actors to child protection issues in these states had occurred from a range of sites. These include the advocacy, advice, and capacity support by international agencies in the field, and donor government pressures on domestic actors to meet benchmarks on areas of governance and rule of law that exposed actors to the standards and expectations of the international community on their domestic reform process. However, unlike much of the literature on norm diffusion that considers the diffusion of norms as a linear (or spiral) process, progress on human protection at the domestic level is far more uneven, both in terms of geographical reach and in various levels and domains of governance.

In Cambodia, for example, the police, with generous government and international funding and capacity support, have had the most success in addressing issues of human trafficking and sexual exploitation in urban hubs, but much less success in marginal rural areas where most of the trafficked children were from. The social welfare sector looks after all of the children who are delivered to them by the police after successful raids. Yet, at the time of my research, this sector received no additional funding from the central government. This was despite the fact that the government enjoyed recognition for its policing successes from the international community, through ongoing increases in donor funding, and being dropped from a Tier 3 to a Tier 2 country in the annual US Trafficking in Persons report.

Many of these children return to cycles of poverty and violence due to inadequate resourcing and a lack of creative options for the livelihoods of the country's most vulnerable children. Here the politics within the state, that privileges the security sector over the social welfare approaches to protection, have resulted in the irregular and short-lived protection of the country's most vulnerable children. The level of awareness of human rights norms and international protection standards within the special anti-human trafficking and juvenile justice unit were far more advanced than in both the severely underfunded social welfare sector, or regular policing units, given the sustained engagement of the international community with this unit, and the willingness of the central government to maintain a significant budget for the security sector. Yet, a failure to take into account the relational dynamics between the various sectors and the importance accorded to them at the elite level, as well as their routine interactions through the child-referral system, significantly undermines this laudable progress.

Given the complexity, and very political nature of protection agendas, approaches to research on human protection therefore requires an engagement with the field being studied, and an identification of how international norms and expectations are mediated on the ground by domestic actors. Local understanding and practices of protection interact with international norms because of the presence of international, donor government, and civil society actors in humanitarian spaces of conflict and post-conflict societies. But these are translated through local practices and repertoires of the professionals responsible for their implementation, and the power relations between these actors play a significant role in carving out the space in which they define protection issues and operate in the field.

CONCLUSION

The promises of the study of practice for the human protection agenda is that it is able to define a field that is not necessarily bound by state borders, and permits transnational conflict issues to be analysed across predetermined political boundaries. In doing so, scholars engaging a practice methodology are able to provide practical insight into the relationship between the two overarching trends discussed in the first half of the chapter. These two trends included the strengthened international human protection norms and the increasingly fragmented and internalized fields of armed conflict that contour the contemporary global security landscape.

At an empirical level, this approach facilitates the identification of routine and patterned behaviour — the "stuff" that constitutes security practice — for a nuanced understanding of the micro-dynamics of conflict-affected society. Yet, in terms of the ethical implications, practice-based research reveals oppressive and unjust power relations, and is therefore also a site for political contestation and social transformation.

A brief final note is then warranted in the conclusion on the ethics of engaging practice theory in research on human protection, given its salience to the core theme of this chapter. Much of the ethical thrust of engaging with practice theory is in the choice of case studies selected, and the decision by the researcher to shed light on practices by state or other elite actors whose routine and seemingly mundane practices could, or should, be the subject of rigorous scrutiny and critique. Indeed the methodological choice, including one's mode of analysis, is largely an ethical choice that the researcher should be cognisant of, and perhaps even deliberative of, from the outset. A commitment to international human protection norms and their advocacy is likewise an ethical decision that is reflected in the tone and mode of analysis.

All theories contain normative judgement (Reus-Smit and Snidal 2008), and the sphere of human protection in conflicted societies is one domain in which the implications of one's research are potentially deeply significant for individual lives. So, while practice theory, like most of the social constructivist research with which it shares close affinities, does not offer a moral philosophy or ethical framework given its rejection of such foundational truths, the subject matter of human protection in conflicted societies is an inherently deeply ethical concern. This is the reason why consensus on the principles underpinning new developments in international civilian protection norms is nearly unanimous among the UN's member states, even if certain states have reservations on their technical aspects. Researchers are therefore encouraged to be both clear and consistent in their ethical approaches to researching human protection in conflict affected societies and in thinking through the practical implications of their research.

Notes

1. For perspectives of individual states, see statements given at the Annual UN General Assembly Informal Interactive Dialogue on the Responsibility to Protect <http://www.globalr2p.org/>.
2. Bourdieu is not the only inspiration of the practice turn in international relations. However it is the most clearly articulated approach by international relations scholars — for example, Adler and Pouliot 2011; Adler-Nissen 2013; and Bigo 2011.
3. This section is based on Jacob 2014a.

SECTION II
Analysing Politics

5

THE DESIGN-BASED REVOLUTION IN COMPARATIVE POLITICS

Paul Kenny

INTRODUCTION

Is aerial bombardment an effective counter-insurgency tactic? Do immigrants depress local wages? Does the presence of natural resources harm democratic consolidation? Answering questions such as these requires the uncovering of general patterns of cause and effect. Social scientists have been attempting to put this search for causal inference on a sure philosophical and methodological footing at least since Émile Durkheim's pioneering research on suicide in the nineteenth century, but progress has been slow, coming in fits and starts. Even the diffusion of computing technology and the modelling revolution it brought about did not solve the problem. However, the last decade or so has seen one of the most exciting developments in the history of causal inference in the social sciences for generations.

The design-based revolution has transformed how social scientists go about their research and the kinds of causal inferences they can now draw from it. Field experiments and natural experiments are at the foundation of design-based inference. A growing body of scholarship outlining the principles, techniques, and promise of this kind of research already exists, but most of it has been aimed at an audience already well versed in comparative analysis and statistical methods (Gerber and Green

2012; Morgan and Winship 2015; Angrist and Pischke 2015; Imbens and Rubin 2015). The logic of design-based inference is actually very intuitive, despite its somewhat daunting technical language. In this chapter, I want to introduce the design-based approach to a non-specialist audience, primarily those who use qualitative rather than quantitative methods.

I first introduce the two main models of causal inference common to comparative politics, the sufficient-component-cause (SSC) model and the counterfactual model. Second, I outline the problem of confounding in traditional qualitative and quantitative methods in the social sciences. Third, I detail the experimental method in its basic form and present some examples of randomized controlled trials (RCTs) in Asia. Fourth, I discuss extensions to the experimental model in the form of natural experiments and again illustrate the method with some examples from Asia. Finally, I discuss the limitations of the design-based revolution and what needs to be addressed going forward.

BACKWARD AND FORWARD INFERENCE

There are two main models of causal inference used in comparative politics, the SSC model and the counterfactual model. These models are sometimes associated with qualitative and quantitative methods respectively, but this understanding is actually incorrect. The difference between the approaches is better thought of in terms of whether the investigator reasons backwards or forwards.

In backward reasoning, we first observe an outcome and then attempt to uncover the processes or conditions that led to that outcome. This approach makes sense for discrete historical problems. Like a detective investigating a crime, the researcher sifts through the available evidence to trace through a sequence of events. This would be the approach used to explain why a particular counter-insurgency campaign failed or why a particular coup occurred. In some cases, this can lead to persuasive and reliable historical inference. However, even though this approach is utilized to answer distinct historical questions, it cannot work without more generalizable models of causal inference. That is, how we infer causality in a particular chain of events is typically shaped by how we believe people should behave on average in a given situation. Thus, even historians cannot fully escape the rules of good causal inference.

The more general form of the backward-looking approach is sometimes called the SSC model. This model of causal inference is based on the search for causes of effects. That is, we know the effect or outcome, and want to elucidate its cause(s). For this approach to work, we need more than one case, so that we can identify sufficient and necessary conditions that might produce the outcome in question.

A sufficient condition is a condition such that its occurrence is always enough by itself to produce the outcome in question. If A is the condition and B the outcome, we can say, *if* A *then* B. Conditions may be jointly sufficient if the presence of two or more conditions always produces the outcome in question. If C is another condition, then *if* A *and* C *then* B. A necessary condition is a condition such that an outcome will never occur unless this condition is present. Simply, B *only if* A. Conditions may also be jointly necessary. B *only if* A *and* C. This approach is thus attractive when researchers are looking to explain the full configuration of factors that caused particular events or outcomes.

In qualitative research, this approach works by applying either the method of difference or the method of agreement. The method of difference works by observing the occurrence of an outcome in one case, and its non-occurrence in another number of cases, where the cases have all conditions in common except one in the former; this one differing condition is the cause of the differing outcome. The idea, in short, is to match treatment and control groups along every dimension except that the former experiences the treatment while the latter do not. The approach attempts to mimic the modelling techniques of regression analysis but on a smaller scale (King, Keohane, and Verba 1994). The method of agreement instead works by observing the occurrence of the same outcome in two or more cases, where the cases have no conditions in common except one; this one similar condition is the cause of the outcome.

An example of this approach is Dan Slater's *Ordering Power* (2010). Slater looks to identify a set of conditions that explain why the authoritarian regimes of Southeast Asia varied in their stability over the late twentieth century. Slater identifies defensive elite protection pacts in response to the revolutionary conditions of the mid-twentieth century as the key condition that separated the authoritarian leviathans of Singapore and Malaysia from the less stable authoritarian regimes of the Philippines and Indonesia.

Problems arise when attempting to formulate a generalizable causal model from one or a few discrete cases. Many outcomes of interest in political research are highly complex, and there is rarely a condition, or set of conditions, that is sufficient to produce them. Moreover, such conditions are especially difficult to identify when working with a small number of cases (King, Keohane, and Verba 1994). However, the search for necessary and sufficient conditions is not the exclusive preserve of qualitative research. Indeed, the SSC model was formally elucidated for research in epidemiology that typically works with much larger data sets (Rothman 1976). The difficulties of inferring causality with this model of inference are thus common to both qualitative and quantitative research. Although a great deal of political and sociological research takes this approach, and while it is consistent from an epistemological and ontological perspective, in practice it is difficult if not impossible to implement without introducing several sources of bias. Bias in this sense does not refer to the prejudices of the researcher. Rather, bias refers to the tendency to over- or underestimate the value of a causal factor because of the way in which the data has been processed. I discuss sources of bias in more detail below.

While it is enticing to search for causes of effects, this research is often most valuable when it suggests avenues for new kinds of forward inference. In this chapter, I am primarily concerned with the latter. The other way of reasoning is to take a particular cause and then measure its effects. Causal inference in this model is established when we can compare two states of the world — a treated state and a non-treated or control state. The difference between the two is called the treatment effect. Of course, we cannot observe both states of the world at the same time, so we have to compare the observed outcome with a potential outcome. This is the counterfactual model of causal inference and it is at the heart of the design-based revolution that I discuss further below.

Counterfactual models of causation underpin a lot of research in both quantitative and qualitative political science. The great difficulty in drawing causal inference from observations of the real world is the presence of confounding factors. This is just as true of forward-looking causal models as it is of backward-looking models. Design-based inference attempts to implement or replicate as closely as possible the experimental method in order to eliminate this problem of confounders.

CONFOUNDING IN COMPARATIVE POLITICS

Confounding occurs when the causal factor in question is not independent of other potential causal factors. If the cause, or treatment, is not independent (or exogenous) from other factors that might have led to the outcome in question, then it is not possible to accurately infer the effect of that cause. The main sources of confounding that arise in comparative politics are selection bias and endogeneity bias.

Selection bias refers to the selection of individuals, states, or other units of analysis such that the sample used is not representative of the population under investigation (Geddes 1990). If we were attempting to study the effectiveness of a particular drug, and deliberately selected only those subjects who evidenced a response to it for analysis, the results would be biased. Similarly, in social science, the arbitrary restriction of the sample of units of analysis, say by geography or by time period, can have a distorting effect on the results of an empirical study.

Take Maya Tudor's recent book on the divergent post-independence regime trajectories of India and Pakistan, *The Promise of Power* (2013). While India has been mostly democratic, Pakistan has been highly unstable, reverting from democracy to authoritarianism and back again. For Tudor, the explanation centres on the political movements that led India and Pakistan's respective independence movements — specifically the relative strengths of the party networks of the Indian Congress Party on the one hand and the Muslim League on the other — and the class basis of the two respective political movements. However, with such a truncated sample (of two), it is impossible to determine whether this explanation is correct. Although India and Pakistan are matched in many respects, there are many sources of underlying variation between them, such that all possible confounders (i.e. additional variables that are correlated with both cause and outcome) cannot be controlled for. Indeed, looking at the same two cases, Philip Oldenburg (2010) comes up with a very different account. Oldenburg also goes back to the contingent historical process that resulted in the greater relative strength of the Congress network in comparison to that of the League, but he is primarily interested in explaining the relative strength of the Pakistani bureaucracy when compared to India. He argues that those areas of colonial India that became Pakistan were governed through a more bureaucratically dominant administrative structure than the areas that became India. If we were to look at more cases, even within British colonial Asia, such as Malaysia, Myanmar, and Sri Lanka, different conclusions would likely emerge. Expanding the sample to all of the British Empire, or to all of the colonies of all empires, would alter the results even further. Even then, however, we could not be sure that there were no further omitted variables that were correlated with both the nature of colonial independence movements and the nature of post-colonial regime trajectories.[1] This leads us to the related but distinct problem of endogeneity.

Endogeneity refers to the problem of including a causal factor in the model that is potentially correlated with other unobservable causal factors relegated to the error term. In other words, it means that some potentially important causal factor that influences both cause and effect is excluded from the model, thus misrepresenting the true effects of those factors included in the model. Omitted variable bias is a common source of endogeneity. In the example of attempting to study the effectiveness of a drug, it could arise from allowing subjects in a trial to choose whether to take the drug or the placebo. Those individuals willing to risk taking a new drug might be sicker, thus influencing how effective the drug would appear to be.

To illustrate its operation in comparative politics, it is easiest to take an example from the literature. Say we want to know the effect of corruption on economic development. In *Crony Capitalism*, David Kang (2002) asks why corruption is sometimes associated with high growth and sometimes with low growth. Comparing South Korea and the Philippines, Kang argues that different types of corruption have different effects on development. The presence of a small and stable network of business and government elites in South Korea meant that corruption functioned to lower transaction costs and promote growth. A dispersed set of conflicting elites and bureaucrats in the Philippines meant that corruption raised transaction costs and inhibited growth. Kang's causal model is certainly plausible. But what if there was some prior condition that simultaneously caused South Korea to have a particular type of business and government elite structure *and* to be more developed, but which caused the Philippines to be less developed? Recent research by Jong-sung You (2015) suggests that the greater equality of landholding in South Korea might have done exactly that. Thus, without taking account of this omitted variable, we would wrongly infer that the type of business and government elite structure caused development when, in fact, this was an intervening factor at best or epiphenomenal at worst.

Endogeneity bias also occurs when the outcome of interest recursively affects the cause of interest. That is, there is a feedback between cause and effect. In her recent historical investigation of the Pakistan military, Christina Fair argues that the strategic culture of Pakistan's army accounts for its persistently belligerent behaviour in the region, even though its actions have brought it limited success (2014). Although Fair is incredibly thorough in her investigation of the relevant sources, there remains the strong possibility that the army's strategic culture, or set of beliefs, is affected over time by the very outcomes Fair is attempting to explain. That is, the relationship between the Army's strategic culture and the outcomes of its military and strategic engagements is circular. This is a widespread problem with observational research, especially research in which the effect of beliefs on behaviour is concerned.

It is important to note that these kinds of confounding can occur in quantitative as well as qualitative research. In quantitative research, investigators attempt to control for potential confounding variables by including a large number of cases so that only like cases are compared. This means that cases are effectively matched on all of those factors that the researcher believes might influence the result. Ultimately, however, the addition of more cases does not resolve the issue, nor does the application of more and more sophisticated modelling techniques. In fact, it turns out that no amount of modelling can really overcome them because the researcher cannot be sure that there is not some unobserved confounder that is influencing both cause and effect. How then can we get around this problem of confounding?

THE EXPERIMENTAL METHOD

The simplest way to overcome the problem of confounding is through randomization. The random assignment of units of analysis to treatment and control groups ensures that the treatment is uncorrelated with possible confounding variables, as the latter average out across the two groups. This implies the use of the experimental method. The experimental method provides very reliable causal inference. Because the treatment is directly manipulated by the researcher, he or she can be confident that it is unrelated to potential confounding variables. For instance, in a drug trial, it means that individual participants are given no choice as to whether they will take the treatment or the placebo. Any potentially important extraneous factors such as genetic variation or underlying sickness should therefore be the same on average across treatment and control groups. The subsequent variation in outcome, if there is one, can thus be attributed to the effect of the drug.

The experimental method typically eliminates confounding by having large enough study samples such that treatment and control groups resemble one another on average. With a very small sample, the researcher could inadvertently assign the more healthy individuals to take the drug rather than the placebo. Most experiments in the political sphere are therefore large-N (number of units of analysis) rather than small-N studies. While they are thus typically quantitative studies, the actual number of units of analysis does not need to be exceedingly large. Moreover, as I discuss below, the principles of counterfactual causal inference translate over into small-N qualitative research.

Randomized Control Trials

In the real world, the experimental method means applying an intervention in the form of a field experiment or RCT (Gerber and Green 2012). Some of the earliest systematic research employing RCTs in political science studied the effect of various kinds of voter mobilization techniques on voter turnout (John 2013). Interventions that involve the provision of information tend to be more common as they are cheaper to implement than other interventions. As the effectiveness of RCTs has come to be appreciated in the policy world, however, recent years have seen the deployment of a large number of ambitious and exciting projects.

An RCT aims to make an inference about the causal effect in a population based on the results from a sample of that population. The first task in an RCT is to select a sample from the population. This is not unproblematic. The sample should resemble the population for whom the treatment is relevant in important dimensions like age, gender, and so on. To ensure this representativeness, there should be randomization in the selection of trial participants. Because of the law of large numbers, randomization ensures that the sample average should approximate the population average. The second step is to select treatment and control groups. Again, randomization is critical. We cannot allow participants to self-select into the treatment. Treatment and control groups should then be checked for balance to make sure that we have not, by some fluke, assigned only people of one ethnicity or gender to the treatment, and only people of another ethnicity or gender to the control. This process ensures that there are no confounding factors that might bias our results. The third step is to measure the average outcome in the control group and the treatment group. The difference in these averages is called the average treatment effect.

Some Examples

In one of the best known examples of an RCT in the political economy field, Benjamin Olken investigated how corruption might be reduced in the infrastructure sector. Olken (2007) randomly assigned 600 Indonesian village road projects to control and various treatment groups. Treatments were of two types: greater top-down auditing of project expenditures and construction, and civil society monitoring of the projects. Corruption was estimated by the difference between actual expenditures on the village road projects and the actual cost of construction based on an experimental road constructed explicitly as a control for the project. Olken found that while top-down monitoring reduced leakage through corruption as compared to the control group, grass-roots monitoring was only effective in very limited circumstances.

In another highly ambitious project, Banerjee et al. (2015) investigated the effects of a comprehensive developmental package for the extreme poor on their subsequent welfare. The package included a productive asset grant, training and support, life skills coaching, temporary cash consumption support, and access to savings accounts and health information or services. The study included 10,495 villagers in six developing countries including India and Pakistan. The researchers measured the impact of this package on consumption, food security, productive and household assets, financial inclusion, time use, income and revenues, physical health, mental health, political involvement, and women's empowerment. The study found statistically significant impacts on all ten key outcomes that persisted in most cases a full three years after the initial intervention. Although the study was expensive to implement, they found that in most countries the extra earnings of participants outweighed the programme cost. This suggests that well-targeted poverty alleviation programmes can actually be very effective.

Critiques of RCTs

RCTs clearly contribute positively to our knowledge of cause and effect in many areas of policy and politics. However, they are not without substantial problems. First, RCTs in the policy space come with major ethical implications (Barrett and Carter 2014). RCTs could have potentially adverse consequences, despite the best intentions of ethics review boards. Second, while RCTs are solid on internal validity, they are necessarily inhibited by a lack of external validity (Garcia and Wantchekon 2010).

That is, even if a policy shows a positive effect in one trial in one location, we cannot be sure it will work in another time and place until further experiments are carried out (Cartwright and Hardie 2012). Third, in the real world, information and resources for individuals fit within a much broader sociological context, so many RCTs find only substantively weak effects. Their impact is deeply contingent on a wide set of factors that are not easily controlled for, even in RCTs. Fourth, interventions can only be contemplated in a restricted set of areas of politics and economics (Rodrik 2008). We cannot use an RCT to study the effect of a war or a new electoral system. Fifth, and more fundamentally, because these are real world interventions, we would often like to understand the mechanism that is generating the outcome (Deaton 2009). To say that the discovery of a new education policy that increases high school completion would be incredibly welcome is an understatement. But we would need to know how it works. What if it increased high school completion rates at the expense of individual health because it was based on the universal prescription of Adderall or some other attention-increasing drug? In short, RCTs, on their own, are no panacea for causal inference without a good understanding of causal mechanisms.

NATURAL EXPERIMENTS

Natural experiments are closely related to field experiments in the way in which they attempt to draw causal inference (Dunning 2012). Although the interventions are not controlled by the researcher, they are selected because they are implemented in an as-if random way. Because such natural experiments are contextually embedded, they offer a chance to see how large-scale projects work in practice. Natural experiments can draw on a variety of sources. Some of them rely on policies delivered by governments in random or quasi-random ways. Others instead draw on exogenous shocks like natural disasters. The key distinction between a natural experiment and a purely observational study is that the treatment (or cause) is uncorrelated with confounding variables that may also affect the outcome.

As with RCTs, there are many good examples. In India, in order to increase women's participation in politics, a 1993 law reserved leadership positions on randomly selected local village councils for women. Using a survey of 8,453 of adolescents aged 11–15 and their parents in 495 villages, Beaman et al. (2012) find that compared to villages that never had a reserved female leader, the gender gap in aspirations closed by

25 per cent in parents and 32 per cent in adolescents in villages assigned to a female leader for two election cycles. Female adolescents in treated villages spent less time on household chores than in non-treated villages, although there was no sustained impact on women's labour market opportunities in reserved villages. The effect of reserving village council leadership positions seems to have persistent political effects also. Bhavnani (2009) finds that the probability of a woman winning office in previously reserved councils is approximately five times greater than the probability of a woman winning office if the constituency had not been reserved for women.

Extensions of the natural experimental approach include regression discontinuity designs and instrumental variables (IV) designs. Regression discontinuity designs rely on exploiting another kind of as-if random assignment to treatment and control groups. A number of studies have attempted to determine the impact of migration on the prosperity of migrants and their families to whom they remit earnings. An obvious problem with many studies would be that the families of those who migrate could be systematically different from those who do not. Michel Clemens and Erwin Tiongson (2014) study Filipinos migrating to work in manufacturing jobs in South Korea through a bilateral agreement under the Employment Permit Scheme (EPS) programme. Because the EPS requires individuals to exceed a certain minimum score on a language competency exam, it is possible to compare the effect of migration on those individuals who just exceed the score to those who just fall short. Because the difference in score is so similar, we can assume that the individuals are on average similar on things that matter like ambition and intelligence. They find that migration has important effects on households' financial behaviour, including tripling expenditure on education and health, reducing borrowing, and raising savings. Interestingly, the shifting of budget allocation decisions from husbands to wives appears to drive much of this change, independent of the effect of remittances.

IV analyses also attempt to overcome the problem of confounding by exploiting exogenous sources of variation in causal forces. However, in this case, the actual causal variables of interest are not randomly assigned. Rather, another variable, or set of variables, that is related to the causal variable of interest but *not* directly to the outcome of interest, is randomly assigned. It is common in such research designs to use factors like weather or other natural events. For example, Yusaku Horiuchi and Jun Saito (2009) revisit the question of whether voter turnout affects election and policy outcomes. A typical observational study would suffer from confounding because of omitted variable bias and endogeneity bias due to the repeated interactions between politicians and voters. Rainfall is known to suppress voter turnout but it is obviously unaffected by policy outcomes. Rainfall thus functions as an instrument for turnout. Using a large, municipality-level data set from Japan, Horiuchi and Saito show that the effect of turnout on intergovernmental fiscal transfers is large and statistically significant.

Although in each of these examples, the researcher has not been able to directly manipulate assignment to treatment and control groups, because the assignment process was not influenced by the characteristics of the subjects in question, we can be quite confident that any variation in potentially important additional factors average out between the two groups. Thus, the observed differences in outcome are due to the effect of the treatment.

DESIGNING COMPARATIVE RESEARCH

Like field experiments, natural experiments draw causal inferences by estimating the average treatment effect across a large number of units of analysis (whether individuals, families, districts, nations, or something else). They thus have a natural affinity with quantitative approaches. Where the experimental design is particularly clean, the statistical analysis might not be much more complicated than a simple difference-of-means test between treatment and control groups. While the counterfactual approach to causality works especially well with quantitative studies, it also has application in qualitative research. In fact, the principles of the design-based revolution suggest that researchers could instead look to identify cases in which causal forces of interest are exogenously assigned.

In fact, there are innumerable historical shocks and policy interventions that can be studied in this way from a qualitative approach. Natural disasters, commodity price shocks, and mass displacements of citizens in neighbouring countries are examples of exogenous shocks that can be used to study the effects of causes in qualitative research. In my own research, for instance, I have studied the impact of an institutional change in centre-periphery relations in India, precipitated by the death of Prime Minister Jawaharlal Nehru (Kenny 2013). Based on an extensive reading of the primary and secondary source material, I argue that Nehru's death acted like an exogenous shock, shifting the power balance away from the Union Government and towards the state governments. Similarly, in another ongoing study, I examine the effect of an Indonesian Supreme

Court decision to open party lists on the power of national parties over their subnational branches.

Such research might entail comparing across units of analysis. For instance, the sudden discovery of oil in one region of a country versus its non-discovery in adjacent regions would allow researchers to explore the effects of natural resources on the local economy and society in a way not possible with simple cross-case comparative research. Inter-temporal comparisons can also play an important role in causal inference. The exogeneity of the treatment is central to causal inference. For instance, economists have been investigating the effects of the 2011 earthquake on the Japanese economy using forecasting methods, but this work could also be done from a qualitative perspective.

This kind of qualitative counterfactual analysis should not be seen as the lesser cousin of quantitative counterfactual analysis. As critics of the experimental method argue, simply establishing a correlation between a treatment and outcome variable should not be the end of the investigation. We need to know how and why such correlations might exist which demands more detailed probing of the causal mechanisms at work. Qualitative research is especially suited to this kind of investigation, whether in the form of in-depth comparative ethnographic research or detailed archival research.

CONCLUSION: THE PROMISE AND LIMITS OF THE DESIGN-BASED REVOLUTION

It would be rash to completely dismiss all research not based on an experimental or quasi-experimental research design. We can learn a lot from observational study. Indeed, experiments are often only suggested by careful attention to causal processes in the real world. However, the design-based revolution cautions all scholars to be much more attentive to the issues of confounding. A well-designed study does far more to mitigate (though not eliminate) the problem of confounding in quantitative research than any number of modelling techniques. Case selection in qualitative research should also be influenced by this discovery. Exogenous shocks can play a useful role in identification of causal factors in qualitative as well as quantitative research. The differential impact of a policy intervention, an external political event, or a natural disaster on otherwise similar political units can similarly inform causal reasoning in qualitative studies. It suggests a slightly different logic of case selection than one based on the method of difference alone.

The design-based revolution thus promises to continue to improve causal inference across the social sciences, but it is not without its potential drawbacks. There is a risk that researchers will tend to favour questions for which natural experiments exist or topics in which field experiments can be carried out. Many problems central to the political world could be ignored if design was to become the only criterion for selecting a subject of study. Much of what happens in the social world is complex. By this I do not mean to say that it is complicated. That is a different matter. Complexity refers to the fact that what we call cause and effect are often not so neatly separable. In the real world, policy interventions are filtered through a maze of institutions, belief systems, and private interests that make their effects difficult to predict. Critically, under conditions of complexity, the totality of an outcome is not simply a result of the sum of its parts. Events, conditions, and processes interact. Thus, as in the disciplines of ecology and climatology, complex systems can only be partially studied through experimentation in which single elements of a system are manipulated. In many cases, whole systems have to study together, often relying on the use of observational data. Observational and experimental studies should be seen as complementary in developing an understanding of cause and effect in the social and political world.

Note

1.   For more on selection bias, see the chapter in this volume by Charles Miller.

6

COUNT ME IN: QUANTITATIVE RESEARCH IN ASIA-PACIFIC AFFAIRS

Charles Miller

INTRODUCTION

Statistical research methods are already very big in many of the social sciences. For decades, it has been well-nigh impossible to get an academic appointment in economics without a thorough grounding in quantitative research. The same is increasingly becoming true in political science (at least in the United States), psychology and to a lesser degree sociology. Even in the humanities, the quants are making inroads — economic history, for instance, increasingly resembles economics more than it does other subfields of history, and some have even sought to apply quantitative analytic tools to the analysis of literature. Nor is this phenomenon confined to the ivory tower. With the exponential growth of marketing opportunities represented by new data-rich companies such as Facebook, Twitter, Linkedin, and Amazon, "data scientist" is, according to the Harvard Business Review, the "sexiest job of the 21st century" (Davenport and Patil 2012). Similarly, the mathematical requirements of financial engineering are becoming so intense that Wall Street, the City of London, and other finance houses are raiding not only economics but also mathematics and physics PhD programmes in order to find analysts with the requisite skills (Lewis 2015).

Statistical and other quantitative methods are powerful tools in the hands of researchers, policymakers, and the public, when used correctly. The first part of this chapter will outline why researchers use quantitative methods in the social sciences. Human brains, even expert human brains, can be horribly wrong in extrapolating general trends from small numbers of events. Where there are multiple cases at hand of a phenomenon in which we are interested, statistics therefore allows us to see the general trend better than anything else. But quantitative methods can be misused. When they are misused, this can be dangerous because a conclusion couched in terms of numbers and endowed with the prestige of science often commands more confidence than it warrants. Costly errors can result, as the 2008 Global Financial Crisis shows us. Good quantitative researchers are aware of such pitfalls, however, and make strenuous efforts to avoid them. In the second part of this chapter, therefore, I will outline some cautions about the application of quantitative research to the social sciences.

First, I will discuss the relationship between quantitative research on the one hand, and culture, ideas, and history on the other. Culture, ideas, and history are undoubtedly harder to measure quantitatively than material factors such as gross domestic product (GDP), population, or military spending, but there is nothing inherent in quantitative research to say that they do not matter. In fact, some of the most interesting recent research in quantitative social science has centred on using creative means to measure such "ideational" variables and found them to matter a great deal. Second, I will discuss the relationship between quantitative methods, multiple causality, and complexity. Any one historical event is bound to be the result of numerous factors — some of which are systematic in the sense that they are at play across many cases, others of which are specific to one particular time and place (often called "stochastic"). A class of events — such as wars, or *coups d'état* — can also have multiple causes. Quantitative research is agnostic as to the relative importance of systematic and stochastic factors in explaining the behaviour we are interested in; that is for the data to tell us, not for us to assume. Thirdly, I discuss the important relationship between quantitative research and policymaking — that is, how can policymakers make the best use of quantitative methods? Finally, I outline some of the areas in which scholars from quantitative and non-quantitative research traditions can work together for mutual benefit.

WHY QUANT?

Learning quantitative research takes time. Understanding statistics deeply, for instance, requires a knowledge of calculus, linear algebra, and probability theory in addition to some skills in computer programing. The cost of this, of course, is that the time spent on this training is time that we could have spent learning languages, reading history, and doing fieldwork. Some scholars can do all of these things, but the fact remains that time is one thing you cannot make more of and an hour spent on instrumental variables is an hour not spent on Indonesia. This time must be justified. Why do some scholars spend their time using STATA (a statistical modelling programme) in a dingy computer room rather than getting their hands dirty in Sumatra?

One of my former professors at graduate school put it to us quite simply — "because you can't trust your brain". In studying the social and political world, we are generally in the position of trying to make inferences about the world around us based on limited information. We want to make general statements about large numbers of units even though it is simply impossible to study every single one of these units (because, again, of that pesky "time being the one thing we're not able to make more of"). In my own research, for instance, I want to find out what people in the Asia-Pacific region think of China, what makes Australians more or less likely to support the alliance with the United States, and whether cultural sensitivity training in the Australian Defence Force (ADF) lowers prejudice against minorities, especially the Muslims amongst whom the ADF is often deployed. I cannot contact every single Australian soldier or voter or Japanese, Korean, or Thai citizen, so instead I have to take a sample.

Now, I could talk to a small number of people in great detail about the issues I am interested in studying. Even assuming, however, that these individuals are indeed a "representative sample" of the population I am interested in studying, the very fact that I am only talking to a few of them is deeply problematic. Here is why.

Let me ask you a question — which of these is most likely to occur?

a) You toss a fair coin ten times and get eight or more heads.
b) You toss a fair coin one hundred times and get eighty or more heads.
c) You toss a fair coin one thousand times and get eight hundred or more heads.

If your answer is that they are all equally likely to occur then you are like the majority of the population as a whole, but you are dead wrong. By far, the likeliest of the three situations is (a). A fair coin has a 50–50 chance of coming up heads. So for 80 per cent or more of coin tosses to come up heads is unusual and, in a sense, "unrepresentative". Unrepresentative outcomes are, moreover, far more likely to occur in small samples (like eight or more heads in ten coin tosses) than in large ones (like eight hundred or more heads in one thousand coin tosses). Yet because we are "intuitively poor statisticians" — as Nobel Prize Winner Daniel Kahneman (2011) noted — we tend to think that the impressions we get from small samples will hold for the general population, when in fact it is quite likely that they will not. This is what my professor meant by "you can't trust your brain". It is why when we are looking to make inferences about phenomena which concern large numbers of units — whether those units are countries or individual voters, citizens or businesses within countries — large data sets give us better answers than small data sets do (all other things being equal). Analysing large data sets, in turn, requires some knowledge of statistics.

In order to move out of the abstract world of probability theory and into the world of politics, let me give two examples to make this point more concretely. In the last Asian Barometer survey, 75 per cent of Japanese respondents said that China has either a bad, or a very bad, influence on Japan. The Asian Barometer survey is a probability sample of over 1,000 Japanese citizens, so we can be pretty sure that a sizeable majority of Japanese citizens hold a negative view of China. If, however, I were to go to Japan and base my assessment of Japanese views of China on a small sample of individuals with whom I came into contact with, I might come to some quite erroneous conclusions. Suppose I speak to twenty Japanese citizens about what they think of China. As in the coin toss example, it is quite possible that (through pure random chance) a majority of these twenty people hold a favourable view of China, even though a majority of the Japanese population (which I want to study as a whole) does not. I will then return to Canberra confidently and incorrectly asserting that the Japanese think China is just great. Of course, this is leaving to one side the possible problem that the Japanese people who are willing to speak to me, a foreigner, about China may be unusually open-minded and cosmopolitan in outlook, and therefore far more likely than average to hold positive views about China. Even if this problem of selection bias does not exist, relying on a small sample to make generalizations about a large population is going to cause problems.

Let us look at a second example. In Figure 6.1, I produce a scatterplot of states' democracy scores (from Polity IV) against their (log) gross national income in purchasing power parity terms (from the Quality of Governance Institute at the University of Stockholm) in the year 2000, with a regression line superimposed. The regression line represents the relationship between wealth and democracy estimated from the data in the plot.

The relationship, overall, is positive — richer countries also tend to be more democratic. But the key word is "tend", as not every country fits this pattern. Some countries — like China and Singapore — are much less democratic than one would expect, based on their wealth. Others — like Bangladesh or Mongolia — are much more democratic than they "should" be, given their level of economic development. If one were to study the relationship between wealth and democracy just by looking at any one of these countries, one would reach the (erroneous) conclusion that wealth and democracy are negatively correlated. Indeed, one could even study a small number of countries and quite easily (and unluckily) select an atypical few. For instance, if one were to investigate the relationship between wealth and democracy by comparing the experiences of Bangladesh, Mongolia, India, Singapore, China, and Malaysia, you would get a relationship as shown in Figure 6.2.

The relationship between wealth and democracy now appears to be the opposite of what it actually is. By looking only at a small sample of the overall population, the analyst would have concluded that the wealthier a country, the less likely it is to be democratic.

How, then, does one know what is a sufficiently large sample to allow one to conclude that the observed pattern is typical of the population? Short of sampling the entire population, one can never be certain. However, probability theory does allow us to state quite precisely how big a sample we need in order to have a good degree of confidence that we are getting the right answer. Pollster Roy Morgan, for instance, notes that to be 95 per cent confident that the proportion of Australians who will vote for a given party lies 1 per cent either way of the poll's sample mean requires a sample size of only 1,500, assuming the sample is chosen at random.[1] In other words, if the Morgan poll of 1,500 Australians says that 47 per cent intend to vote Labor, there is a 95 per cent chance that between 46 and 48 per cent of *all* Australians really do intend to vote Labor.

FIGURE 6.1

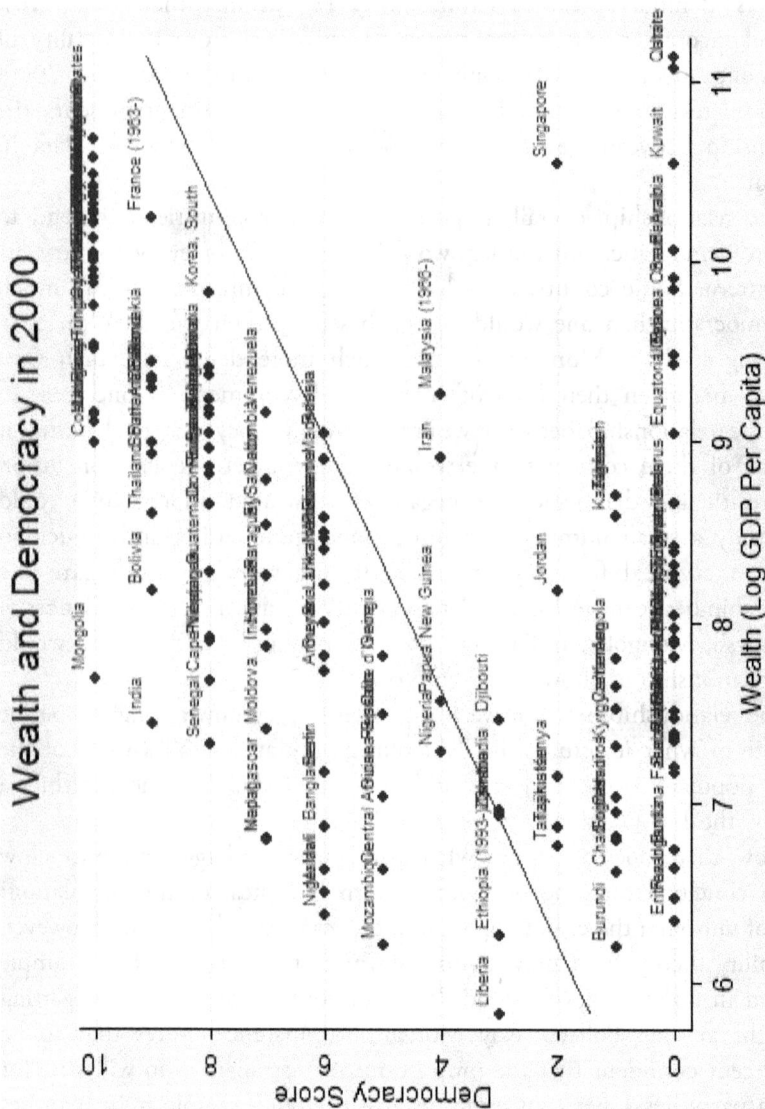

Wealth and Democracy in 2000

Source. Teorell, Jan, Stefan Dahlberg, Sören Holmberg, Bo Rothstein, Anna Khomenko and Richard Svensson. "The Quality of Government Standard Dataset", version January 2016. University of Gothenburg: The Quality of Government Institute. <http://www.qog.pol.gu.se>. Doi:10.18157/QoGStdJan16.

FIGURE 6.2

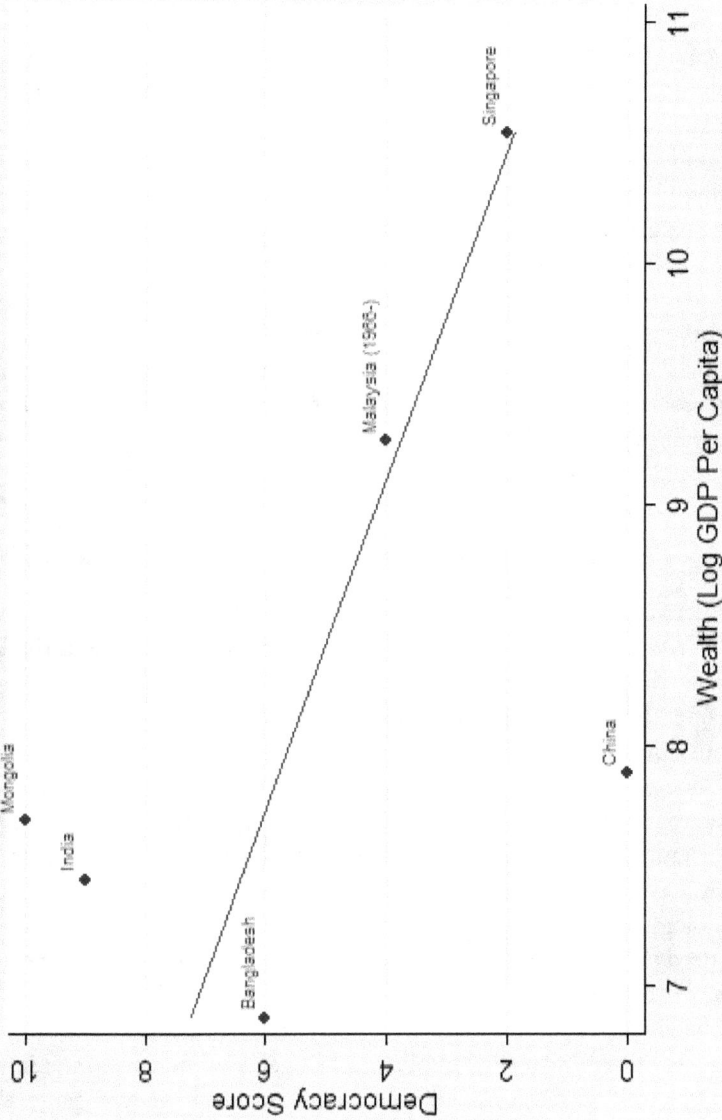

Wealth and Democracy in 2000

Source: Teorell, Jan, Stefan Dahlberg, Sören Holmberg, Bo Rothstein, Anna Khomenko and Richard Svensson. "The Quality of Government Standard Dataset", version January 2016. University of Gothenburg: The Quality of Government Institute. <http://www.qog.pol.gu.se>. Doi:10.18157/QoGStdJan16.

Of course, it is *possible* that the true proportion (that is, the proportion of all Australians, not just those who were surveyed) who intend to vote Labor is actually 39 per cent, or 56 per cent, or in fact anything between 0 and 100 per cent. It is just very unlikely that it is currently outside that narrow 46–48 per cent band (specifically, there is a less than 5 per cent chance that it is). That is why many complaints about "the polls" are misplaced. If the actual election result is outside of the polls' margin of error once, that does not really tell us very much about whether the polls are good or not. By design, the margin of error of five polls out of one hundred will not contain the true level of support in the population. Only if we see a repeated pattern of errors can we conclude that there really is a problem with "the polls".

Quantitative research exists to give us an eagle's eye view of social phenomena. It is designed to give us a general picture of some phenomenon in which we are interested, provided there have been sufficient instances of the phenomenon at hand. As with most powerful tools, though, it can go wrong. In the second section of this chapter, I list a number of common misconceptions and pitfalls that surround quantitative research.

CULTURE, IDEAS, NORMS — AND NUMBERS

The recently deceased John Nash is one of the figures most associated with the "*Homo economicus*" assumption. Nash was one of the early leading lights in the development of game theory (Nasar 1998). Beginners' classes in game theory will usually teach students to solve games such as the famous "prisoner's dilemma" by assuming the individuals who are playing the game are perfectly rational and care only about their own well-being, rather than that of others. A common critique of game theory, voiced for instance by Lawrence Freedman (1998) or the documentary maker Adam Curtis (2007), is that this is not a realistic account of human psychology. Human beings, in fact, care about other people and have wants and needs that are shaped by history, culture, and normative expectations. Game theory has little value, in this view, because it imposes an overly narrow vision of human nature which, some speculate, may have been related to Nash's own well-publicized struggles with schizophrenia (Curtis 2007). A self-deprecating joke favoured by some of my game theorist friends goes something like this. An engineer, a doctor, and a game theorist are stranded on a desert island. The doctor worries that if they do not build a shelter soon, they may contract hypothermia and die. The engineer gets together scraps of wood to build something and finds some nails washed up on the beach to put them together with. To their mutual frustration, however, the doctor and engineer note that they do not have a hammer to hit the nails with. "I have a solution," the game theorist says — "assume a hammer".

There are a number of problems with this line of critique, however. First, it is inaccurate even as a description of modern day game theory. Game theorists today do not believe or assume that human beings are perfectly rational or motivated only by money. The common thread running through game theory is not the idea that human beings are intrinsically materialistic, but rather the idea that we are intrinsically *strategic*, that we anticipate others' likely reactions when formulating our own plans and that others do likewise (Gintis 2009). Modern game theorists are agnostic about what people want or why they want it (known as the principle of *"de gustibus non est disputandum"* which means "in matters of taste, there can be no disputes") (Brennan and Tullock 1983). They merely point out that because our decisions and those of others are interdependent, you cannot simply infer that a particular social outcome came about just because people wanted it to. Game theory is then a mathematical tool for mapping individual preferences onto social outcomes by taking into account the fact that we base our decisions on what we think other people will do (when, of course, they are basing their decisions on what they think we will do). The key insight of game theory is that, because of this interdependence, we can arrive at social and political outcomes that none of the actors might have preferred if they had not had to take into account the actions of others.

Moreover, game theory is just one type of quantitative research method in the social sciences. It is quite distinct from statistical modelling, even though both methods employ mathematics as a tool for understanding the social and political world. Game theory creates ideal-typical models of the real world from which it attempts to deduce results. Statistical modelling draws conclusions inductively from analysis of empirical data. Many game theorists therefore shun statistical modelling and vice versa (Signorino 2002).

Quantitative researchers who primarily employ statistics rather than game theory as their mode of enquiry are, if anything, even less likely to hew to a view of human beings as perfectly rational, materialistic *Homines oeconomici*. Opinion poll and survey research, for instance, includes extensive questions on values and beliefs. For instance, the Asian Barometer includes questions such as "you have to choose economic development or democracy, which do you think is more important?" and "do you agree that political leaders are like the head of a family? Should we follow their decisions?" If statistical researchers did not believe values to be important, there would be no need to collect data on questions about them.

The equation of quantitative research with *Homo economicus* assumptions may also stem from the fact that material variables (e.g. GDP, military capabilities, resource exports, and so on) are more easily measurable and quantifiable than ideas, culture, history, or norms. There is an old joke about an economist who is out with a friend and loses his wallet. He immediately starts to look underneath a lamplight. "But," says his friend, "you didn't lose it underneath the lamp". "I know," says the economist, "but that's where the light is." The joke, of course, is that just because something is hard to observe does not mean that it is not important. For many years, this was a valid critique of quantitative social science in general.

But the incentives of the academy are changing. Precisely because material variables are easy to measure, they have been a part of the best known data sets for a long time (e.g. the Correlates of War project) (Sarkees and Wayman 2010). However, because they have been around for a long time, all or most of the good research which could have been done with them, already has been done. Quantitative scholars, if they want to earn their spurs in the modern academic job market, have to stand out and one of the ways to stand out is to find ways to measure things previously thought unmeasurable — especially culture, history, norms, and ideas. Among the more striking examples of this genre of quantitative research include:

1) United Nations diplomats from countries with a strong rule of law are more likely to pay local parking fines in New York even though they have diplomatic immunity and so do not have to (suggesting that the rule of law is, at least in part, determined by internalized cultural values) (Fisman and Miguel 2006).
2) African child soldiers who are randomly assigned to receive cognitive behavioural therapy to reassess their own self-image are less likely to return to fighting than those who receive straight cash payments (Blattman, Jamison, and Sheridan 2015).
3) Areas of Germany with large numbers of anti-Semitic pogroms in the Middle Ages recorded a higher Nazi vote share in the 1930s and are more likely to harbour anti-Semitic attitudes even today (Voigtlander and Voth 2011).

4) East Germans are systematically more likely to cheat others than West Germans, suggesting that the Communist political and economic system fundamentally changed the way in which individuals conceived of interpersonal relations (Ariely et al. 2015).

5) American Southerners have a different physiological response to insult than Northerners, providing evidence for the existence of a Southern "culture of honour" (Cohen et al. 1996).

6) Individuals coming from areas of Eastern Europe today which were once part of the Habsburg Empire, exhibit systematically higher trust in clean government than individuals from the same states of the same countries today which were under Russian rule, suggesting that history can continue to play a role in individuals' political attitudes for generations (Becker et al. 2011).

7) Deaths of Afghan civilians at the hands of NATO (North Atlantic Treaty Organization) increase support for the Taliban in Afghanistan, but deaths of Afghan civilians at the hands of the Taliban do not increase support for NATO, suggesting that civilian populations respond differently to violence against civilians when they share an identity with the perpetrators than when they do not (Lyall, Blair, and Imai 2013).

In short, quantitative research does not rely on any assumptions about what motivates human beings. Rather than relying on an overly materialistic view of human nature, quantitative social scientists, in recent years, have produced a slew of interesting studies demonstrating convincingly that culture, norms, ideas, and history matter.

QUANTITATIVE RESEARCH, MULTIPLE CAUSATION, AND COMPLEXITY

Many eighteenth-century physicists and mathematicians believed that perfect prediction of all motion in the universe was possible, in principle, if all of the initial conditions were known. However, by the end of the nineteenth century, this view of the universe had come to be abandoned in the natural sciences (Mitchell 2009). Instead, natural scientists now talk about probabilities and relative risks. Quantitative social science is similarly probabilistic rather than deterministic. A quantitative social scientist who claims that "wealth causes democracy"[2] is not saying that all wealthy countries are democracies or that if you become wealthy, then you will definitely become a democracy. Instead, they simply mean that wealthy countries are more likely to be democracies than poor countries, and they acknowledge that there can be exceptions to this rule, as we saw in Figure 6.2. But these exceptions do not invalidate the rule itself, any more than the existence of a healthy ninety-year-old man who has smoked and drunk alcohol his entire life invalidates the proposition that drinking and smoking are, in general, bad for you.

Similarly, quantitative social scientists do not tell the government that "if you do X, you will get Y". This is overly simplistic. When a quantitative social scientist gives policy advice, what they are saying is "if you do X, you will be more likely to get Y, *ceteris paribus*". This is a crucial nuance. The key phrase "*ceteris paribus*" — or "all other things being equal" — is a caveat always attached to quantitative social science findings. This caveat invites the obvious rejoinder — "well, when are all other things equal?" The answer to this is, of course, rarely if ever, but that is not the point. *Ceteris paribus* does not mean that we believe all other things to be equal in any one particular case; nor does it mean that the finding is only valid in the event that "all other things are equal". Another medical analogy should help to clarify what "*ceteris paribus*" means. We know that — *ceteris paribus* — smoking increases your risk of heart disease. Now, it could be that if you smoke, you might manage to avoid a heart attack if you have the right genes, exercise, and eat well. It is just that you will be even less likely to have a heart attack if you have all of these things and quit smoking, too. Conversely, if you do not smoke, you might end up clutching your chest if you have the wrong genes, live on a diet of fried chicken and Coke, and never leave the sofa. It is just that you will be at even more risk of a heart attack if you have all of these risk factors and also smoke. Therefore, *ceteris paribus* just means "regardless of the values of the other variables which might have an important effect on Y, you are more likely to get Y if you do X than if you do not". From this discussion, it should be clear that quantitative social science is not monocausal — we recognize that events have multiple causes. A quantitative researcher may focus on the impact of one particular variable, but this does not mean to say that this is the only variable which he or she thinks matters for the outcome in question. If a quantitative social scientist claims that wealth causes democracy, for instance, this does not mean that other things do not also cause democracy. Resource endowments, religious heritage, and human capital could all have effects on whether a state is a democracy quite independently, without invalidating the claim that wealth causes democracy. Moreover, it is quite possible that in any one given case, a state could have everything that the literature suggests should lead it to transition to democracy — wealth, education, modern social values, or something else — and still remain autocratic for some random, stochastic reason. For example, a promising pro-democracy campaigner is hit by an unanticipated scandal, or the price of the country's main export on global markets suddenly soars, giving the regime the wherewithal to buy off discontent — any number of things could happen. A good quantitative researcher has to be prepared for the fact that something outside of the systematic variables in the model can cause things to pan out differently than he or she had expected.

A new and fascinating area of study which bridges the natural and the social sciences looks at the types of scenarios I have outlined in the preceding paragraph. Complex systems analysis, or "complexity science" examines systems in which small changes to initial conditions can have outsized effects further down the line (Mitchell 2009). A street trader in Tunisia sets himself on fire, triggering the Arab Spring, which leads in turn to civil conflicts in many states, into which vacuum Daesh/Islamic State steps. The United States is drawn in, once more dragging its attention back to the Middle East and complicating any attempt to "rebalance" to the Asia-Pacific. This, in turn, affects the downstream calculations of states such as the Philippines or Japan whose connection to Tunisian street traders might be tangential. Any social phenomena which exhibit "tipping points" are likely to exhibit complex systems effects (Schelling 1978). For instance, once a certain critical mass of people have joined a riot, protest, revolution, or coup, the number of people who join subsequently may rise much more quickly than it did before the tipping point, resulting in a non-linear relationship.

Complex systems are a fact of political, social, and economic life. The technique of agent-based modelling is a powerful tool which helps us to think through the implications of complex systems (Miller and Page 2007). Statistical models exist which can capture most, if not all, types of non-linear relationships among variables (Cedermann, Warren, and Sornette 2011). The existence of a non-linear relationship between two variables may make a particular type of statistical model inappropriate, but it does not make statistical methods per se inappropriate.

QUANTITATIVE RESEARCH AND POLICY ADVICE

Policymakers in the fields of international affairs and defence tend to be trained in qualitative disciplines, especially history and languages. Partly as a consequence of this, they are less likely to engage with quantitative scholarship than with other types of social science scholarship (Avey and Desch 2014). Even in international politics, however, the gap between the policy world and quantitative scholarship is being broken down. Randomized controlled trials (RCTs), which are becoming increasingly common in domestic policy, are also becoming routine in development policy and even in certain conflict situations (Lyall, Blair, and Imai 2013). The beauty of RCTs, as Paul Kenny (this volume) notes in his chapter, is that the basic logic behind them does not involve much in the way of complicated mathematics. Moreover, the statistical tools which one needs to analyse a properly designed experiment are, in fact, among the simplest in the statistician's toolbox.

Parallel, though separate to this development, is the growth of what is variously termed "predictive analytics", "big data", or "artificial intelligence". Big data is often erroneously used as a synonym for any kind of statistical analysis. However, big data refers to data sets consisting of millions or more observations along potentially thousands of dimensions, not a few thousand observations along one hundred dimensions, as in the Asian Barometer or the Australian Election Study. The rise of "big data" has been enabled by three trends — the availability in digital format of increasing amounts of information, the growth of computer power, and the development of sophisticated methods for making sense of this raw information.

The growth of social media and the Internet is simply one of the new sources of information available. There is also an increasing effort on the part of researchers around the world to collect all kinds of data and to make it available in open source format. For instance, there are a number of projects — funded both by the U.S. Government and by private companies such as Google and Lockheed Martin[3] — designed to pinpoint and classify all significant newsworthy events from around the world for the last few decades, intended eventually to span back to the beginning of the nineteenth century. The power of modern computers makes analysis of this data feasible in a way that would not have been the case only a few decades ago. If a researcher wants the dates and latitude/longitude coordinates of all reported attacks on Myanmar's Rohingya minority in 2014, or all incidents of verbal jousting between China and Japan in 2010, they are just a few clicks of the mouse away.

At the same time, techniques such as machine learning (Lantz 2013) and Bayesian Model Averaging (Montgomery and Nyhan 2010) make it possible to extract actionable intelligence from this data. Researchers using this technique will focus on a type of event which we might be interested in predicting — say, for instance, military coups. These researchers will create algorithms (lines of computer code) which systematically explore as many different variables as possible that might be a leading indicator of the event of interest. They will then divide the "historical data" into discrete time periods and ask how well each algorithm would have fared in predicting events that actually did happen in the past (cross-validation). The algorithms which do best are then applied to forecasting the future. Their performance is then evaluated again and adjusted accordingly to improve their future accuracy. This represents an almost Darwinian process in which the algorithms that most effectively make sense of the data survive and thrive, and those which do not are abandoned, leading to progressively more accurate classifications and forecasts.[4] The results so far are impressive, at least for short-term predictions. The analysis of personal "metadata" by intelligence agencies, such as the U.S. National Security Agency (made famous by the Edward Snowden case), tries to predict involvement in terrorism using similar methods, although obviously the success or failure of this approach is far harder to gauge (besides the obvious ethical implications it raises with respect to civil liberties). In all, the increasing popularity of predictive analytics and the amount of money that the U.S. Government is prepared to spend on it suggests that there is no inherent conflict between policy relevance and quantitative research, where policymakers can see a clear benefit.

Yet there is a danger of hubris in this, too. Excessive confidence in one's own conclusions is a dangerous trait in a policymaker. Former U.S. Secretary of Defense Robert McNamara, for instance, has been seen by many historians as bearing more than his fair share of the blame for the disaster in Vietnam. Fortified by a range of quantitative data on all manner of issues, but especially kill ratios, McNamara is alleged to have been immune to the type of self-doubt which might have caused him to change course and potentially save lives (McMaster 1997). McNamara is, moreover, by no means the only example of the phenomenon. Some analysts have, for instance, pointed to excessive confidence in quantitative risk models as a key factor behind the global financial crisis (Taleb 2007; Silver 2013). Because bankers and politicians trusted the models too much, they took too many risks and loaded both companies and governments with excessive debt. Proponents of this point of view can even point to evidence from social psychology by Professor Kimmo Eriksson which suggests that putting a mathematical equation — even a nonsensical one — into a journal article leads individuals to rate it more highly (Eriksson 2012). Do numbers, then, promote excessive certainty?

The risk is present, but ironically, the best antidote to excessively confident policy advice stemming from quantitative research is a good foundation in quantitative research! In Eriksson's (2012) paper, the experimental subjects who were least likely to be fooled by the nonsense equations were those who themselves came from quantitative disciplines. Similarly, one of the first individuals to note the failure of America's strategy in Vietnam was Stanford's quantitative researcher Jeremy Millstein. His analysis of the performance of the Vietnamese currency, Vietcong attacks, and President Lyndon Johnson's approval rating made it clear that the U.S. strategy was failing many years before it became apparent to policymakers (Milstein 1974).

Hubris about our ability to know the effects of our policies on society is a widespread phenomenon, not limited to quantitative researchers. Guarding against such hubris does not mean uncritically accepting (or rejecting) any research simply because it contains numbers. Rather, it has to consist in judging research on a case-by-case basis. In quantitative research, this means we especially need to look out for the following issues:

1) Is the correlation, which the researcher has identified, genuinely causal (Kenny, this volume)? Is there something else which might be causing both the independent and the dependent variable, leading to a spurious correlation? How was the sample that we are studying selected? Could the way in which the sample was selected have affected the outcome you found (selection bias, as we discussed above)?

2) Is the functional form of your model correct given the nature of the data? This question is rather technical and probably the most specific to quantitative research. One of the major problems with the risk models used by economists was that they relied on functional forms which assumed very large losses to be much less likely than they really were.

3) Are we measuring the correct outcome? Or are we just measuring what is convenient to measure (like McNamara's kill ratios)? Do the measures you are using in your model match up well with the concepts you are testing? If you are running a survey, are your respondents being truthful, or do they have incentives to mislead you? If so, what is your strategy for dealing with it?

4) How strong is the effect which has been identified? How robust is it? Did you just pick the one model that gave you the result you wanted out of the many other models you could potentially have chosen (the technical term for this is "p-hacking")?
5) How good are the predictions which are based on your model?
6) Even if the predictions on which your model is based are good, what are the costs of being wrong? What can we do to hedge against the possibility that it is wrong? If there is one thing the global financial crisis should have taught us, it is that we need to have a good back up plan for very unlikely but hugely costly contingencies. In my field of international politics, that description fits large-scale, interstate war very well.
7) If we used your findings as the basis for policy advice, how long would it be before people would start adapting their behaviour to it and so defeat the point of the recommendation?

This list is by no means exhaustive, nor should it be limited to quantitative research methods.

BENEFITTING FROM COLLABORATION

Quantitative methods can give us unique insights into the political and social world of Asia and the Pacific. Moreover, many of the critiques levelled at such methods per se are unfounded. However, this most certainly does not mean that quantitative scholars can ignore the work of area specialists and historically minded scholars. In fact, collaboration is essential. For one thing, many of the most important data sets which quantitative social scientists use would be impossible without context-specific knowledge. The Polity data set, for instance, which is a staple of cross-national quantitative research, relies on a survey of country experts to classify political systems along a number of dimensions. For instance, what meaningful constraints exist on executive power? Are there legal restrictions on participation in politics? If so, on what grounds might one be excluded from the system? The Correlates of War data set relies on the judgements of historians as to the participants, initiators, winners, and losers of the wars contained within it. Similarly, many analyses of text as data require an initial stage in which human area specialists attempt to use their judgement to sort chunks of text according to a set of classifications (i.e. is this Tweet or Facebook post "liberal" or "conservative" ideologically?).

Computer algorithms are then "trained" to replicate the performance of human coders in a small sample before being let loose on a larger sample of text. The only reason why computers are used for the remaining amount of text at all is because they are cheaper and faster than using humans (Lantz 2013). But for the whole process to get started, we need to have human coders with area specific expertise.

Moreover, there are a large number of issues in international politics in which there are very few past observations to study and far fewer "natural experiments" which can allow us to infer causal relationships with a great degree of confidence. But this does not mean that these issues are unimportant. In fact, these are some of the most important issues in international politics today. For instance, only eleven states have ever acquired nuclear weapons, only one has ever used them, only one has ever given them up, and no one has ever retaliated against a nuclear strike with a nuclear strike of its own. This makes quantitative analysis of the causes and consequences of nuclear weapons rather tricky!

Finally, the natural experiments which, as Paul Kenny (this volume) points out in his chapter, are so valuable in modern quantitative research, also arise from an intimate familiarity with specific times and places. In order to correctly analyse a natural experiment, and even more especially to find one in the first place, statistical training by itself is not enough. For instance, the idea for one of the most celebrated natural experiments in political science in recent years — Jason Lyall's analysis of the effects of Russian bombardment of Chechen civilians on insurgent violence in the war — resulted from Lyall's extensive knowledge of the Russian language, Russian/Soviet military tactics, and extensive in-country fieldwork. Young scholars looking to replicate his work in an Asia-Pacific context need to combine a strong understanding of causality and statistics on the one hand, with intensive area specific knowledge on the other. If these attributes are not combined in one person, as will often be the case, then scholars with expertise in the one area should seek out co-authors in the other.

If quants, area specialists, and historians can therefore work together, based on a genuine understanding of each other's methods and where their respective strengths are complementary, we can produce more research that is casually valid and rigorous, but that is also sensitive to context and appropriately humble in its conclusions. If we can do this, then we can help, bit by bit, to make our region and the world a better place.

Notes

1. See <http://www.roymorgan.com/findings/6292-morgan-poll-federal-voting-intention-june-15-2015-201506150528>.
2. Leaving aside, for one moment, the question of whether the correlation between wealth and democracy is really causal. For more on causality, see Paul Kenny's chapter in this volume.
3. See <http://www.lockheedmartin.com.au/us/products/W-ICEWS/iData.html> and <http://www.gdeltproject.org/>.
4. Indeed, a subset of AI (artificial intelligence) research, known as "genetic algorithms", consciously sets out to mimic the process of natural selection, "breeding" algorithms as though they were natural life forms.

SECTION III
Shaping a Region

7

HISTORY, CONFLICT, AND CONTEXTS: REMEMBERING WORLD WAR II IN ASIA

Joan Beaumont[1]

I have dreamed in my life, dreams that have stayed with me ever after, and changed my ideas; they have gone through and through me, like wine through water, and altered the colour of my mind.

—Emily Brontë (1818–48)

As in Emily Brontë's dreams, war has flowed through Asia in the past century like wine through water. Be they interstate conflicts, inter-communal violence, social revolutions, or struggles for sovereignty, wars have transformed political structures, changed territorial boundaries, and reshaped the regional order. In particular, World War II, which strides the twentieth century like some malignant colossus, had a profound impact on the region. Estimates of its human cost vary, but it probably caused at least twenty-three million deaths in the Asia-Pacific (Wikipedia 2015*a*).[2] Politically, it shattered the hold of the European powers on their colonial subjects, triggered the wave of post-war decolonization, and established the bipolar balance which dominated international and regional relations for almost fifty years.

In a less tangible but equally important sense, World War II and other violent conflicts transformed the cultural imaginations of the peoples and societies of the region. Not only did the defeat of the European powers in 1941–42 make a world beyond imperialism imaginable, but in recent decades, the memories of past wars have come to play a central role in the domestic politics and interstate relations of the region. Asia is not alone in this. The memory "boom" which has swept the globe since the 1970s or 1980s has seen a turn to the past in many countries. In both established and emerging states, war memory has become "a key element in the symbolic repertoire available to the nation-state for binding its citizens into a collective national identity" (Ashplant, Dawson, and Roper 2000, p. 7). Across the globe also, the politics of war memory have been used by various substate agents to justify their claims to greater recognition or compensation for past grievances and injustices.

MEMORY IN THE ASIAN CONTEXT

The study of the memory of World War II in Asia faces particular challenges. Firstly, this war is commonly depicted by English-language historians as "a binary clash between Japan and the United States and its allies" (Fujitani, White, and Yoneyama 2001, p. 6). This framing shapes the temporal scope of the war: the start date being the 1941 Japanese attack on Pearl Harbour, not the 1937 incident at the Marco Polo Bridge (Lugouqiao), which is often taken to mark the beginning of the Sino–Japanese war. The end date in such a framing, meanwhile, is the Japanese surrender on 15 August 1945, an event which, as Arif Dirlik puts it (2001, p. 301), has "the decisiveness of an end-marker for Japan alone. … For others [China, Korea, Vietnam], wars were beginning before the war had ended".

Moreover, such teleological representations of World War II reduce the peoples of the Asia-Pacific to the background. Military historians ignore "wholesale the people living on the islands over which the armies were 'hopping'" (White and Lindstrom 1989, p. 6), while Asian landscapes are remembered as little more than battlefields for the major powers. However, within the context of the titanic Japanese–American clash, there were many other subregional conflicts: the civil war between Communists and Nationalists in China and the Thai–French border clashes (1940–41) being only two examples. For the populations caught up in these subsystem conflicts, these were the wars that mattered. These were "our", not "their" wars, as the battles between the Japanese, the Americans, and the European imperial powers generally were. Hence, although it can be argued that there were "genuine thematic commonalities in the legacies of war that cohere across the Asia-Pacific region" (Twomey and Koh 2015, p. 6), there was no single "pan-Asian" experience of World War II. Nor was there one "Asian" memory of this war.

A further complication is the dominance in memory studies of European scholarship. Not only have the general models and theories been Western in origin, but the multiple studies of the intersection between memory, history, and politics have drawn largely on Europe and American case studies (Lunn 2007, p. 81). This does not mean that memory making in the countries of the Asian region has been completely neglected. In the last two decades, there has been considerable scholarly analysis of issues such as: the disputes between Japan, China, and Korea about the nature and scale of the 1937 Nanjing massacre (for example, Seaton 2007; Yang 1999, 2001; Yoshida 2006); the representation of World War II in Japanese and other school textbooks (for example, Duus 2011; Nozaki 2008; Seaton 2007; Tohmatsu 2011); and the enforced prostitution of "comfort women" (for example, Hicks 1997; Yoshimi and O'Brien 2000; Min 2003; Sand 1999; Soh 2008). In recent years also, there has been a growing interest in Asian war heritage, the sister of war memory (for example, Beaumont 2009; Henderson 2007; Logan and Reeves 2009). But relative to studies of European memories of World War II, and especially the Holocaust, our understanding of Asian memory formation remains undeveloped. In particular, the academic community has yet to engage strongly with the question of how national and other collective memories shape the conduct of international relations within the Asian region; and whether the practices of what might be called transnational "memorial diplomacy" are different in Asia as opposed to Europe (Bell 2006, pp. 1, 3).

WORLD WAR II MEMORY IN
ASIAN NATIONAL FORMATION

Despite this, it is clear that collective memory performs a similar function within the societies of Asia as it does in the West. Asian peoples clearly embrace group identities arising from "a relatively widely shared understanding of history and its meaning, [and] the construction of a narrative tracing the linkages between past and present, locating self and society in time" (Bell 2006, p. 5). Hence, memory has played a core role in the construction of national identities and nationalisms across the region.

However, as one would expect, the content of these memories varies, not just because of the specific historical experiences, but because of different cultural contexts.

In the case of World War II, as Kevin Blackburn (2010, p. 5) has shown, some Southeast Asian countries have incorporated this conflict into their processes of nation building, while others have "a national amnesia" on the subject. Among the instances of "amnesia" are Indonesia, Vietnam, and Thailand. During the Sukarno period (1949–67), for example, Indonesian official history privileged the narrative of the independence struggle of 1945–49, the conflict that invested Sukarno's role as national leader with enduring legitimacy. Events prior to this were remembered only as a prelude, especially as the Japanese occupation involved some "difficult" memories, such as Sukarno's role in recruiting Javanese workers to work for the Japanese, a practice which resulted in many of them dying of malnutrition and maltreatment.[3] Under the subsequent Suharto regime (1967–98), when the national narrative evolved to incorporate the historic achievements of the Indonesian army and Suharto himself, the struggle for independence continued to be of central importance. As Anthony Reid says, the Japanese wartime occupation was important as a prelude to that event, but "to commemorate its portentous happenings as turning points in their own right would risk diluting the transcendent quality of 1945, and giving the Japanese a share in the glory that belongs to Indonesians themselves in asserting their independence" (Reid 2005, pp. 173–74).

In Vietnam, too, memories of World War II, when the country was subjected to "protection" by the Japanese, have been subordinated to narratives which give pre-eminence to the leadership of the Communist Party in the post-war struggle for independence. The war may have offered Ho Chi Minh, the leader of Viet Minh, the chance to establish a power base, but there was nothing, in the complex political manoeuvrings of 1941–45, to match the later defeat of the colonial power, the French. Since 1954, Dien Bien Phu has been considered "as among the most important public events in Vietnam" (Logan and Binh 2012, p. 53). The subsequent war against the United States and its allies in the 1960s inevitably affirmed this triumphalist narrative of a small nation under Communist leadership proving capable of defeating the greatest military powers of the West.

In Thailand, meanwhile, the amnesia about World War II is more profound. Unlike Singapore, the Philippines, and Myanmar, Thailand does not mark World War II by any national day (Blackburn 2010, p. 28). Rather, when war is remembered in the national political culture, it is war against the historic enemy the Burmese, and iconic events like the fall of the historic capital Ayutthaya in 1767 (Raymond 2015, ch. 2). Such narratives serve to affirm the political consensus built around the three pillars of the Thai political culture: nationalism, Buddhism, and the monarchy. In contrast, the World War II collaboration of the Phibun Songkram government with the Japanese, which involved its declaring war on the Allies in January 1942, was best "forgotten" in the post-war years, when Thailand quickly realigned strategically with the West. Moreover, although Thailand's survivalist diplomacy could be rationalized as a pragmatic accommodation to the realities of the power balances in the Asia-Pacific in 1941–42, it masked an uncomfortable complicity with the Japanese in the building on Thai sovereign territory of the Thai–Burma railway, on which 12,000 Allied prisoners of war and perhaps 100,000 Asian labourers died (Beaumont and Witcomb 2015, pp. 67, 77).

Yet, if Thailand, Vietnam, and Indonesia have marginalized the memory of World War II, Malaysia and Singapore have positioned this conflict at the heart of their national memory formation. In both cases, this is a relatively recent phenomenon, coinciding with the global memory boom. For some fifty years after 1945, the Malayan (from 1963 Malaysian) state engaged in "memory repression" of this conflict (Blackburn and Hack 2012, p. 5). Remembering the Japanese occupation meant conceding some historic role to the Malayan People's Anti-Japanese Army (MPAJA), a largely Chinese force that was associated with the traumatic communal violence of 1945–46 and with the communist-inspired Malayan Emergency. It was the Emergency itself that took centre stage in postcolonial national memory making (Koh 2015, p. 20). Memories of the wartime massacres of the Chinese and the deaths of many Malay Tamils and Indians on the Thai–Burma railway, meanwhile, were consigned to local commemorative practices, if they were remembered at all. In later decades, state policy imperatives, including then Prime Minister Mahathir Mohamad's (1981–2003) "Look East Policy", meant that the traumas of the Japanese occupation continued to be downplayed. The Japanese were even told, in 1994, to "stop apologising for wartime crimes committed about 50 years ago" (Blackburn and Hack 2012, p. 260).

A more complex memory of World War II did begin to evolve in the 1980s, and with this, the war became constructed as the crucible of Malay nationalism. In a considerable feat of ahistorical imagination, those who had collaborated with and those who resisted the Japanese were both represented as exemplars of Malay martial prowess. Yet, for all this, the memory of World War II in Malaysia has been what Blackburn and

Hack (2012, p. 9) have termed "plural commemoration", in that the state narrative continues to privilege mainly Malay memories while tolerating, but not fully incorporating, the other unsettling voices from the past.

Singapore, in contrast, has generally chosen to forge the memories of all its citizens, whatever their ethnicity, into a unifying story of "a shared past" of common suffering during World War II (Blackburn 2001, pp. 8, 15–16). Less than two years after the foundation of the nation, in February 1967, a memorial was installed at the centre of the city to commemorate the victims of the Japanese occupation. Notably, this memory was not limited to the Chinese, even though this ethnic group had been the victims of the worst atrocity, the Sook Ching massacre of early 1942. Rather, at the government's insistence, the memorial commemorated all victims of the Japanese, thus in effect "nationalizing" the Chinese memory and "homogenizing" the national memory (Koh 2015, p. 20). Local and individual memories of communal conflict between Malays and Chinese were also silenced.

In the 1980s and 1990s, when the ruling People's Action Party sought to buttress its legitimacy (Koh 2015, p. 23), the Singaporean state made even more explicit attempts to subsume ethnic memories into a unifying narrative, according to which Singapore was forged by the suffering of Japanese occupation into "an embryonic multiracial nation-in-waiting" (Blackburn and Hack 2012, p. 9; Koh 2015, p. 15). In 1995, a new monument to the pro-Japanese Indian National Army was installed (replacing an earlier one), while in 2002, a museum commemorating the Malay Regiment's role in Singapore's defence in 1942 was opened on the sixtieth anniversary of the fall of Singapore. (Incidentally, this sparked a controversy about whose memory this actually was, with the Malaysian government pointing out that many of the soldiers were originally from the Malay peninsula and that to claim them as Singaporeans was anachronistic [Koh 2015, p. 27]). Meanwhile, in 1998, the date of the British surrender in 1942 — 15 February — was renamed "Total Defence Day", in an explicit invocation of the past to warn Singaporeans about the need for constant vigilance, national unity, and uncomplaining national service on the part of its young male population.

It is worth noting, as Ernest Koh has pointed out, that this focus on the Japanese occupation as the centrepiece of Singapore's creation myth, is deeply ahistorical — as, for that matter, is most national memory of war. It has meant that the transnational nature of Singapore's Chinese community, and their service in military units beyond the now national boundaries (for example, on the China–India–Burma front), has been excluded from national memory. Singapore's war "is thus situated exclusively in a particular geographical space with boundaries defined by postcolonial borders, and defined through the nation's ultimate end — that is, state sovereignty" (Koh 2015, p. 16). The logic of this is to deny that there were multiple experiences of World War II for Singaporeans, while reminding today's communities that, unlike some of their forebears who fought for Nationalist China or even the British Empire, "their allegiance should be to the nation" (Koh 2015, pp. 14, 29).

MEMORY AND ASIAN INTERNATIONAL RELATIONS

In Singapore's case, this positioning of World War II at the centre of national memory was not driven entirely by internal processes of identity construction. Like much of the memory boom elsewhere, it was part of a wider process, in which war memory became internationalized, some would say, "globalized". The growth of war memory in the West in the late twentieth century spawned an explosion in "pilgrimages" to battlefields and war cemeteries across the globe. Many sites of war memory thereby acquired a transnational or universalized quality (Lunn 2007, p. 8), as veterans, their families, and the governments that represented them claimed, if only informally, some "ownership" over what might be called extraterritorial war heritage. In particular, they claimed the right to visit and to perform commemorative rituals on key anniversaries at these sites. This, in turn, placed on host states an obligation to be custodians of a heritage that owed its significance not to their own citizens' memories of war but those of other nations. Such developments, of course, were not necessarily resisted by the host countries. There are considerable commercial benefits in war tourism, and across the globe, sites of trauma and the memories of war have been intensely commodified for this reason.

Beyond this, national leaders have come to recognize the considerable political capital in projecting national memories of war onto the stage of international relations. In the past two decades, we have seen the emergence of "memorial diplomacy": that is, "carefully choreographed public ceremonies [held] on the anniversaries of historic occasions at s elected sites of memory, long established or of recent invention, typically on the margins of international summits or intergovernmental forums" (Graves 2014, p. 170). The seventieth anniversary of the D-Day landings, in 2014, for example, was attended by the United States' Barack Obama, Russia's Vladimir Putin, Britain's David Cameron, France's François Hollande, and, more improbably, Australia's Tony Abbott (only 3,300 Australians participated in the landings!). Whether such "memory summits" actually speak to a new shared memory of past wars — beyond a transnational minimalism which professes a commitment to peace and "never again" — is doubtful; but clearly the leaders involved assume that the theatre of memorial diplomacy plays a positive role in enabling wider bilateral and multilateral relationships. For example, Hollande invited the Ukrainian president-elect Petro Poroshenko to the 2014 Normandy ceremony, as his personal guest, in an effort to break the ice between Moscow and Kiev as fighting continued in eastern Ukraine between government forces and pro-Russian separatists. Memorial diplomacy also provides national leaders with an international stage on which to play to interested audiences at home.

Such memorial diplomacy is notably absent in the Asia-Pacific region. Yes, there are some commemorative events attended by the politicians and members of the public from multiple countries: for example, anniversaries of the fall of Singapore attract not only dignitaries of Allied countries but also local Singaporean officials. However, with the notable exception of the recent seventieth anniversary of the end of World War II in Beijing, these are rarely on the scale of comparable European ceremonies. Moreover, whereas in Western Europe memorial diplomacy has become more inclusive in recent years, in that it incorporates former enemies as well as allies, Prime Minister Shinzo Abe of Japan was not among the thirty political leaders who attended the recent commemorations and military parade in Beijing on 3 September, China's newly named Remembrance Day. Abe had been invited to the ceremony but did not take up the invitation, supposedly because of his parliamentary schedule (Zhang 2015). The former Japanese Prime Minister Tomiichi Murayama, however, did attend.

Rather than China and Japan embracing a European-style memorial diplomacy, in recent years, they have projected onto the stage of international relations, memories of World War II that divide rather than reconcile. This is a relatively recent development. In earlier decades — indeed from the 1870s on — the Chinese viewed Japan as a potential or real threat, but also recognized it as a model of successful modernization and an exemplar of how the modern and the traditional could be fused, borrowing from the West but not losing what was best of the East (Rozman 2002, pp. 99–100). Even during Communist rule, Japan provided economic inspiration, as well as highly significant levels of aid and investment (King 2016a, 2016b). Under Mao Zedong, Chinese memories of WWII drew a distinction between the small number of "imperialistic" military leaders who had led Japan into war, and the millions of ordinary "peace-loving" Japanese citizens. Ultimately, the memory of Japan's role as an aggressor in the region took secondary place to an ideologically-framed view of international relations which gave primacy to the struggle between communism and U.S.-led imperialism. As Amy King and Brendan Taylor have put it, "There was no real 'history problem' in Northeast Asia during the Cold War" (King and Taylor 2016, p. 111).

From the mid- to late 1980s, however, Chinese authorities began to articulate a far more critical memory of the Japanese role in World War II. The early 1980s, as it happened, marked the start of the long-running Japanese textbook controversy: that is, the debate (which continues to this day) about the attempts of Japanese educational authorities and right-wing lobby groups to relativize Japan's aggression — on the grounds that other powers were imperialists too — and to downplay the criminality of Japan's occupation of Asia (Nozaki 2008, passim). The associated denial by Japanese conservatives of the scale of, and intent behind, the Nanjing massacre of 1937 (Tohmatsu 2011, pp. 115–18) also gave the Chinese good cause to assert a counter-narrative of the Sino–Japanese war. Even though Japanese opinion was not unitary — progressives such as Ienaga Saburō mounted a decades-long legal challenge to the right of the Japanese authorities to demand revisions to more critical texts — more exposure was given internationally to the continuing self-censorship of educational publishers and the ambiguity of the Japanese Liberal Democratic Party on the subject of Japan's war record (Duus 2011, pp. 110–13).

However, if the Japanese gave ample cause for offence, the Chinese government had its own domestic reasons for re-remembering World War II. Faced with the profound social dislocations of the opening of the Chinese economy, and a crisis of communism's legitimacy as the Cold War ended, the Chinese leadership became concerned with maintaining national cohesion. With Mao Zedong no longer possessing the symbolic power that he had in the early days of the People's Republic, the "War of Resistance to Japan" offered an alternative focus (Mitter 2000, p. 280). As Charles S. Maier has said, "the surfeit of memory is a sign not of historical confidence but a retreat from transformative politics in an age of failing expectations, particularly of socialism" (quoted in Müller 2002, p. 16). In 1985, therefore, the Nanjing Memorial Hall was opened by the Nanjing Municipal Government. Consisting of outdoor exhibits, skeletal remains of victims, and an exhibition hall of historical documents, the memorial proclaimed a toll of 300,000 victims — a statistic which many in Japan contest. Two years later, in 1987, a new War of Resistance Museum was opened in Beijing, to mark the fiftieth anniversary of the Lugouqiao (Marco Polo Bridge) incident (Mitter 2000). Replete with a Hall of Martyrs displaying reliefs of heroic incidents during World War II (including one, incidentally, of Nationalist forces who have been reinstated in the national narrative), the museum positioned China's wartime struggle within a global anti-fascist war, represented China as a leader of a global diaspora, and gave voice to Chinese nationalism in a way that was unusual in the People's Republic of China. Most importantly, the museum reinserted "the formerly taboo subject of the Sino-Japanese war into official political and educational discourse" (Mitter 2000, p. 293). However, while condemning the Japanese military, the museum did not lay blame for the war and its atrocities at the feet of the entire Japanese people.

The memory wars escalated in the 1990s, when the changing regional strategic balance, China's rapid economic growth and Japanese economic stagflation all combined to fuel what was becoming a reciprocal and self-fuelling exchange of recrimination.[4] South Korea joined the increasingly internationalized dispute when its democratization and the emergence of civil society brought the question of "comfort women" to national and global attention (Goh 2013, pp. 189–94). Increasingly, South Korea and China embraced what Jie-Hyun Lim (2015, p. 708) has called a "victimhood nationalism": a deeply emotive positioning which not only challenged the Japanese long-standing claim to be privileged victims by virtue of the nuclear bombing of Hiroshima and Nagasaki in 1945 (Lim 2015, pp. 708–09) but also resurrected demands for compensation which the Japanese claimed had been settled by earlier post-war treaties.

Every memory war has key tropes and, in this case, they included, firstly, the ambiguity about Japan's apologies for its wartime aggression and war crimes. There have, in fact, been many so-called "apologies" — a diligent Wikipedia entry lists some forty-one between 1990 and 2015 (Wikipedia 2015*b*) — but only one, the 1995 statement by Prime Minister Tomiichi Murayama on the fiftieth anniversary of the war's end, came close to being acceptable to Japan's former victims. Murayama used the all-important words "colonial rule and aggression" and offered his "heartfelt apology" rather than the softer "remorse", "regret", or "deep sorrow". The failure by later politicians to explicitly repeat Murayama's formulations provoked regular public protest in South Korea, China, and beyond. Abe's equivocal speech on the seventieth anniversary of Japan's defeat in August 2015, in particular, was criticized by the Chinese press as "linguistic tricks" (McCurry 2015), and has been seen by one Australian commentator as "a massive step back" (Morris-Suzuki 2015).[5] Even Murayama declared it "meaningless" (*Asahi Shimbun* 2015).

The second deeply symbolic issue has been the visits by conservative Japanese politicians to the Yasukuni shrine, Tokyo, at which the wartime leader, Hideki Tojo, and other "Class A" war criminals are honoured. Beginning in 1985, with a visit by Yasuhiro Nakasone in that year, these inflammatory events have continued to this day. Abe visited the shrine in December 2013, followed by his wife in May 2015, the latter visit provoking Beijing's foreign ministry to urge "the Japanese side to face up to, and deeply reflect upon, its history of aggression and make a clean break with militarism" (*Straits Times* 2015).

Such visits, of course, are not made with the international community as the primary audience. Like all political leaders, the Japanese are constrained by domestic lobby groups. Memory making here, as elsewhere, is not simply a matter of "top-down" government orchestration. It is the product of a continuing negotiation and contestation between multiple agencies at different levels of society. Hence, Abe is positioned, Janus-like, between his critics overseas and those within Japan who oppose "apologetic" histories of the past. Similarly, in China and Korea, the explosion at the level of popular culture of anti-Japanese sentiment — manifested most recently in films and television series which exploit the "Japanese demon" trope — both validates and constrains the governments' anti-Japanese rhetoric in the international domain.[6]

WHERE TO FROM HERE?

What will be the future of these memory wars in North Asia? If the history spiral is, as is commonly accepted, a feature only of the last two or three decades, can it be unwound? The answers to these questions depend on how we understand the nature of political processes and memory formation. From a traditional realist perspective, the current memory wars might be seen as little more than a rationalization, for domestic and international consumption, of a conflict anchored in underlying national interests, those interests being defined in essentialist terms as disputes over power transitions, territory, and resources. In other words, the memory wars are a function of the changing regional balance. Faced with the prospect of the United States China's assuming a strategic role that is commensurate with its growing economic power, China is signalling that World War II showed that "of all the countries in the world ... Japan was the only one that had forfeited the moral right to be a political or military great power because of its record of brutality in Asia" (Rozman 2002, p. 103). In other words, the lesson of "history" is that Japan should never be permitted to remilitarize; nor to amend its constitution to allow the deployment of Japanese defence forces in roles beyond peacekeeping.

Similarly, China and Japan both exploit the memory of World War II and its legacy to validate their claims to the disputed Senkaku/Diaoyu islands. China cites the 1943 Cairo and 1945 Potsdam declarations which revoked sovereignty over territory seized by the imperial Japanese government between 1895 and 1945. The Japanese, in turn, quote the 1952 San Francisco Peace Treaty under which the United States gained administrative control over the Senkaku islands, control which was then transferred to Japan under the 1972 United States–Japanese Reversion Agreement. This version of "history" presents Japan as a defender of the rule of international law and the regional order, while China is not (King and Taylor 2016).[7] For a realist, therefore, the memory wars of North Asia will not end in the foreseeable future because the conflicts of interests arising from a major power transition within the region are deeply intractable and, as yet, not capable of resolution.

However, a constructivist — and all memory scholars are such — would argue that those national interests are not immutable. They are open to redefinition and reshaping, not just in the face of new geostrategic conundrums and evolving norms, but also changing perceptions of the past. Here, then, memory becomes critical. It has both symbolic and structural power — as Jan-Werner Müller says, it has "the power to define what is put on the political agenda, in what terms political issues are framed and which conflicts get avoided" (Müller 2002, pp. 26, 29). In other words, memory is more than a tool; it infuses political cultures and shapes how individuals and governments respond to changes in their environment, understand the character and conduct of other elites, and form their perceptions of policy options.

If we revert, then, to memorial diplomacy in Western Europe, it might be argued that it is the redefining of national interests by the key protagonists of the two world wars, Germany and France, that has made these performative occasions possible. Germany has renounced any aspirations to dominate central and eastern Europe and in multiple gestures — ranging from support for Israel to the installation of a vast Memorial to the Murdered Jews of Europe at the very heart of the political culture, next to the Brandenburg Gate, Berlin — it has manifested an abject contrition for its past crimes against peace and humanity. Moreover, this Franco–German redefinition of interests has generated a common discourse, in the form of a "progressive narrative" which sees the two world wars as "a saga of ruinous nationalism eventually transcended in internationalism as the bloody first half of the twentieth century gave way to a second half characterized by peace and prosperity" (Reynolds 2015, p. 227). Hence in Asia, if the memory wars are to cease, there needs to be a comparable of interests and a reshaping of the discourse about the past. This would require significant political will but it is possible. Memory, after all, is not an agent in itself. Memory is constructed; and those who created the history spiral in North Asia have the capacity to reverse it, and imagine alternative futures. Even though certain elements of national narratives may have gained such a hegemonic power within particular domestic contexts and international relations that they constrain the choices of governing elites, they can be reshaped with skilled leadership and political will.

Imagine, for example, what might happen to Sino–Japanese relations if Japanese prime ministers ceased to visit the Yakusuni shrine. Or if, even more dramatically, Abe fell to his knees before the Nanjing Massacre memorial, as German Chancellor Willy Brandt did, in a stunning act of contrition, before the Warsaw Ghetto in 1970. Various critics have proposed such a gesture, and there is a recent precedent for it. In August 2015, former Japanese Prime Minister Yukio Hatoyama knelt at the Seodaemun prison, Seoul, in a gesture of apology to those who experienced harsh treatment during Japan's colonial rule.

Such a gesture would be performative, but performance is integral to transformative politics. A deeply symbolic act of contrition on the part of the Japanese would profoundly unsettle the dominant memory narrative, promulgated constantly by China and South Korea, in which Japan never shows appropriate contrition for its criminal history. Moreover, it would place the onus on the Chinese and South Korean governments, and those civil society groups who make it their business to keep anti-Japanese sentiment alive in those countries, to articulate what restitution for past wrongs would, in fact, bring the memory wars to an end. As Japan has argued, with some justification, the resolution of past grievances requires the victim as well as the perpetrator to change how it views the past and its aspirations in the present (see the "Report of the Advisory Panel on the History of the 20th Century and on Japan's Role and the World Order in the 21st Century" 2015, pp. 20–21).

Yet, such a dramatic act of contrition on the Japanese part might be counterproductive to reconciliation. As Jennifer Lind (2008, 2009) has argued, national apologies elsewhere have often triggered polarizing domestic political debates. While placating international critics, they ignite nationalist backlashes at home. These, in turn, lead foreign observers to ask what the popular outrage might reveal about the hidden, unspoken government agenda. Perhaps then, as Lind argues, Japanese leaders should not emulate Willy Brandt's *kniefall* but look to the model of Konrad Adenauer (Chancellor, 1949–63) who found "a safer middle ground between denial and contrition" (2009, p. 133) by acknowledging Germany's atrocities, yet emphasizing the country's post-war achievements and the potential for future collaboration.

Whatever the merits, or otherwise, of one specific symbolic gesture, it seems clear that the question for the future is whether any of the parties in the memory wars in North Asia can find the will — and the capacity domestically — to accept that the past can be remembered in a different way. The memory of World War II will never cease to flow through their political cultures, like wine through water, but so far as international relations at least is concerned, it might become, to quote W.G. Sebald, "something that can be left behind" (quoted in Bell 2006, p. 8).

Notes

1. This chapter was developed and completed while the author was Lim Chong Yah Professor in the Department of History, National University of Singapore, in 2015.
2. The number of deaths is impossible to determine precisely. The Wikipedia entry cited draws on reputable sources.
3. Similarly in Burma, the collaborationist leader Ba Maw conscripted many thousands of his own people to work on the construction of the Thai–Burma railway; the Burmese made up perhaps 44 per cent of the deaths of Asian workers on this project (Beaumont and Witcomb 2015, pp. 74–75).
4. The Chinese created a Patriotic Education Campaign in the early 1990s with the aim of bolstering popular nationalism and support for the Chinese Communist Party (CCP) by invoking memories of its role in the defeat of Japanese imperialism and fascism. Gilbert Rozman (2002, p. 106) dates, from 1993, a significant shift in official Chinese criticism of Japan, especially the strengthening of its alliance with the United States and its friendly relations with Taiwan. The Nanjing Memorial Hall museum was enlarged and renovated in 1995 and a second stage of the Beijing War of Resistance Museum was opened in 1997.

5. Abe also caused outrage in 2007 when, under his first administration, the cabinet declared that there was no documentary evidence of coercion in the recruitment of comfort women. In 2014, he signed an advertisement in a New Jersey newspaper protesting a memorial to comfort women in the town of Palisades (Kotler 2014).

6. More than seventy anti-Japanese series were screened on Chinese television in 2012 (Murong 2014) while the Nanjing massacre was the subject of a 2011 movie, *The Flowers of War*, which — in a transparent effort to globalize the issue — starred Oscar-winner Christian Bale. In Korea, the drawing power of movies depicting the Japanese as villains has been evident in the box-office hit *Assassination*, and the patriotic blockbuster *The Admiral: Roaring Currents* which depicts the defeat of the Japanese fleet in 1597 (St. Michel 2015).

7. All textbooks approved in the latest round of the Japanese government's screening process promote Japan's claims on the disputed Senkaku/Diaoyu Islands, as well as the Takeshima/Dokdo Islands (controlled by and disputed with South Korea) (Pollman 2015).

8

REGIONALISM AND GLOBAL POWERS

Evi Fitriani

Asia has faced multiple drivers of regionalism in the post-Cold War era. These include states' needs to cooperatively tackle new regional challenges, and a growing desire to pursue common interests regionally. Regionalism is defined as formal state-sponsored regional projects, as distinct from the more informal process of regional building led by non-state actors and commonly referred to as "regionalization" (Nair 2008, p. 111). In regionalism, elites and/or state leaders in the region play important roles in region-building processes, regional integration, and regional movements and initiatives. They push forward regionalism and, to some extent, create regional institutions. However, their efforts are not always successful. One of the big challenges for regionalism is the presence of global powers — states whose power can impact globally — that exist both within and outside the region.

This chapter discusses the relations between regional institutions in the Asia-Pacific and several global powers, namely the United States, China, and Russia. While located in the region, these three great powers have not always been included in regional initiatives. The chapter delves into the interaction of these global powers within several regional institutions such as the Asia-Pacific Economic Cooperation (APEC), the Association of Southeast Asian Nations (ASEAN), ASEAN Plus Three (APT), and the East Asia Summit (EAS). The chapter first provides a short history of the relationship between regionalism and global powers in the Asia-Pacific, before turning to a contemporary picture of regionalism in the region. It then investigates the role of global powers in the development of regionalism by focusing on the four aforementioned regional institutions. Finally, the chapter provides a brief review of the key methodological approaches to studying regionalism and global powers in Asia.

HISTORY OF REGIONALISM IN THE ASIA-PACIFIC

It is often said that APEC was the first form of regionalism in the Asia-Pacific because it drew together countries on both the Pacific-side of Asia as well as the Pacific-side of North and South America. However, regionalism in Asia has a much longer history, originating with Japan's military campaign in Northeast and Southeast Asia in the lead up to the Second World War. Japan's military campaign was underpinned by its vision of "Pan-Asianism". Pan-Asianism reflects the early movement of regionalism in the Asia-Pacific and is a precursor of contemporary Asian regionalism (Saaler 2007). Japan-led Pan-Asianism was based on cultural unity (and particularly East Asian societies' use of Chinese characters and a common religion), the "racial" kinship of East Asian peoples and ethnicities, the geographical proximity and historical legacy of the Sinocentric order, and a vision of common destiny (Saaler 2007, p. 10). Thus, it was an early attempt to create an "Asian identity". It was also intended to develop an exclusive regionalism — to liberate East Asian peoples by standing up against the West. At the same time, Japan-led Pan-Asianism was also developed in opposition to China, Japan's powerful neighbour and the region's previous hegemonic power, despite the fact that Japan itself had relied on Chinese heritage (Saaler 2002, p. 14).

The idea of Pan-Asianism developed in the Meiji Period as "an idealist-culturalist movement" responding to the spread of European colonialism in East Asia (Saaler 2002). But in the early decades of the twentieth century, this cultural regionalism was transformed into a more political and economic movement when Japan tried to create a Japan-centred regional order and sphere known as the "Greater East Asian Co-Prosperity Sphere". Yet like Napoleon's military campaign in Europe, Japan's military-based attempt to foster regionalism in East Asia was unsuccessful. Japan was not only defeated in the Second World War, but the legacy of this war has also ensured that Japan has been remembered for having been aggressive toward its Asian neighbours. Subsequently, Japan's war image has become a key hindrance to the development of regionalism in Northeast Asia.

In the early years after the Second World War, another type of Pan-Asianism emerged in South and Southeast Asia. India hosted the Asian Relations Conference in New Delhi from 23 March to 2 April 1947 (Agung 1990, p. 23). It was attended by statesmen from twenty-five newly-established Asian countries, such as Indonesia and Sri Lanka, as well as leaders from still-occupied countries, such as India. In this context, Pan-Asianism took place as a solidarity movement among Asian peoples as well as a transnationally-connected nationalist movement to support the decolonialization of Asian peoples (Acharya 2012). In this regard, Asian regionalism, at this time, excluded Western countries.

Later, with the onset of Cold War, the newly independent Asian countries faced the challenges posed by competition between the Western and Eastern blocs. The Asian solidarity movement progressed into the trans-regional movement of the Asia-Africa Conference in 1955, and the establishment of the Non-Alignment Movement (NAM). Newly sovereign countries across Asia and Africa shared a common interest in not being entangled in the bipolar Cold War conflict. Despite the end of the Cold War, the NAM has survived but its relevance and substantive achievement have been questioned, given the fact that many of its members are now involved in alliances or special relations with global powers.

In the last couple of decades, the cultural element of Pan-Asianism has emerged in politics and international relations, not only in Northeast Asia, but also in Southeast Asia. Some leaders have promoted what they call "Asian values"; others have called for the creation of an "East Asian Community". Pan-Asianism also spilled over into the economic realm and boosted economic integration through the proposal of an "East Asian Economic Group" by Malaysian Prime Minister Mahathir Mohamad in 1989.

These brief historical descriptions show that Asian peoples have had various experiences and motivations in establishing regionalism. However, attempts to build an exclusive regionalism — Pan-Asianism — have not been successful. Arguably, this is due to competition among regional countries and the long history of global powers' engagements in the region. Indeed, a global power which is also a country in the Asia-Pacific, namely the United States, has helped to foster regionalism in Asia by providing either a direct or indirect security umbrella. After the establishment of the North Atlantic Treaty Organization (NATO) in Europe in 1947, the United States sponsored the Southeast Asian Treaty Organization (SEATO). It was established in 1954, in response to the fear of the spread of communism in Southeast Asia following the defeat of France by Communist Vietnam in Indo-China. SEATO consisted of the United States, the United Kingdom, Australia, New Zealand, France, Pakistan, the Philippines, and Thailand. But, unlike NATO, no military command structure was assigned; so, rather than a security alliance, SEATO became a form of political cooperation that represented the United States' containment policy in Southeast Asia (Weatherbee 2009, pp. 65–66; Acharya 2012, pp. 131–38). Furthermore, it is difficult to categorize SEATO as an example of regionalism in Southeast Asia because only two regional states were members of the organization and the initiation and operation of the organization was almost always determined by the United States, an extra-regional, global actor.

There were also a couple of initiatives by regional actors before the establishment of ASEAN, including the Association of Southeast Asia (ASA), which was initiated in Bangkok on 31 July 1961 by Thailand, Malaysia, and the Philippines. This association was first proposed by Malaysia and aimed to develop cooperation in the economic, social, cultural, scientific, and administrative fields (Broinowski 1982, p. 9). Indonesia rejected Malaysia's invitation to join this regional initiative (Leifer 1986, p. 172). Nevertheless, ASA had a short life because the three member countries were preoccupied with efforts to build their nation states rather than develop regional cooperation. ASA was abandoned in 1963, after Malaysia and the Philippines could not solve their territorial dispute over Sabah in North Borneo. Another regional institution emerged shortly after ASA deteriorated. The Philippines initiated a regional grouping called "Malindo" to promote "Greater Malay Confederation", which included Malaysia, the Philippines, and Indonesia. This regional project was also short-lived because its objective of fostering a region based on common Malay origin was limited and not relevant to other countries in the region (Broinowski 1982, pp. 9–10).

Thus, historically, regionalism that involved countries from both the western and eastern halves of the Pacific was an uncommon phenomenon. Instead, subregional institutions were more apparent, particularly in Southeast Asia. By contrast, regionalism in Northeast Asia has been underdeveloped due to the problems of mutual animosities and historical tensions among Japan, China, and the Republic of Korea. Although deeply interdependent, these three countries have lacked the political will necessary to forge further regional cooperation. On the eastern rim of the Pacific Ocean, the United States, Canada, and Mexico established the North American Free Trade Agreement (NAFTA) in 1994. However, NAFTA seems to be an economic regional institution dominated by the United

States, rather than a "genuine" regional cooperation that treats members equally.

The post-Cold War period provided a more favourable environment for regionalism in the Asia-Pacific. Recent developments in the region show a new dynamic of East Asian regionalism as the result of pressures from national, regional, and global changing environments. These changing environments include regime change and democratization in some East Asian countries, the Asian financial crisis, and the "global war on terror" (Katzenstein 2006). Again, ASEAN and the Southeast Asian countries have been most active in this endeavour. However, due to their limitation, they can no longer focus solely on Southeast Asia as they need to engage countries in Northeast Asia and beyond. This phenomenon has created not only numerous regional initiatives in the Asia-Pacific but also complicated networks of regionalism.

A COMPLEX PICTURE OF REGIONALISM
IN THE ASIA-PACIFIC

Regionalism in the Asia-Pacific is a complex picture. This complexity appears in the great variety of regional architectures that have evolved over the last two decades. The variety does not only extend to the geographical coverage of regional initiatives, but also extends to the membership of different institutions. Decisions to place countries within "in-groups" and "out-groups" in regional institutions are strategically determined. APEC, ASEAN, APT, and EAS each have different geographical scopes and memberships. In addition, their memberships overlap with one another, indicating different strategic choices in the grouping of countries.

APEC has the largest geographical coverage and includes twenty-one economies from both the eastern and western halves of the Pacific, but does not involve all countries located in this wide geographical area. This regional initiative, which started in 1989, has conducted regular summit meetings since 1993. APEC also has three global powers — the United States, China, and Russia — in its membership. APEC accepted the admission of China, Taiwan, and Hong Kong at the same time in November 1991 and, to avoid the political complication associated with doing so, APEC members are therefore described as "economies" rather than "countries". From the beginning, APEC was intended to focus on economic integration and liberalization but it adopted a wider agenda in the 2000s, including anti-terrorism (in 2001), health (in 2003–4), emergency preparedness (in 2005), and climate change (in 2006–7) (Panennungi et al. 2014, p. 7). APEC's focus on the economy has strengthened since 2008, but the United States' interest in focusing on wider political and security issues has continued.

Another example of regional cooperation in the Asia-Pacific is ASEAN. It was established in 1967 and has become the longest surviving regional institution in the Asia-Pacific. This institution covers the smaller geographical area of Southeast Asia, making it a subregional grouping. Unlike APEC that has global powers in its membership, ASEAN consists of ten regional countries that can be categorized as "small" and "middle" powers. However, the global powers have engaged in this subregion since before the Second World War. Global power engagements have varied across the ten countries, depending on each country's position in the Cold War. As a result, regional countries like Thailand, the Philippines, and Singapore traditionally have closer security relations with the United States, while Vietnam used to be a part of the Soviet Union's alliance. ASEAN was established as a form of regional cooperation to create stability and prosperity in Southeast Asia. It increased its membership from five to ten member states in the 1990s, despite the fact that its new members had very different political systems, ideologies, and levels of economic development. Consequently, ASEAN member countries have neither a common security threat, nor a common system of politics and economic advancement. In the last decade, the ten member countries have agreed on the pursuit of a more ambitious goal of creating an ASEAN Community. In addition, the regional institution maintains close relations with the global powers, and has "dialogue partners" from outside the region. The European Union (EU) became ASEAN's first dialogue partner in 1977, and currently, ASEAN has ten dialogue partners.

In 1997, the ten ASEAN members and three countries in Northeast Asia — Japan, China, and South Korea — founded the ASEAN Plus Three (APT) as a way to expand and deepen cooperation between Southeast and Northeast Asian countries (EAVG 2002). All of the Northeast Asian countries had been ASEAN dialogue partners. This cooperation, referred to as "East Asian regionalism", was driven by ASEAN interests to build a more sustainable and regular platform with these three major Asian countries. Following the 1997 Asian financial crisis, the APT mechanism was useful in bringing about a regional response to the crisis, namely the Chiang Mai Initiative (CMI). Learning from the disappointing response to the financial crisis by the World Bank and International Monetary Fund, the APT countries insisted on the establishment of the CMI as a bilateral swap agreement in 2000. In March 2010, CMI was further developed into a multilateral swap agreement called "Chiang Mai Initiative Multilateralization" (CMIM), with a standby fund amounting to US$240 billion (MOFA 2014). While being labelled as a form of economic regionalism, CMI has contributed to the rise of a deeper regional awareness among East Asian countries (Fitriani 2014). The East Asian Vision Group (EAVG) — established by APT after the financial crisis — recognized that the need for mutual cooperation in overcoming the crisis provided momentum for an East Asian identity and drove the institutionalization of cooperation in the political-security, the economic-financial, and the sociocultural sectors. Furthermore, the EAVG claimed that the process encouraged community-building in East Asia (EAVG II 2012). The ASEAN countries have also managed to maintain the APT despite the sometimes tense political and security relations among the three Northeast Asian members. In fact, ASEAN has been able to take advantage of these uneasy relations to advance an ASEAN-driven agenda within the APT.

The EAS is yet another group stemming from ASEAN. This group was initiated and driven by ASEAN member states not only to enhance ASEAN significance beyond Southeast Asia but also to create "balance" or — to borrow the words of former Indonesian Foreign Minister Marty Natalegawa — a "dynamic equilibrium" in East Asia. When it was inaugurated in 2005, EAS comprised of the APT countries, and Australia, New Zealand, and India (ASEAN plus three plus three). While the EAS has achieved few substantial outcomes, global powers and other important actors have shown a strong interest in joining. In large part, this is because the EAS is comprised of countries undergoing rapid economic development and because East Asia is now the most economically dynamic region in the world, especially following the impact of the Global Financial Crisis in the United States and Europe. After intense lobbying, the United States and Russia were admitted to the EAS in 2011, but attempts by the EU and India to join the organization have so far failed.

The development of EAS has indicated that it is almost impossible for Asian countries to develop an exclusive regionalism due to regional dynamics and indispensable engagements of global powers in the region. Apart from the four regional institutions mentioned above, there are other regional initiatives that have been proposed, such as a Northeast Asian Free Trade Agreement, East Asian Community, and Asia Pacific Community, to name a few. However, due to political problems and lack of support, these regional projects are characterized more by rhetoric than by reality. Indeed, there has been tension in the region regarding the direction of East Asian regionalism as to whether it should include the United States (Asia-Pacific regionalism) or if it should be limited to the Asian countries (Pan-Asian regionalism) (He 2004; Higgott and Stubbs 1995).

As in Europe, regionalism in East Asia has developed among previously adversarial countries. However, it has different characteristics from the European model of regionalism. East Asian regionalism has been referred to as "new regionalism", and has the characteristics of being less institutionalized and more informal and open than Western forms of regionalism (Wyatt-Walter 1995, pp. 74–121; Fawcett 2004, pp. 429–46; Hettne 2005; Acharya 2006). East Asian regionalism has had to adopt such characteristics because of internal and external challenges. Internally, severe disparity in levels of economic development between countries, diversity in political systems and cultural backgrounds, and bitter historical experiences are serious problems that have hindered regional cooperation in East Asia. But, the most fundamental obstacle is the strong centrality on the nation state (Öjendal 2004; He 2004; Acharya 2006; Ba 2003). This assertion of sovereignty has led to a strong attachment to principles of consensus, non-interference, and non-intervention within ASEAN and, coupled with distrust and politically inharmonious relations in Northeast Asia, has resulted in both the absence of an Asian framework for East Asian security (Hettne 2005; Katzenstein 2006; Acharya 2006), and an unreliable safeguard against regional financial crisis (Aggarwal and Koo 2005, pp. 189–216). Externally, the biggest challenge to East Asian regionalism is the strong presence of the United States in regional economic and political-security affairs (Shin and Segal 1999, pp. 73–83; Ruland 2000; Ba 2003; Öjendal 2004).

Despite many studies that point to the role of global powers — especially the United States — as an obstacle to regionalism in Asia, deeper observations reveal that global power support is needed in order for East Asian regionalism to develop. Thus, the picture of regionalism in the Asia-Pacific embodies close trans-Pacific relations. However, the increasing role of China and Russia, and continuing presence of the United States shape the dynamic of regionalism in the Asia-Pacific currently. These circumstances encourage further discussion on the role of global powers in Asia-Pacific regionalism.

THE ROLE OF GLOBAL POWERS IN
ASIA-PACIFIC REGIONALISM

The role of global powers, like the United States, has been very important in the development of the EU. European regionalism has been institutionalized within the liberal international order guarded by the United States, despite the lack of a formal structure between the EU and the United States. In addition, despite frequent uneasy times between EU member states and the United States, the former depended on the latter for security (Hiesser 1991, pp. 27–47). The Soviet Union also played an important role in initiating regional cooperation among the Western European countries as it became their common threat (Nelson 1991, pp. 48–66). So, without a formal admission to the EU, the global powers helped shape the European regional integration. One may argue that global powers, either directly or indirectly, play important roles in regionalism. This section discusses the role of global powers, namely the United States, China, and Russia, in Asia-Pacific regionalism.

In the ASEAN and EAS examples, the role of the United States cannot be denied as this global power's engagement in East Asia dates back to the Second World War. In the last decade, however, relations between China and ASEAN member countries have intensified and this phenomenon has also affected relations between the Southeast Asian countries and other global powers.

There is no formal association between ASEAN and the United States except for the fact that the latter has been one of ASEAN's ten dialogue partners since 1977. However, since its inception, ASEAN has been thought of as part of the United States' effort to contain the spread of communism in Southeast Asia. The five ASEAN founding states shared the United States' threat perceptions against communism as all were ruled by anti-communist regimes at that time. In addition, Thailand and the Philippines were allied with the United States, while Malaysia and Singapore were members of the Commonwealth countries led by the United States' close ally, the United Kingdom. Moreover, like the EU, ASEAN also developed within the context of the liberal international order led by the United States. ASEAN member states are also members of the Bretton Woods institutions built by the United States toward the end of the Second World War. In the post-Cold War era, ASEAN member states have maintained close relations with the United States. Despite the superpower's limited engagement within the region in the 1990s, it continued to be a key participant in ASEAN's initiative for a regional security framework, namely the ASEAN Regional Forum (ARF). Today, ASEAN–U.S. dialogue relations focus mainly on political and security issues in which ASEAN member states recognize the key role played by the United States in maintaining peace, security, and stability in the region (ASEAN 2016). The United States has also been involved in a series of consultative meetings with ASEAN such as the ASEAN Defence Ministers' Meeting Plus (ADMM Plus), EAS, and the Post Ministerial Conferences (PMCs). Additionally, the United States acceded to the ASEAN Treaty of Amity and Cooperation (TAC) on 22 July 2009. This enhanced engagement with ASEAN encouraged the United States to establish a dedicated diplomatic mission to ASEAN in 2010, and it has posted a Resident Ambassador to ASEAN since 2011. U.S. engagement with ASEAN has been driven by its understanding of the strategic importance of Southeast Asia, and by the role of individual ASEAN countries in Washington's wider Asia-Pacific strategy (Goh 2013, pp. 34, 65–66; Cook 2014, pp. 37–52). Two factors have been particularly important in enhancing Southeast Asia's strategic importance to the United States in the post-Cold War era. The first relates to the U.S.-led "War on Terror", dating back to 2001. Home to a number of important radical Islamic groups, Southeast Asian countries such as Indonesia and the Philippines were engaged by the United States as a way to counter and combat terrorism. This led the United States to propose political and security cooperation with these two countries, as well as with ASEAN more generally.

The second factor that has driven the U.S. "pivot" back to the region is the rise of China. China's approach to Southeast Asia started in the mid-1990s when the rising power agreed to support the ASEAN countries in conducting an interregional forum with the EU, namely the Asia-Europe Meeting (ASEM). A bolder step southward was taken by the China Government in supporting the establishment of the APT in 1997. The engagement between countries in Southeast Asia and China was driven by China's impressive economic development, and its need for both raw materials and export markets in Southeast Asia. China was the first dialogue partner admitted to the ASEAN Treaty of Amity and Cooperation (TAC) in 2003. The negotiation of the ASEAN–China Free Trade Agreement (ACFTA) was concluded in 2003 and became effective partially in 2010 and fully in 2015. China also offered the Early Harvest Programme (EHP) to ASEAN countries, which reduced export tariffs of agricultural and manufactured products to China from early 2004. In the political field, the heads of governments from China and the Southeast Asian countries signed and issued the Joint Declaration on Strategic

Partnership for Peace and Prosperity at the 9th ASEAN Summit in Bali, in October 2003. Through this strategic partnership, the parties agreed not only to increase their trade and investment relations, but also to hold a regular forum for security related dialogue. A Chinese official portrayed China's approach to the region as "good neighbour, safe neighbour, and enrich neighbour" (Breckon 2004).

Building on this record, China has now become the biggest trading partner for almost all Southeast Asian countries. Nevertheless, these close economic ties have also created tensions between China and ASEAN countries. Although the growing interdependence between ASEAN and Chinese production networks and markets has been of great economic benefit for ASEAN countries (Fitriani 2015, pp. 65–84), the vast influx of Chinese products — which are usually cheaper and of lower quality — have also threatened local ASEAN producers. Additionally, research has revealed that ACFTA has reduced export income from ASEAN countries (Aslam 2012, pp. 43–78). Thus, China has provided opportunities as well as challenges to ASEAN.

Furthermore, this economic cooperation has not spilled over into the political and security realm. For example, ASEAN countries have not successfully persuaded China to commit to the principles contained within the 2002 Dec.aration on the Conduct of Parties in the South China Sea. Deteriorating territorial conflicts between China and the Philippines, Vietnam, Malaysia, and Brunei are now the most pressing problem facing China–ASEAN relations. Despite its claim for a peaceful rise, China has become more assertive in the last decade by conducting military patrols, unilaterally establishing an Air Defense Identification Zone (ADIZ) in the East China Sea, and building structures in the conflicting territory. Some incidents have taken place, resulting in the use of naval forces and coast guards between China and the Philippines, and between China and Vietnam (Cook 2014; Cho and Park 2013). As a result, concerns and fears toward China have increased in Southeast Asia.

Yet, perhaps the greatest problem for ASEAN in its relations with China is variance in ASEAN member states' views of and relationship with China. Consequently, ASEAN rarely achieves a common position toward China, especially on problems in the South China Sea. Indeed, for the first time since its inauguration, the ASEAN Foreign Ministers' Meeting in 2012 failed to produce a joint declaration. This was due to disagreements between the host country, Cambodia, and the Philippines over the position that should be taken towards China. Like their relationships with the United States, ASEAN countries also have varying levels of engagement with China, depending on both historical ties and on contemporary issues, such as the degree of competition in gaining access to Chinese markets. Therefore, China has also created an obstacle for Southeast Asian regionalism.

In addition, China's aggressiveness in the South China Sea has driven some ASEAN countries to strengthen their relations with the United States. It has also become a window of opportunity for the United States to pivot to the region in the last several years under a policy of "rebalancing to Asia". Due to their engagements with various external regional powers, ASEAN countries have welcomed the involvement of global powers and tried to prevent domination by a particular power. Similarly, ASEAN countries agreed to admit the United States and Russia to the EAS in 2011. Aware that the United States "rebalance" to Asia is appealing to many Southeast Asian countries, China has responded by taking steps to try and maintain its attractiveness among ASEAN countries. In particular, over the past two to three years, China has adopted "a neighbourhood policy", and has offered ASEAN countries three initiatives: an up-graded ACFTA; the "One Belt, One Road" (OBOR) Initiative, which includes both the 21st Century Maritime Silk Route and the land-based Silk Road Economic Belt running from China to Europe; and membership in the Asian Investment and Infrastructure Bank (AIIB). So far, ASEAN countries have been divided in their response to these Chinese offers. Moreover, it is not only China that has sought to reach out to the ASEAN countries. Because of the region's growing economic and strategic importance, other important international actors — such as Japan, India, and the EU — have also tried to strengthen their presence in Southeast Asia. All of these external regional powers approach ASEAN based on their global strategic interests respectively, which are not always in line with those of ASEAN countries.

In the wake of the ASEAN Community's creation in 2015, global powers and important actors are increasingly reaching out to ASEAN. On the one hand, the involvement of these external countries in Southeast Asian regionalism is needed and invited; ASEAN alone can hardly develop economically or play key roles in the Asia-Pacific, let alone take on international roles, as it consists of small and medium powers. On the other hand, the involvement of global powers hinders ASEAN from taking common positions and actions. In fact, the engagement with global powers has caused ASEAN countries to strive for solidarity which, in turn, affects their regional building. Thus, there is a risk that ASEAN efforts to pursue a holistic and comprehensive regional community — such as the

ASEAN Community — will not be achieved in the face of global power engagement and competition in the region. Alongside its internal dynamics, Southeast Asian regionalism continues to be shaped and reshaped by global powers.

Finally, Asia-Pacific regionalism has also faced problems of divergence within other institutions such as APEC over the last several years. APEC's pursuit of trade liberalization, as declared in 1994's Bogor Declaration, has been challenged by the entrenched preference for mercantilism, not only by the United States but also by other economies in East Asia. Like the EAS and ARF, APEC's institutional mechanism has also been criticized for taking an "ASEAN way" approach, such that "consensus" and "less institutionalization" have become more prominent than "binding mechanisms" and "substantive realization" (Nair 2009). These circumstances have driven the United States, as a part of its pivot to East Asia, to strengthen its relations with several economic partners in the Trans-Pacific Partnership (TPP). With strong support from this global power, the TPP has been built as a high-standard Free Trade Agreement in which the United States, as the world's largest economy, and Japan, the third largest economy, are negotiating with ten other countries in the Asia-Pacific. Notably, however, major regional economies such as China and Indonesia are not included within the TPP. At the 2011 APEC Summit, the TPP group held a separate meeting, which sparked concerns of the emergence of a split within APEC. In response, ASEAN and its six dialogue partners established the Regional Comprehensive Economic Partnership (RCEP) in 2012, an initiative that has been strongly supported by China. RCEP does not have the depth or scope of the TPP, though it could provide a model and alternative vision for a Free Trade Area of the Asia-Pacific (FTAAP) (Miller 2015). Thus, APEC has been challenged from within as its members are divided between the U.S.-led economic cooperation in the TPP and Chinese-led economic cooperation in the RCEP. Despite efforts by Russia, Indonesia, and China (the three APEC host countries between 2012 and 2014) to revive APEC, the institution has lost momentum in deepening Asia-Pacific regionalism.

METHODOLOGICAL APPROACHES TO RESEARCHING REGIONALISM AND GLOBAL POWERS

Both quantitative and qualitative approaches have been used to research the relationship between Asia-Pacific regionalism and global powers. Research on intra-regional and extra-regional trade relations, trade diversion, regional economic trends, and regional economic integration typically applies quantitative methodologies. In these approaches, researchers use econometrics, statistical regression, or other quantitative instruments to explain regional phenomena and their relations to global powers. Economists and scholars of international political economy usually undertake this kind of study.

For international relations scholars, however, qualitative methodology has been more commonly used to study regionalism and the global powers in the Asia-Pacific. There are several qualitative methods that can be applied, including the use of historical analysis and case study-based approaches. In a case study, researchers typically take a particular regional institution — such as ASEAN, APEC, or EAS — as the primary analytical unit. To date, case studies on Asia-Pacific regionalism and global powers have been dominated by observations on interactions between ASEAN and the United States (Beeson 2003, pp. 251–68; Beeson 2009; Acharya 2012; Koo 2012; Goh 2013). To a lesser degree, there have also been studies on the relationship between ASEAN and Japan. In recent years, we have seen growth in case study-based research focusing on ASEAN–China relations, in large part because of the increasing interactions between China and the Southeast Asian countries since the 1990s (Goh 2013). In contrast, studies on ASEAN–Australia relations, or ASEAN–India relations, remain very rare.

Another potential qualitative approach is comparative regionalism, or within-region comparative studies. For example, one might compare the relationship between a great power and two or more regional institutions, such as China's relationship with ASEAN and APEC, or the United States' relationship with ASEAN and the EU. Alternatively, comparative approaches could also be used to compare two or more great powers and their relationship to a particular regional institution, for example a comparison of ASEAN–U.S. relations and ASEAN–China relations.

In this chapter, a comparative approach was adopted in order to observe four regional institutions — namely APEC, ASEAN, APT, and EAS — in their relations with the United States and China. Further research could undertake similar comparisons with the EU. In doing so, one could draw conclusions about the extent to which Asia-Pacific regionalism is a "special case", or whether it shares similarities in the relationship between regionalism and the great powers in other parts of the world. Such a comparative approach would assist us in observing both the opportunities and challenges for region building posed by great powers in the Asia-Pacific region and beyond.

CONCLUSION

Regionalism in the Asia-Pacific dates back to the early twentieth century, and the engagement of global powers in the region predates region-building initiatives. The evolution of Asia-Pacific regionalism presents a complex picture, consisting of regional institutions with different geographical scope and different conceptions of what the region actually is. Asia-Pacific regionalism has also been challenged by the domination of, and competition between, global powers, in particular the United States and China. Within Southeast Asia, for example, the global powers may serve as economic partners and play significant roles in ASEAN countries' economic development. Global powers can also strengthen regional countries' bargaining position vis-à-vis other global powers and important actors. They may also pose economic and/or security threats to particular ASEAN countries. But more fundamentally, the global powers have hindered the development of ASEAN common positions and actions, thereby limiting further region building. Hence, the ASEAN case reveals the problems of new regionalism in Asia and of open regionalism in Southeast Asia

SECTION IV
Conflict and Order

9

WAR AND ORDER: THINKING ABOUT MILITARY FORCE IN INTERNATIONAL AFFAIRS

Hugh White

MILITARY ORDER AND INTERNATIONAL RELATIONS

The study of international relations today faces a formidable methodological problem: how to understand the role of power in relations between powerful states, and especially in the creation, maintenance, and decline of the international orders which frame those relations within groups or systems of states from time to time. The problem extends to explaining the role of power in general, but it is most acute in relation to power in its starkest form — military power. That is the focus of this chapter. It explores the role of military power in shaping orders in systems of states.

This is hardly a new question. Military power has been central to the conduct and study of international relations since states and state systems first emerged. But today it is poorly understood and its influence on current developments is generally underestimated, especially perhaps by analysts and decision makers in the West. This has big implications for our understanding of the choices that countries of the West now face, and of the risks they may confront at a time when, it is now generally accepted, we face a significant shift — or set of shifts — in international order. These choices and risks bear upon Australia as much as on any Western country, and perhaps more than on most. It therefore seems important, for very practical reasons, to make sure we refresh our understanding of the role of force in shaping international orders.

This chapter suggests a simple way to see this issue: an international order in a system of states is framed — its boundaries are defined — primarily or ultimately by what the great powers within the system are willing to go to war with one another over. Or, to be a little more precise, an order is framed by what the great powers can *convince one another* they are willing to go to war with one other over. One obvious example is the bipolar global order of the Cold War era, which was framed by the clear conviction on each side of the other's willingness to go to war to defend their established spheres of influence in the key European and Northeast Asian theatres. Another is Europe's nineteenth-century order, the Concert of Europe, which was framed by the conviction among all the great powers that each of them would go to war to defeat a bid for hegemony by any of the others. In both cases, the order broke down when these core convictions could no longer be sustained.

As these examples suggest, there is nothing at all profound or original in the idea being suggested here. It is in a sense self-evident, at least up to a point, that states' willingness to use force defines the boundaries of the order within which they manage their relationships without the use of force — the boundaries of diplomacy, in other words. I think this view of the relationship between war and order is at least one of the ideas which underlie the intriguing opening passages of Henry Kissinger's *A World Restored* (1957). "Those ages which in retrospect seem most peaceful were least in search of peace", he wrote. "Whenever the international order has acknowledged that certain principles could not be compromised even for the sake of peace, stability based on an equilibrium of forces was at least conceivable." In other words, a stable order other than hegemony can only be sustained when two or more powers both recognize that the others are willing to go to war to defend some element of the order.

But being self-evident does not make it unimportant. To the extent it is true, this account of the relationship between order and military power has clear implications for the way the world's key international orders will evolve over coming years. The shape of the new orders, and the role contending great powers can expect to play in them, will depend on what they can convince other great powers they are willing to go to war over. An associated thought — not bearing directly on the key focus of this chapter but perhaps useful to note in passing — is that apart from defending itself against a direct attack, securing its place in a strategic order is, perhaps, the only reason a great power will accept the costs and risks of going to war with another great power.

Bluff has a part in a country's ability to convince others of its willingness to go to war, but not a decisive one: history suggests that it is hard to fool others about one's willingness to go to war over the long run. But that willingness itself depends not just on a state's military power — its ability to go to war — but also on its resolve: its readiness to pay the costs of war against another great power. The interaction between these factors is important, too. The greater the advantage in military power enjoyed by one side over the other, the lower the costs and risks of conflict, and the less resolve is required to go to war. Conversely, the greater a state's resolve, the greater cost and risk it will accept and the less relative military power it needs to make its willingness to fight credible. On the account offered here, then, these factors and their interaction are most important in determining the evolution of international orders.

One important caveat to this general position might be the idea explored by John Ruggie (1982) that the content of an order depends not just on the fact that a group of great powers agree on the constitution of an order, but also critically on which countries end up having the biggest say, and the objectives, interests, and values they bring to bear on the task of order building. So, for example, whether a regional order in Asia is primarily shaped by China or the United States has big implications for the kind of order it is. This is true, but I do not think it detracts from the basic point I am making here: how much influence each country has on the content of the order will be determined ultimately by their relative evident willingness to go to war to maximize that influence. And, of course, whether there is a peaceful order at all depends on whether they end up being willing to go to war over the same things.

Before we go any further, it might be helpful to clarify a few concepts. First, by "system" I mean a group of states whose principal strategic concerns relate to other members of the group. Second, by "order" I mean the shared expectations that shape the way states in a system relate to one another — expectations which may or may not be encapsulated in any formal agreements or institutions. This is close to the austere concept of order laid out by Hedley Bull in *The Anarchical Society* (1977, pp. 3–5) but not quite identical to it, if only because my concept of the primary or elementary goals to which order is a means might be even more austere than Bull's. That is because it does seem to me that peace between states is a higher-priority goal than any other, and the more catastrophically costly war threatens to become, the more the avoidance of war stands alone as the primary goal of order. But not the sole goal, especially in light of Kissinger's point above. And third, by "great power" I mean a state that is powerful enough relative to other states in the system to have a decisive influence on the shape of the order in that system. Some implications of these definitions will become clearer in what follows.

LOOKING BACK

There is a good reason why we have tended to overlook the role of military power in shaping international orders in recent decades. For twenty-five years since the end of the Cold War, we have been living through — or at least it seemed we were living through — a period of remarkable stability in what was primarily a global international system. This era began with the still-astonishing and probably unprecedented transition from a bipolar global strategic system framed primarily by strategic rivalry between two global powers to one framed by the uncontested power of the United States. The old Cold War strategic order was, of course, profoundly shaped and, in most respects, virtually defined by military power as reflected in the military balance between the superpowers. But military power had no role in its collapse.

Nor did military power have — at least apparently — anything like the same role in the new, unipolar order that replaced it. That order seemed to be based on the willing acceptance by all the world's strongest and most important states of a global order led by the United States. This order was not, it seemed, framed by military power; no country with anything approaching the military potential to challenge the U.S. global primacy had any interest in doing so, because the U.S.-led order seemed to work so well in the interests of all the world's strongest states.

Moreover, it was assumed that if any of these strong states had been tempted to think differently, they could be in no doubt that the United States was both willing and able to use its massive preponderance of armed force to crush any challenge to its leadership of the global order. It was, in turn, based on a view that U.S. military preponderance was so overwhelming that it could prevail over any adversary anywhere at relatively low levels of cost and risk, so the question of a military challenge to the post-war global order hardly arose. This did indeed seem, from a classic strategic perspective, like the end of history. More realistically, however, we could say that the post-Cold War global order was characterized by a clear set of expectations about the use of force by the global system's great powers. Every state seemed convinced that the United

States was willing to go to war with any other state to preserve its leadership and all other key aspects of the unipolar order, and no other major state was willing to go to war to challenge any aspect of it. Thus, the role of force in framing the order was rendered largely invisible.

This image of a stable, uncontested, and demilitarized global order among the world's strongest states was, if anything, reinforced by challenges to that order emerging from the periphery of the global power structure. Rogue states, weak states, and non-state actors posed significant problems for the United States and its partners, but they did not threaten the order itself. On the contrary, these peripheral challenges seemed, if anything, to consolidate consensus in support of the U.S.-led order among the strongest states, and made the order seem even more robust. Coral Bell (2007), for example, argued that what she called the "Jihadist threat" would reinforce strategic cohesion between the world's major powers. The more the unipolar order was troubled by these peripheral disruptions, the less chance there seemed that it would be riven by differences among the core of powerful states.

In this setting, it was easy for both analysts and practitioners to believe that war had ceased to be a significant factor in the relations between major powers. Instead, future strategic challenges were seen mainly in terms of bringing the disruptive periphery in line with the order accepted and upheld by the core of powerful states (Freedman 1998; Smith 2005). This was, in turn, reinforced by a view that the state itself was becoming less significant in an increasingly globalized world, suggesting that long-term secular trends were rendering irrelevant the interstate strategic rivalries that had shaped the international orders in the past. Thus, it appeared this shift was no passing phase but a new normal (Bobbitt 2002).

Governments, in the West especially, tended to be ambivalent about this view of the shifting and declining role of force. They talked a lot about a new post-Cold War strategic environment in which traditional symmetrical state-on-state conflicts had been replaced by non-traditional and asymmetric challenges as the main focus of their aired forces. At the same time, few, if any — perhaps New Zealand under Helen Clarke the only clear exception — significantly changed the kinds of armed forces they were building by shifting investment from capabilities clearly suited mainly to traditional old-fashioned wars to those more suited to the new wars. They did, however, allow the development of capabilities suited to traditional major wars to slow down, as defence budgets dropped while attention and resources were diverted to operations in the war on terror and other similar "new" tasks. And that, of course, has made these governments all the more eager to believe that traditional major wars are no longer a serious possibility, even as they continued half-heartedly building capabilities that only made sense if they were.

NEW REALITIES

There were always analysts who doubted this view of the role of force in international affairs (Gray 2005; Mearsheimer 2001). But only over the past few years has it started to become widely accepted that the assumptions about the post-Cold War international order were being challenged by events in several parts of the world, and the significance of this for our thinking about the role of military power has hardly begun to be considered.

There are several ways to analyse the trends and events driving these shifts in perceptions, but perhaps the best place to start is with the erosion of two supposed foundations of the unipolar order: the preponderance of U.S. military power, and the willing acceptance by other major states of a U.S.-led global order. It has become clear that neither of these are as robust as was widely supposed, because several countries have emerged which seem to have both the power and the desire to challenge U.S. leadership.

The realistic assessment of contemporary U.S. military power is a major subject in itself, but suffice it to say that sobering reality has punctured the illusion of U.S. military omnipotence in several places. It has become clear that while the United States has, as is so often said, by far the world's greatest military power overall, that does not mean that it can achieve swift, cheap, and decisive military victories over any adversary anywhere, at any time. The United States does clearly exceed every other state in its capacity to deploy and sustain conventional armed force globally, but it cannot necessarily deploy and sustain enough force in distant theatres to win such victories against capable adversaries operating in or near their own territory. This has been shown most obviously in the Middle East, where it has also become plain that the U.S. military is ill-suited to operations involving the control of territory and populations rather than the destruction of an adversary's armed forces. But more to the point for this chapter, it has become clear that in conventional conflict scenarios against major regional powers, the United States has much less capacity to prevail than had generally been assumed.

This has been most starkly demonstrated in Eastern Europe. Russia's 2008 incursion into Georgia was an early warning, but Russia's 2014 seizure of Crimea and support for separatist forces in Eastern Ukraine, and the evident unwillingness of the United States to respond to Russia's use of force with force of its own has been seen as a clear challenge to the European order, and to the United States' role, and especially the role of U.S. military power, in underpinning it. This challenge has had both conventional and nuclear elements. At the conventional level, it has become clear that the United States, even with help from NATO (North Atlantic Treaty Organization) allies, simply lacks the capacity to achieve an easy victory over Russia in a continental conflict on Russia's borders, deep in the heart of Eastern Europe.

This should come as no surprise: the United States has, after all, never been a match for Russia in land warfare on the Eurasian continent. But in addition, the Georgian and Ukrainian crises made it clear that the United States' nuclear forces cannot provide the overwhelming military preponderance that its conventional forces do not, unless the United States is clearly willing to risk an escalating nuclear exchange carrying real risks of nuclear attack on U.S. targets, including cities. It has quickly become clear that there is no question of the United States being willing to accept such risks to respond to Russia's challenge to the old order in Eastern Europe. On the other hand, Russia's willingness to use force in the ways it has done has shown it is willing to run a risk — slight, but not negligible — of conflict with the United States as a means to change the regional order in its favour. Russia, it seems, is more resolved to change the regional order in Eastern Europe than the United States is to preserve it.

This has clearly come as a surprise to many people in the United States and Europe. In part, that has been because they have underestimated Russia's dissatisfaction with the U.S.-led order, and in part because they have overestimated the United States' advantage in the regional military balance on Russia's borders. That, in turn, reflects a tendency to focus too much on comparisons of global rather than regional power, which in turn reflects a preoccupation with global rather than regional orders. Again, this is understandable in view of the experience not only of the past few decades but of the past few centuries. Since the late eighteenth century, there has been a series of global strategic orders framed primary by the major North Atlantic countries — the United States, Russia, and the Northern Europeans — whose preponderance of power and spread of interest have made their strategic influence decisive across the globe. But the fleeting unipolar order of the post-Cold War decades might come to be seen as the last of these global orders, because the world is reverting to a more equal distribution of wealth and power around the globe. As that happens, the United States, the last of the old "global powers", has lost its ability to shape events in regions far from the Western Hemisphere against local states that are weaker than the United States overall, but comparable in their own region. An era of integrated global strategic system shaped by the comparative weight of a number of global powers is giving way to an era of more discrete regional systems, shaped by the weight of regional great powers, and that the United States, as the only remaining global power, can bring to bear in each region. This is, in fact, a reversion to the pattern that prevailed throughout history until the industrial revolution's "great divergence" created an unprecedented asymmetry in the global power distribution.

Hitherto, analyses of the relative military power of the United States and its various potential adversaries have tended to go no further than the fact that none of them has anything like the capacity to challenge the United States as a global power. That is true, of course, but becoming less and less relevant to judgements about the relative weights of great powers in regional systems in which U.S. power is increasingly counterbalanced by the weight of regional great powers. It does not matter much to the emerging order in Eastern Europe that Russia cannot compete with the United States globally; what matters is the balance of military capability in the region in question. So the tendency of the United States and other Western analysts and policymakers to focus on the global level has concealed the more equal distribution of power in a number of regional systems.

The second factor which underpinned perceptions of an unchallengeable U.S.-led order was the idea that major regional powers around the world had no reason to challenge it, because the order worked well for them. Many people believed, for example, that Russia was basically committed to working within the U.S.-led European order because that seemed to offer, by far, the best prospects for the political and economic development that Russia's people have so obviously desired. Likewise, it has been easy to assume that despite its growing assertiveness, China is not really serious about challenging U.S. primacy in Asia because China itself benefitted so much from the peace and stability that it provided. That assumption rested on two others: that Beijing shared the West's belief that U.S. primacy offered the only possible basis for stability in Asia, and that countervailing impulses, such as nationalism, would play no major part in shaping its approaches to regional order. Both turn out to be wrong. China, like Russia, turns out to be deeply committed to changing its regional order in its favour and, in view of the regional balances of military power already described, both have options to pursue these ambitions by challenging the U.S. militarily in their own regions.

Many Western analysts have, nonetheless, remained confident that the United States' still-formidable nuclear capabilities guarantee that it would ultimately prevail in any contest of wills with regional competitors over the shape of regional orders. They have assumed that no regional power would dare to question the United States' willingness to use its nuclear forces to counterbalance conventional forces and restore its overall military preponderance. The United States' reliance on nuclear forces in this role is implied by its continued refusal to adopt a "no first use" policy (US DoD 2010; White 2010). But the credibility of the United States' willingness to use nuclear forces to preserve regional orders cannot be taken for granted, especially where regional rivals have the capacity for nuclear retaliation against the United States itself, as China and Russia, of course, both do. It depends on the strength of the United States' commitment to preserving its primary position in the orders of regions remote from the United States itself. Back during the Cold War, the United States was willing to go to war with the Soviets involving a high risk of nuclear attack on the United States itself in order to prevent Soviet gains which it believed would threaten the U.S. position in the global order. There is no reason to assume that the United States today would be equally willing to risk a nuclear attack, even on a smaller scale than when threatened during the Cold War, to preserve the regional order in Eastern Europe or Asia. In the end, there is no reason to assume that the United States is more committed to preserving U.S. primacy in East Asia or Eastern Europe than China or Russia are to changing those orders in their favour. On the contrary, it is a fair assumption that China and Russia care a lot more about what happens in their own regions than the United States does, just as the United States cares more than they do about the order in the Western Hemisphere.

This means there are a number of states which, though they cannot contest the United States globally, can challenge it diplomatically and especially militarily as a regional power. Russia in Eastern Europe, China in East Asia, and eventually perhaps Iran in the Middle East, are now capable of raising the costs and risks to the United States of conflict in their own region to the point that the United States can no longer dictate the shape of their respective regional orders. And that, of course, is exactly what they are doing. As we watch this happening, the role of military power in shaping regional orders becomes once again central to our understanding of international politics.

THE EAST ASIAN EXAMPLE

Against this background, let us look more closely at the idea that international orders are framed by the willingness of great powers to go to war with one another, by looking at the most important contemporary example of an order in flux — East Asia. The old regional order emerged in the 1970s with China's acceptance of U.S. strategic leadership in Asia. That meant, in practice, that China was not willing to go to war to contest the United States' position on Asian strategic questions, especially maritime questions, with the single and important exception of the status of Taiwan. China maintained that position for almost forty years, but in the last five years or so, that has changed. Beijing has begun to challenge the regional order based on U.S. primacy, and it has done that specifically by creating situations in which its willingness to risk war with the United States over regional strategic questions was demonstrated, and the United States' willingness to risk war with China was called into question.

China has found opportunities to do this, both in the East and the South China Seas. Consider the East China Sea example. U.S. primacy in Asia depends on its alliances and friendships with a number of regional partners, of which the alliance with Japan is the most important. The health of that alliance depends ultimately on Japan's confidence that the United States would be willing to go to war to help protect Japan from any serious attack. For many years until recently, that confidence has been hard to question seriously. China's assertive challenges to Japan's position over the Senkaku/Diaoyu Islands has changed that. By taking actions that have clearly increased the risk of a military clash with Tokyo, it has raised questions about the United States' willingness to incur the costs and risks of a confrontation with China in order to fulfil its obligations to Japan.

Those questions have not been answered by President Barack Obama's declarations that Washington regards the Senkaku Islands as falling under Article 5 of the Mutual Defence Treaty (The White House 2014). Real uncertainty remains about whether, in the event of a confrontation, Washington would really be willing to go to war with China over the

Senkakus, in view of the significantly increased cost and risks involved in such a course compared with even a decade ago. Today, as is now widely understood (Heginbotham et al. 2015), the United States cannot expect a swift and successful victory to a conflict with China in the East China Sea. The best it could expect would be an untidy exchange in which the United States as well as China would take substantial loses, leading to an inconclusive draw and heightened tensions dragging on indefinitely. The economic as well as strategic and political costs of this to the United States would be immense. These costs would be, in no way, made easier to bear by simply acknowledging that the costs to China would also be immense, because there is no reason to assume China would blink first. And there are much worse possibilities, too: an escalating conflict in which the nuclear threshold would be unclear and might be quite low, leading to the potential for a U.S. president to face the choice between accepting either a humiliating back down or the real risk of a nuclear attack on U.S. cities.

Of course the stakes for the United States are very high, because a failure to support Japan even over the Senkakus would seriously weaken and might actually destroy the U.S.–Japan alliance, and hence the entire basis of U.S. strategic leadership in Asia. No one can assume that a U.S. president would not accept the costs and risks of war with China to defend all that. But no one can any longer be sure that he or she would, and the uncertainty is likely to grow as China's power grows relative to the United States'.

Naturally, the same questions arise for China. Its adventurism in the East China Sea suggests quite strongly that it believes the United States would abandon Japan over the Senkakus to avoid a war with China, but if it is wrong, then China too would face a terrible choice between a humiliating retreat and the risk of an unwinnable war. We cannot yet know which, if either, of them would prevail in such a battle of nerves, which makes their respective roles in Asia's future order so uncertain. What we do know is that the outcome would have huge consequences for the future Asian order one way or the other. If the United States backed off, China would be well on its way to displacing the former and, perhaps, even replacing it as the leading regional power. If China backed off, U.S. leadership would be confirmed and reinforced.

We can see some of the same issues at work in the South China Sea. There, the United States has been trying to reassert its leadership in the face of China's blatantly challenging conduct over contested maritime territories. Washington has hoped to do that by "imposing costs" on

Beijing large enough to moderate Beijing's behaviour, but it has been very careful to avoid actions which might lead to a confrontation because it is not willing itself to accept the costs that that would entail. The result, as shown by the ineffectual Freedom of Navigation transit of late October 2015, was to demonstrate U.S. weakness rather than strength. It suggested that Washington will only be able to show its leadership in Asia if it shows it is indeed willing to run a serious risk of confrontation with China, and can convince China that it is sufficiently determined to protect its position in Asia, to allow a confrontation to lead to conflict if necessary.

These specific instances lead to a broader question: what in Asia today is the United States willing to risk war with China over, and vice versa? If it is willing — and if it can convince China it is willing — to risk war over the Senkakus or the Spratlys, then the United States has a good chance of preserving its position as Asia's leading power. But if China can convince the United States that it is willing to risk war with them over these issues, then U.S. leadership is in big trouble. By the same logic, the United States will ultimately only be able to constrain China's power in Asia over issues which it can convince China it is willing to go to war with China over, and vice versa. The United States will only have a significant strategic role in Asia if it can convince China it is willing to go to war over something, and China can only expand its role at the United States' expense if it can convince Washington that it will go to war over something other than Taiwan. And, in every case, the calculations of cost and risks must encompass the possibility, real but uncertain, that a war between them could cross the nuclear threshold.

THE RETURN OF POWER POLITICS

This is a strange and unfamiliar way to talk about international affairs. It suggests a return to concepts of realist power politics which had seemed to be definitely passé. We are, perhaps, in a position not unlike that faced by the theorists of the post-World War II era, and so brilliantly foreshadowed on the war's eve by E.H. Carr (1946). For a few decades after 1918, the role of force seemed to be eclipsed, and accounts that emphasized other factors — rules and norms, institutions and identities — came to the fore. After 1939, the realist reaction to these ideas exemplified by Morgenthau (1948) created a crude set of concepts which have proved quite inadequate at explaining the complex pattern of international politics since then, though they have often offered an excuse for lazy thinking by analysts and policymakers alike.

We need to do better than that. Among the refinements to realism which have emerged since those early post-war days, the ideas that seem, to me, to offer the most promising starting point for a more sophisticated and accurate understanding of the role of forces in international affairs in the situations we have sketched here, are those of the early English School — the era of Martin Wight and the group of thinkers who worked with him including, of course, Hedley Bull and Coral Bell. These ideas are, perhaps, best reflected in the edited volume *Diplomatic Investigations* (Butterfield and Wight 1966) as well as Bull's *The Anarchical Society* (1977).

The key insight of these thinkers at this time was that states operating in an anarchical system mediated by power could, nonetheless, negotiate with one another to establish sustainable orders among them which provided a way to manage their relationships peacefully. They recognized, I think, that the boundaries of order in a system were set by the great powers' willingness to go to war against each other, but they also understood that it was not necessary to go to war to discover where those boundaries lay. Much could be achieved by negotiation, in other words. But those negotiations would not succeed if they did not always keep in mind the reality of military power and the risk of war that loomed if negotiations failed. Indeed, it was the seriousness of the alternative, especially in the nuclear age, which made the peaceful negotiation of new orders possible, as well as so desirable. Any conception of international relations which underestimates the role of force and the risk of war is apt to underestimate how important negotiations are over the shape of new orders where change becomes, as it seems to be today, inevitable.

This leads to some rather straightforward observations about the priorities for further reflection and analysis. First, it would be helpful to explore how Asia's great powers could, and should, define those core issues about which they would be willing to go to war with one another. For example, much more work could usefully be done on questions about U.S. strategic objectives in Asia over coming decades. This has been neglected because for so long. it has been so readily assumed that the United States would have no trouble in maintaining primacy in the region, ultimately because it has been so readily assumed that its military preponderance would remain unchallengeable. As it becomes more and more clear that the United States will have to step back from primacy, at least to some degree, questions about where and how far it should step back become critical.

Second, the analysis offered here suggests the value of work on a key set of questions concerning the way in which states signal to one another their willingness to go to war. The recent rash of studies into the crisis of July 1914 suggests very clearly that a key cause of the war that followed was the propensity in each capital to misread and underestimate the resolve of the other parties to the crisis. The greatest risk of war in Asia today may well be the tendency of both the United States and China to underestimate one another's willingness to go to war over their differing visions of the regional order. The issue here is not just the well-studied one of communication and signalling within a crisis, but the broader one of pre-crisis signalling. How can the two sides signal to one another both their willingness to compromise over the future order, and the limits to that willingness? The future of Asia may well depend on this question.

10

POWER, PRESTIGE, AND ORDER

Nick Bisley

This is a good time to study Asia's international security setting. The biodiversity is astonishing. Scholars and analysts have become accustomed to what were once termed "new" security threats being core business. In the past, considerable energy and effort was spent trying simply to make the case that problems like transnational crime or the spread of infectious diseases warranted the distinctive analytic and policy lens of "security". Today, the range of issues in the region that present clear, immediate, and significant challenges to the well-being, indeed existence, of states and peoples is huge. Equally, the old fashioned security challenges which many had thought we had left behind — rivalry between states over territory, resources, and influence — have become recharged. Flying in the face of the complacent platitudes of liberally-minded globalization enthusiasts, the growth, wealth, and interdependence of Asia's states and societies has fuelled tensions, not caused a binding of interests or fostering of a sense of common cause.

But it is not just the range of security issues — both conventional and non-traditional — it is the sense of change and the rate with which such changes are occurring which makes the field so engaging and challenging. There is a palpable sense that the current period is experiencing a high level of "plasticity" (Mahbubani 2008). The mix of moderate foreign policies and a stable military balance, that kept the traditional security concerns from centre stage for over forty years, is changing. Moreover, the global financial crisis of 2007–8 and its recessionary aftermath has accelerated the sense of transformation. The structures which gave confidence in the past are eroding, future trajectories are uncertain, and state goals and ambitions similarly unclear. Therefore, it is a good time to study Asia's security landscape.

One of the notable features of the Asian security literature, both scholarly and policy-focused, is the absence of a shared vocabulary about that with which we are trying to grapple. Perhaps more precisely, there is no clear intellectual consensus about the meaning of central concepts and ideas. One must feel a degree of sympathy for the defence planner tasked with having to determine what kit to buy to advance their defence and security interests in the future; as they look to the literature to anticipate how China might behave or what role security of energy supply will play in state strategy, they see conflicting (if not downright) opposing views as to what to expect — and that is before they even try to grapple with the more scholastic analysis such as that coming from "critical security studies" scholars. Why do some think conflict between China and the United States is inevitable while others think it is unimaginable? At the heart of the debate about security in Asia lies a range of subtly different ways in which core concepts are used and, indeed, understood. One of the region's most important features is the rapid economic growth of a number of very large countries, most obviously India and China. But what does having more wealth actually entail for how a state will behave? Then there is the question of rank and behaviour — do states with certain attributes behave in particular and predictable ways? Much of the debate about China's future is predicated on the assumption that it will follow certain predetermined models as it becomes a bigger power. Yet, often left out of such discussion is the question of motivation — why do states act as they do? Does the force of their location in the structure of the system determine their future, as many realists insist? Yet any explanation of the current parlous state of Sino–Japanese relations must recognize the powerful role played by nationalism and ambition in their respective political systems.

One of the reasons why studying the social sciences is so engaging, is the inherently contested nature of the subject matter. In debates about Asian security, this is clearly part of the intellectual frisson, yet we need to have a better sense of the implications of these differences because the consequences of research findings and policy recommendations in this field can be a question of life and death. The purpose of this chapter is to explore these issues and, in particular, to examine how a number of key concepts in the study of Asian security are understood in different ways by scholars and analysts, as well as the implications of these differences for scholarship and policymakers. The first part of the chapter looks at the question of power and, in particular, unpacks the assumptions about the link between size and influence in international politics and then considers the expectations about how certain kinds of states behave.

Clearly, the traditional understandings of categories like great powers and middle powers do not fit the current circumstances, yet are often invoked as if they were laws of nature. The chapter's second section explores the tensions between more structurally oriented accounts of how states behave and the more protean, but nonetheless crucial, political forces that must be factored into analysis, such as nationalism, prestige, and ambition. The chapter concludes by exploring how these ideas intersect in differing accounts of the region's future security order.

POWER AND POSITION

For some time it has been evident that power in world politics has been shifting away from the North Atlantic hub where it has resided for the bulk of the past three hundred years or so. Scholars were debating the security implications of the rise of China and power diffusion from the early 1990s (Friedberg 1994; Brown et al. 2000). But it was not until the economic calamity of the global financial crisis that scholars and analysts realized just how significant this power transition had become. Until the financial meltdown of 2007–8, no one argued that China was not a global economic heavyweight nor that India was not also beginning to realize its potential and play a greater role, but as Fareed Zakaria put it, it was not so much "the decline of America but the rise of everyone else" (Zakaria 2009, p. 1). Yet with the onset not only of the crisis but the Great Recession, the rise of the rest was indeed met by the decline of the rest, with most of the economies in the Organization for Economic Cooperation and Development (OECD) shrinking in the five years following the crisis.

More than any other factor, it is the recognition of the shifting locus of power that has sparked significant scholarly and public debate relating to traditional security concerns. China's economic revival, alongside America's evidently waning power, has prompted great speculation about a range of issues, most prominently, the likelihood of conflict in the region (Friedberg 2012), the need to restructure regional order to avoid conflict (White 2012), its implications for regional order (Goh 2013), and indeed, the global system of international relations (Ikenberry 2011). But it is not only China's remarkable transformation that is prompting the broader sense of "plasticity". India has become a much more important power than in the past and Indonesia is tipped by many analysts to become a top four global economy within a generation (PwC 2015). When one adds to that the revival of Russian power and the presence in the region of Japan, the world's third largest economy, Asia is a place where significant concentrations of economic power seem destined to butt up against one another.

Few question that Asia is home to many states that are or are on their way to becoming very significant economic powers. But what is much less clear from the literature is what one can expect, in terms of security policy behaviour, from states that have large amounts of wealth. Put simply, there is no consensus at all in the scholarly literature about the link that exists between economic power and influence and behaviour at the international level. At one end of the spectrum, the link is thought to be straightforward and direct. As states get richer, they become more powerful. As they gain more power, they carry a greater weight in the international system and eventually, the most powerful are fated to struggle for dominance. Structural incentives impel powerful states to expand until they eventually must fight. Thus, for scholars like Mearsheimer (2001), the only thing that will prevent an eventual hegemonic contest between the United States and China is the unlikely prospect of China's economy falling into a sinkhole. A second common position in the literature is to see a direct, albeit complex, link between wealth and power (White 2012). Rather than seeing wealth inexorably prompting competition, this line of thinking sees wealth as a key driver of assertive behaviour, but one which alone does not determine things. Other forces are needed before states are prompted to act in ways liable to bring about conflict. In particular, the international milieu in which states find themselves — Do they feel threatened? Can they find satisfaction? — alongside domestic political pressures, determine how states behave. Wealth alone is not a necessary and sufficient condition, but in the right circumstances, scholars — predominantly from the realist tradition — see a reasonably direct line between wealth and power at the international level.

A third group is much more agnostic about the determinants of international behaviour. Citing the examples of Japan and Germany in the post-war period, they argue that states can have very significant concentrations of wealth, they can be in uncertain and dangerous geopolitical contexts, yet can still opt out of an assertive posture in security and defence policy. Here, it is the choices states make about how they think about their interests and the nature of the foreign policy instruments they choose to adopt at the international level that determine their behaviour (Katzenstein 1996). Variations on this argument see more liberally-inclined scholars, like John Ikenberry (2008), argue that China's interests and the broader constraints of the existing liberal international order make it unlikely to adopt behaviour that is destabilizing. While others argue that configurations of power matter, particularly preponderances, the means through which power is managed determine their impact. Perhaps the clearest statement of this approach, elaborated by Evelyn Goh (2013), is one that argues that Asia has enjoyed a "layered hierarchy" of power organizing its international relations in which the region is at its most unstable when there are uncertainties about the United States' position atop that order. Thus China's wealth and capacity alone does not prompt a challenge — it is the way in which it raises doubts about the United States' role, and challenges the thinking about order among Asian states, that matters most.

Debate about how the dramatic accretion of power by China and the relative decline of the United States will affect the region has not generated a clear consensus in the scholarly literature (on this see Bisley 2014). Most agree that, at least in the past, U.S. military predominance kept the region stable (whether due to a realist style balance or hierarchy or, indeed, hegemony), but what we can expect from changing power configurations is unclear. If this is true in the scholarly world, then it is equally true in real world international politics. Emerging powers are grappling with how to comport themselves as they become more important players on the international stage (see Narlikar 2013). That China and India would seek to have greater influence at the international level is entirely understandable, but what this will entail is far from clear. Of one thing we can be almost certain: no one is seeking to emulate the model set by the United States in the post-1945 period. None of the emerging powers has either the interest or the capacity to build and underwrite international institutions with a global remit and to deploy huge amounts of military capacity abroad on a long-term basis.

Central to any security-focused discussion of the re-emergence of Asian powers is the sheer scale of Asia's states, societies, and economies. Over the next generation or so, it is expected that China, India, the United States, and Indonesia will be the world's four largest national economies (PwC 2015). This has led many, particularly of a more realist variety, to conclude that the link between scale and power in international relations has returned. From the emergence of the modern international system in 1648 through roughly until the nineteenth century, power was closely correlated to size and scale. To become powerful at the international level, states needed to become larger. To have the population to create the wealth and resources to drive economic growth and the military capacity to expand and hold your expansion, you needed to have scale both in terms of territory and population. This is the orthodox international historical understanding of the development of Europe's international system through until the nineteenth centuries. Political power in Europe was concentrated ultimately in five "great powers" because of the inability of any one to gain sufficient capacity to become properly hegemonic (McKay and Scott 1983).

But from around the end of the Congress system until today, the traditional link between scale and power at the international level seemed to break down. Where in the past international dominance was the preserve of the very largest societies and states, now smaller powers began to prevail on the back of technological and political developments. That Britain was the world's pre-eminent power in the late nineteenth century is perhaps the clearest statement of how financial and technological sophistication, mixed with no small amount of self-confidence, could produce decisive advantages at the international level. With just under 2 per cent of the world's population, it controlled over a fifth of the planet's territory.

Yet, this relationship is changing once more. As the Asian giants revive economically, it would appear that the period of North Atlantic dominance will be but an interlude, as the tight correlation between size and power returns. Nevertheless, even if the prognostications of economists are right — that Indonesia will become among the world's largest economies, and that India will overtake China at some point to be the largest economy on the planet — there are a number of reasons to think that the link between size of economy and global power is not as clear cut as more conventional realists believe. As many observers, and indeed Chinese officials, often point out, even as China has an aggregate gross domestic product (GDP) of just over US$9 trillion, when that number is divided by its 1.35 billion people, wealth drops away considerably. In per capita GDP terms, China generally ranks around 80th in the world, depending on the method used. But emerging powers face challenges other than just long division. One of the frustrating elements of much contemporary scholarship and analysis is the tendency to assert or assume fairly clear links between wealth and power. Aggregate GDP figures are used by those who tend to predict that China (or others) will be disruptive to the current international setting. Per capita figures are used by those who tend to argue the opposite.

There is a real "per capita problem" but it is not simply that a large number becomes a much smaller one when divided by another large number. The Democratic People's Republic of Korea (DPRK) turns a very meagre economic scale into considerable military heft because it chooses to immiserate its population. But few states have this option any more. A country that has a low GDP per capita can still marshal considerable resources if it wants. Rather, there are a range of particular circumstances which will mean that emerging powers are unlikely to adhere to traditional expectations of how states with large populations and wealth are supposed to behave. The per capita problem for emerging powers is, in essence, that states are no longer able to extract resources from society and translate that into international weight, as was the case in what might be considered to be the "golden age" of great power politics. Even though not all states are democracies who have obvious electoral constraints on state autonomy, nonetheless the nature of the relationship between state and society in a globalized international system means that growing wealth brings with it growing expectations of capacity and service delivery at home. China is perhaps the ultimate example of this. Even though the Communist Party has no intention of subjecting its grip on power to the ballot box, its form of domestic regime legitimacy means that the state cannot heedlessly plough resources into military and diplomatic wherewithal. Equally, as Chinese officials are acutely aware, China has a host of very significant domestic problems, from the need to adjust its economic model, serious environmental degradation, disenchantment, and economic resource misallocation caused by corruption among many others. The state has a lot on its plate at home. But the point is not only that China is unlikely to behave like a great power of old, the link between its raw economic scale and the kind of role it is likely to play at the international level is not reverting to the kind of straight line connection that comes from the past. The link is complex and strongly influenced by domestic economic, political, and social expectation. The per capita problem means that not only will we increasingly see what might be called poor great powers, they will behave in ways that will be, in many ways, quite different from how major powers acted in the past.

The other problem with this broader literature relates to the notion that there are roles that states take on because they achieve certain concentrations of power. The idea that there is a distinctive role played by great powers is perhaps the most famous of these. Here, states with the highest concentrations of power are expected to have not only a right to behave in ways that others could not, but they also have a responsibility to manage aspects of the system (see Bisley 2012). Inspired by the idea that there are categories of states, scholars began to identify an ostensibly distinctive group of "middle powers". Perhaps the key contribution to the broader debate from the middle power scholarship is the observation that a middle power is distinguished not merely by its standing in international league tables, but by a particular set of attributes and behaviours which mark them out from others in the international herd (Cooper, Higgot, and Nossal 1993).

Yet the problem of the emerging powers is that they show no signs of wanting to adhere to pre-existing models or patterns of behaviour. In the past, great powers tended to follow two broad paths: they would either provide a kind order management function to the international system requiring a degree of consensus and cooperation between themselves, or they would be in competition with one another. In the current era, there seems to be little sign that either pattern will be followed. States with growing wealth and capacity, like China and India, show little appetite for taking on the traditional managerial leadership role, nor do they wish to contest U.S. power in any meaningful sense.

This reflection on scholarship examining the security and broader international consequences of the dramatic economic transformation of Asia leads to two observations. First, the link between power and international impact is neither direct nor straightforward. The simple fact of being a very large state with a considerable GDP may imply a great deal about what one might expect, but on closer inspection, translating wealth to power is a function of a complex array of processes involving domestic and international factors. Second, even when one can determine how wealth is transmuted into power in the contemporary period, states are defying expectations about modes of behaviour. This is, in part, due to the inability of much security scholarship to come to terms with the political forces motivating state behaviour and policy choice. Equally, it is also, in no small part, the result of the fact that much theoretical work has often made unreasonable generalizations about state behaviour based on a limited sample size with behaviour shaped by historically specific factors that have been ignored or forgotten.

FEAR, HONOUR AND AMBITION

Why states act the way they do in the security realm is among the main questions in international relations scholarship. At one end of the extreme, structurally-oriented theorists focus on how large-scale impersonal forces impel states to act in certain ways. Perhaps most famously, Waltz (1979) argues that the structure of the international system produces an unceasing contest between great powers who may not ultimately fight but who will be rivals. At the other end of the scale are accounts that focus heavily on the role of individuals, particularly leaders, in shaping state policy. Here, personalities loom large while more mundane factors, like bureaucratic politics and gaps between formal and substantive policy, are of much lesser concern.

Determining what balance one strikes between structural determination and the freer play of agency helps explain why we see such different interpretations of current events and policy recommendations. But for most analysts, the considerations that feature predominantly in decision-making or, indeed, explanation, are largely material and rational. That is, concern is predicated on the assumption that states act in an instrumentally rational way, informed by a consideration of tangible factors such as military capability, economic resources, and other concrete goods. But, as the figure who is often looked back upon as embodying the earliest insights into the causes of war — Thucydides — famously put it, the cause of the war in the Peloponnese was fear — the fear that the rise of Athenian power prompted in Sparta. The material was important — Athens' growing wealth — but the key was the intangible, yet nonetheless, powerful notion of fear. So not only do security scholars need to focus on their traditional concerns, questions of power and influence, the projection of force, and the complex cut and thrust of a shifting military balance, but they also need to focus on intangible protean forces which are a key part of the security setting in Asia. Of particular salience in the region are nationalism and ambition.

Before I discuss the important atmospherics of nationalism, we need to consider the structural factors which are thought by many scholars to be the most significant drivers of security policy in the region. Here, states are thought to be propelled by large-scale processes that emanate from the structure of the international system, such as the dynamics of the balance of power, and these drive states to act. Yet, scholarship informed by this perspective does not adhere to the same view, either as to the nature of structural forces at play or in the relative weight such forces have on state behaviour.

Perhaps the most prevalent notion among those informing analysis of the region's security dynamics is the set of behaviours associated with the security dilemma (Snyder 1984). The dilemma relates to the choices states make when faced with the security actions of others, normally neighbours. If a neighbour opts to modernize its defence force and acquire cutting-edge capabilities, how should you respond? The neighbour insists that it is simply seeking to defend its interests as it is allowed to do under the United Nations Charter. But what if they are not telling the truth? Or what if circumstances change and a new, more assertive government comes to power which could do you harm? That you do not know and can never know what they intend means you are faced with a choice; this is the security dilemma. In a region like Asia that has a wide range of security challenges combined with rapidly growing economic capabilities, security dilemmas play a significant role in shaping scholarly and policy debate (Christensen 1999). Yet, even though it is an approach involving a degree of agency, the security dilemma is nonetheless a structural form of analysis because it is animated by operations at the international level and, more importantly, because it prefigures the kinds of choices that states make.

At a larger scale of analysis, debate has focused on the extent to which the underlying structural conditions of the region, that have prevailed since Sino–U.S. rapprochement in the 1970s, are being challenged by shifts in the relative balance of power between Asia's great powers (Khong 2014). The order, variously described as primacy (White 2011), off-shore balancing (Walt 2006), or a form of hegemony (Mastanduno 2003), had as its central load-bearing pillar U.S. military power. As the relativities of power shift, so goes the argument, the order must change (White 2012). From this perspective, it is not especially important whether one has a hawkish leadership in Beijing or a more cautious Washington because the forces impelling action are operating at an almost tectonic level.

A third approach finds something of a middle road between the choices of the security dilemma and large-scale debates about security order. Here, scholars identify differing ways in which states can opt to navigate the security challenges they face. When faced with a neighbour whose behaviour is prompting a security dilemma, states do have options. Equally, shifts of large-scale structures do not produce mechanistic reactions from an international system that follows Newtonian-like laws. Scholars have identified a range of ways in which states can navigate the shifting shoals of regional security settings. Often associated with international relations theory's "neo-classical" school, scholarship has argued that when power shifts, states can opt to balance new configurations of power (Cha 2000; Sorenson 2013). That is, sets of lesser states can group together in alliances to offset the power and capacity of a larger player or they can "soft balance" against power concentrations (Paul 2005). States can also bandwagon as a reaction to shifts in the military balance. That is, rather than balancing by combining power (and more than likely taking on increased burdens and risks themselves), they can join an existing coalition that is underwritten by a major power. Certainly, in the enthusiasm with which Vietnam is approaching its links to the United States, one sees a version of this at play in the region. Finally, states can also "pass the buck", that is, they can convince a state that has a large stake in the overarching international status quo to take steps that advance a lesser state's interest (Christensen and Snyder 1990).

Structural approaches are perhaps most notable for their impersonal qualities. The push and pull of domestic politics, the identity and psychology of leaders and decision makers and the role of ideas is not especially important. Yet, while influential, such accounts are, by no means, the only ones which compete to shape scholarly and policy debate. Indeed for many, it is precisely this impersonal quality that makes structural depictions frustrating or limited. From this perspective, the nature of the leadership matters enormously for how states operate. For example, some argue that China's more expansive approach to its maritime interests in the East and South China Sea is directly a result of the attitudes and approach of Xi Jinping (Heydarian 2014). If the chair of China's military commission were less hardline, then China's policy in these disputes would be different. Equally, the role of Prime Minister Shinzo Abe in the continuing transformation of Japan's security policy cannot be underplayed, while many anticipate that India's Prime Minister Narendra Modi will usher in distinct changes in the country's foreign and security policy (see discussion in Hall 2015).

Beyond the place of individual leaders, scholars also emphasize the important role of domestic political structures in policy formation and implementation. In particular, attention is paid to the ways in which the institutional division of labour in foreign and security policy shape decision making. Whether this relates to traditional bureaucratic competition for influence or the differing interests that various groups have on the form and function of security policy, these scholars argue that attention must be paid to the influence of these domestic forces on regional security. For example, Linda Jakobson (2014) has described the ways in which various layers of the party state in China — including local government, state-owned enterprises, the coast guard, and the People's Liberation Army — each have distinct interests in maritime issues and sufficient localized autonomy to have created a condition in which state authority is "fractured". Attempts to grapple with or respond to China's maritime security policy, so this approach avers, must take into account the role of these forces in shaping policy outcomes.

But arguably the most challenging factor at play in the region, and one whose complexity is matched by its importance, relates to a group of protean ideational elements. The role of nationalism, ambition, and prestige in driving states to act has arguably never been more important. Nationalism has been a vital part of the Asian states' postcolonial evolution. Although often associated only with its more atavistic or competitive dimensions, it has also played a vital role in uniting often ethnically and tribally diverse peoples into coherent and largely peaceful polities. Nonetheless, the postcolonial legacy of nationalism, at least in its political impact on security policy, is the way in which it encourages destabilizing behaviour and constrains the room to manoeuvre to manage disputes and regional flash points. For example in 2012, the Japanese government reluctantly nationalized islands in the disputed Senkaku/Diaoyu group, in part because of a desire to strengthen the nationalist credentials of the teetering Democratic Party of Japan-led government. This precipitated the most recent tensions in Sino–Japanese relations as China accused Japan of reneging on an agreement not to change the strategic status quo. Equally, the role of nationalism, in various guises, within the domestic political discourse of many Asian countries, narrows the policy aperture in many aspects of security policy. The disputed territories in the South China Sea have a particularly intractable quality because they have been politically elevated to be a "core" territorial interest of China's and compromise on their status is thus almost impossible to achieve because such actions simply cannot be squared with the national redemption strand of the Communist Party of China's political programme. Also, the poor bilateral relationship between the Republic of Korea and Japan is often thought to be hamstrung entirely because of the role of nationalism in the respective political platforms of President Park Geun-hye and Prime Minister Abe.

One of the features of the current period of plasticity in world politics derives not only from the remarkable growth in economic welfare among many emerging powers but also from their clearly stated aim to carry an international weight more in keeping with their scale. Ambition, particularly among Asia's more sizeable states, is palpable. As with nationalism, this notion — which fits uneasily within instrumentally rational theoretical frameworks — has links to the colonial experience of many states. Having only relatively recently acquired sovereignty and having experienced life at the receiving end of the international system, these states have a desire to shape their circumstances. This does not mean they will replicate how this has been done in the past, but it means that the kind of thinking that is influential in Washington and other capitals — that the current international arrangements serve everyone well — is probably misplaced. Ambition is also often linked with nationalism. That is, nationalism is often understood to be actualized when states stand up for their interests, making the political management of compromise hard to achieve. To be clear, ambition in the region should not be mistaken for aggression, nor indeed does it have a common formation across Asia's many societies. Equally, how particular leaders act on or seek to mobilize ambition within states varies. But when analysing security dynamics, one must consider the impact of how ambition shapes the political process.

Asia's security landscape — both the policy formulation and decision-making process as well as the broader dynamics of security order — is produced by the interplay of structural and agential factors. The precise ways in which wealth and power intersect with domestic political institutions and powerful emotive forces like nationalism, varies in place and time. Those scholars and analysts who opt to emphasize one side over the other are often doing so for heuristic reasons. This can be intellectually reasonable and a function of their broader theoretical endeavour, but when one is trying to make policy based on scholarly insight or conversely to make sense of policy, there is a need to grapple with this complex reality. Of course, one can never integrate all of the variables that shape social reality into an intellectually coherent depiction — the one-to-one model of the world is the world; instead one must recognize the inherent strengths and limitations of the particular analytical frameworks one adopts.

CONCLUSION: POWER, PRESTIGE AND ASIA'S SECURITY FUTURES

In this chapter, I have sought to explore some of the competing ideas and concepts that shape the analytical warp and woof of Asia's security setting. I began by noting that there is no meaningful consensus about core ideas and, unsurprisingly, no general agreement about what states should do to maximize the prospects of stability and prosperity and reduce the chances of conflict and war. By way of a reflective conclusion, it is worth thinking about the differing futures that we might anticipate and what these tell us about the implications of the differing concepts and causal emphasis that they make.

In the best traditions of the social sciences, the first possible future is a vision of regional muddling-through. Here, the basic pattern of security threats and challenges established over the past decade remains in place over the next generation. Rather than challenging U.S. influence or the underlying international context, China continues to seek advantage in a low risk manner, but invests the bulk of its energy on internal economic and social development. Here, the region will be marked by the mix of cooperation and contestation that has been a feature of the region's security setting since around 2010. The second possible future canvassed entails a regional order in which the key powers collaborate to manage the region's security affairs in a cooperative manner. Whether imagined as a G2 (Group of Two), a concert of Europe retooled for the twenty-first century Asia, or the linguistically unlovely "Chimerica", much would hinge on Beijing and Washington establishing a modus vivendi so as to develop a shared way for managing regional order. Although perhaps the most optimistic of possible futures, it is one in which very considerable set of changes would have to have been accepted, most obviously by the United States and its allies.

The third future is one in which Asia's security setting is dominated by contestation. Here, the dominant setting of the region's international relations is one of conflict, perhaps not dissimilar in a basic sense to the underlying structure of the Cold War. Not every issue during that period led to unmanageable friction and outright war between the Soviets and Americans was avoided, but the tenor was one of competition for influence, both in the immediate sense and in the longer term, in which both sides saw the other as not only a threat to their interests, but to the basic structure of the international system that they sought to advance. A final possible future for the region is systemic transformation. This would involve a fundamental shift in the locus of power and influence leading to a radically different set of rules, principles, and operating procedures for the region's security order. A possible way in which this may occur would involve the withdrawal of U.S. power from Hawaii and the creation of a new, explicitly hierarchic regional order dominated by China — a kind of Sino-centric tributary system for the twenty-first century.

The reasons for concluding that Asia's security order will trend in one of these four directions depend on the relative weight one attributes to the factors discussed in this chapter. The impact of distributions of power among sovereign states is among the foundational questions in international relations. Yet, while few would dispute that it retains its conceptual centrality, its impact on state behaviour and, in turn, on the structure of international order remains a point of contestation. For some, Asia's security order is going to be marked by conflict because shifting distributions of power among great powers inevitably brings this about. Yet others argue that a concentration of power is not a necessary condition for a state to throw its weight about. Instead, power provides the capacity, but it is a mix of other factors that are required. And here, advocates for a more benign regional future argue that comfort is to be found. The balance of considerations — particularly among emerging economies dependent on Western consumers and investors for their success — means that even though they may have become much more powerful, they will not challenge the status quo; they simply have too much to lose. Yet, many others point out that states do not always form their preferences entirely rationally. The role of emotive and non-instrumentally rational forces like nationalism and ambition may well skew the way in which costs and benefits are considered. Thus China and the United States may well be headed on a path to conflict, not simply because China is being propelled down a path by impersonal forces, but because of the role that nationalist redemption and ambition plays in the Communist Party of China's world view and domestic legitimation strategy. Because of this, potentially, China's world view cannot be reconciled with the United States' views of an acceptable regional security order.

Even though the role of international institutions, and multilateralism more generally, has a rich tradition in international relations and there are strong advocates for their pacifying effects, in spite of the proliferation of regional institutions over the past decade or so, few scholars and analysts feel that they are going to matter greatly to the region's security setting. Not only is there little confidence that they will shape state preferences in any significant sense, there is scant belief that they will have an influence in shaping the evolution of the region's security setting. Given the number, scale, and influence of the region's major powers, this is perhaps not entirely surprising. Nonetheless, it is striking given the relative importance of multilateralism in virtually all other corners of the globe.

The region is experiencing a profound period of transformation. The old order is plainly fraying, new challenges abound, and we have few precedents from the past to guide our expectations. Asian states' scale, their per-capita power challenges, and the ahistorical quality of so many efforts to find analogues in the past mean that it is an especially challenging and rewarding period to be focusing on questions of security. Indeed, given this, there has never been a more important time for researchers to generate new and useful insights into the emerging landscape as a great deal will depend on the decisions that are made over the coming years.

11

STRATEGIC CULTURE IN THE ASIA-PACIFIC: PUTTING POLICY IN CONTEXT

Peter J. Dean and Greg Raymond

One of the most well-used quotes from Sun Tzu states that "if you know the enemy and know yourself, you need not fear the result of a hundred battles. If you know yourself but not the enemy, for every victory gained you will also suffer a defeat." Thucydides — who like Sun Tzu is a member of the "classical cannon" of strategic studies from the fifth century BCE — argued, in a not too dissimilar vein, that scrutinizing the political and cultural differences of the ancient Greek city states was critical in understanding their motivations and behaviour during the Peloponnesian War.[1] For both writers, appreciating the strategic culture of the protagonists is essential to understanding war, and crucial in the formulation of strategy.

Shifting forward a mere 2,300 years to the 1960s in Southeast Asia, the concept of understanding thy enemy and knowing thyself had not changed. A lack of understanding of the region, and especially its culture and political make-up, was to prove fatal to the efforts of the United States to prop up successive South Vietnamese governments in the face of a communist led insurgency. Robert McNamara, U.S. Secretary of Defense in the Kennedy and Johnson administrations, noted that in accounting for the U.S. defeat in South Vietnam, one of the key reasons was that "we [the United States] viewed the people and leaders of South

Vietnam in terms of our own experience ... we totally misjudged the political forces within the country ... our misjudgements of friend and foe alike reflected our profound ignorance of the history, culture, and politics of the people in the area, and the personalities and habits of their leaders" (McNamara 1995, p. 322). A decade later, Lawrence Sondhaus applied McNamara's analysis of the failings of U.S. policy in South Vietnam to the miscalculations and misjudgements evident in the U.S. invasion of Iraq: an observation that looks increasingly prophetic (Sondhaus 2006, p. 130).

What these insights from the ancient world and modern times reinforce is the continual failure of neorealist and traditional rationalist-materialist approaches to explain strategic behaviour. As Rashed Uz Zaman has noted, the need for understanding ourselves, our potential adversaries, our allies, and the world we live in has not changed over time (Uz Zaman 2009, p. 84). As such, in this chapter, we argue that despite definitional debates and various conceptual problems, the basic premise behind the importance of studying the strategic culture of the Asia-Pacific remains paramount, especially when dealing with such a complex and diverse region. Specifically, we argue that in the researching of Asia-Pacific affairs, the concept of strategic culture is central to putting strategic policy into its national and regional contexts.

In order to account for the ongoing relevance of strategic culture in enhancing our understanding of the Asia-Pacific, this chapter is divided into three key sections. Firstly, it explores the evolution of the modern concept of "strategic culture" from its beginnings in the 1970s through to today. It lays out the definitional and conceptual problems, traces the concept through its development from first to fourth generation debates and focuses on the discourse that has revolved around whether or not the concept should be seen as a form of context setting or a falsifiable theory. It then outlines recent endeavours to modernize the concept and join together the two areas of the "schism" that has characterized the development of strategic culture. Secondly, the chapter provides a focused assessment of the literature of strategic culture in the Asia-Pacific, detailing the depth and breadth of this field of study today. Finally, the chapter outlines a new research agenda for strategic culture in the Asia-Pacific region, arguing for the need for greater depth of study — particularly for the states of Southeast Asia — and for new studies that transcend state boundaries and single cases to consider regional and subregional groupings in order to provide a greater depth of understanding across strategic Asia. Ultimately, this concept is critical in understanding "context", that is, the circumstances that form the setting for events, statements, and ideas so that they can be fully understood. Context thus remains a critical element in the setting of any policy.

WHAT IS STRATEGIC CULTURE?

The modern concept of strategic culture has a rather short but heavily contested history (Sondhaus 2006, p. 6). The concept first appeared in the 1970s and situated itself around the debates on nuclear policy and deterrence. Specifically, this early work revolved around the Cold War and attempts by North Atlantic Treaty Organization (NATO) countries, especially the United States, to understand the motivations and behaviour of the Soviet Union. The first significant work of this kind was released by the RAND Corporation in 1977. This study by Jack Snyder argued that unique elements to Soviet (Russian) history, political institutions, and strategic situation gave it a distinctive strategic culture, one that contrasted with the orthodox understanding of Soviet strategic behaviour in the U.S. military at the time. In particular, Snyder argued that the Soviet Union was less inclined to use tactical nuclear weapons compared to what the U.S. military had previously assessed. However, Snyder also warned that a state's strategic culture was not "cast in concrete for all time" (Snyder 1977, p. 40).

Snyder's foray into a new cultural understanding of strategy was soon expanded upon during the late 1970s and early 1980s by the strategist Colin Gray. In particular, Gray defended the concept in relation to the problems of rational choice theory and game theory in explaining Soviet strategic behaviour. In expanding the concept further, Gray argued — in his 1999 work *Modern Strategy* — that, in fact, all dimensions of strategy are cultural (Gray 1999a, p. 136). Like Snyder, Gray also argued that a particular strategic culture was a "semi-permanent influence on policy shaped by elites and socialized into distinctive modes of thought" (Lantis 2006, p. 7). In addition to Gray, another early proponent of the concept was Ken Booth. Booth argued that strategic culture offered a balance against ethnocentrism, and could help analysts to understand a nation state on its own terms and to better understand irrational state behaviour (Sondhaus 2006, p. 7).

During the late 1970s and early 1980s, the concept seemed to be evolving in a clear, if somewhat iterative manner. However, by the 1990s, strategic culture had become hotly contested amongst strategic studies and international relations scholars. Snyder returned to the field in 1990 to argue that, in the intervening years, the concept had been applied much too broadly. He questioned the relationship between national culture and political culture and argued that the concept of strategic culture was only relevant when "a distinctive approach to strategy becomes ingrained in training, institutions, and force posture" (Snyder 1990, p. 7).

Around the same time, a major shift occurred within the field led by Alistair Iain Johnston. In his work on Chinese strategic culture, Johnston criticized earlier work in the field which he divided into a series of "generations" of scholars, around which the concept had developed (Johnston 1995a). In particular, Johnston identified three generations: the *first generation* (1970s) consisted of Snyder's original work and Colin Gray's studies along with some other scholars, notably Carnes Lord and David R. Jones; a generation that Johnston argued was too broad and simplistic in its approach. Johnston's *second generation* of scholars (1980s and early 1990s) included Robin Luckman and Bradley Klein whom he claimed had focused too much on instrumentality. Finally, he outlined a new, *third generation* of which Johnston emerged as the leading acolyte, which pushed for a much narrower definition of the concept that also sought to achieve a falsifiable theory (Sondhaus 2006, p. 8).[2] For Johnston, strategic culture is, in short, an "ideational milieu that limits behavioural choices" in which strategic behaviour is the dependent variable (the outcome) and cultural traits independent variables (something which causes outcomes) (Johnston 1995b, p. 46). Other third generation scholars, such as Thomas Banchoff, developed a path-dependent model whereby "decisions taken at critical historical junctures have shaped the development of foreign policy over time" (Banchoff 1999, p. 2). This, it is argued, is a process that "predisposes societies in general, and political elites in particular, towards certain actions and politics over others" (Lantis 2006, p. 11).

Johnston's work, especially in the field's conceptual development, created a schism between the third and first generations' scholars — in particular, Colin Gray (Johnston 1995b). This was, in essence, the difference in the use of the concept between Johnston's "positivist" approach and Gray's focus on "interpretivism" (Bloomfield 2012, p. 437). The debate largely centred on the role of state behaviour; Gray argued that behaviour is both an independent and a dependent variable, while Johnston and others dismissed this approach as tautological, claiming behaviour can only be a dependent variable. In response, Gray argued that Johnston and others' attempts to achieve a falsifiable theory was a fundamental mistake as it separates culture from behaviour. He argued that "strategic culture is both a shaping context for behaviour and itself a constituent of that behaviour" (Gray 1999*b*, pp. 49–69).

While the Gray and Johnston debate raged, they both came under criticism by other scholars as being focused far too much on continuity in strategic culture at the expense of accounting for change. Johnston and the third generation also came under criticism for their approach being too difficult to operationalize, especially in trying to assign "definitive, quantitative values to things like preferences and ideas" (Bloomfield 2012, p. 445). One of the more positive outcomes of Johnston's work on China, something which has taken hold in the now emerging fourth generation, is the notion that a state may, in fact, hold several competing strategic cultures that change over time (Uz Zaman 2009, p. 81).

The result of the Gray/Johnston schism, which in many respects seems to be roughly divided along a line that splits international relations (Johnston et al.) and strategic studies (Gray, Ball, Booth, Mahnken et al.) scholars, has been vitriolic and has meant that it makes the concept especially difficult for many scholars and practitioners to grasp.[3] In 2009, Rashed Uz Zaman noted that understanding strategic culture is not unlike "navigating an unmarked minefield on a dark night" (Uz Zaman 2009, p. 69). Developments in this field of study over the last six or so years, after this analogy, means that it could easily be extrapolated: one could well argue that what we now see is an overlapping series of unmarked maritime minefields sown at variable depths by these different theorists that have created an intricate web of complexity. If one was able to map this minefield, it may, in many respects, look like an intellectual and conceptual overlapping of ideas that is not too dissimilar to the cross-cutting territorial claims present in maps that highlight all of the competing claims to the South China Sea.

THE FOURTH GENERATION AND THE UTILITY OF STRATEGIC CULTURE TODAY

While Gray and Johnston disagree on most aspects of this concept, they can agree on the fact that strategic culture exists as ideas or preferences that direct a state's strategic policy and behaviour, and which are used and applied, even if scholars are divided on how this can be conceptually understood. Despite their differences, each of these authors is also attempting to achieve an explicit understanding of behaviour — whether this is contextual or predictive. As Colin Gray argued recently, cultural perspectives on strategy may well be "seriously flawed" but they are, nonetheless, both "helpful" and absolutely "essential" (Gray 2014, p. 92).

In more recent times, a fourth generation of scholars has made claims for the field of strategic culture to come together, to map the minefield *and* chart a course through it. This has been most prominently advocated by the Australian academic Alan Bloomfield and was recently applied by two young emerging academics to the Australian context. Bloomfield has called explicitly for a "re-conceptualizing" of the debate, arguing that it is time to move on from the Gray/Johnston schism. Bloomfield's call is based around Gray's idea of context merged with an extrapolation of Johnston's idea of the development of competing strategic cultures. Bloomfield notes that in accepting the premise of competing subcultures, "we can [then] begin to solve the excessive continuity problem by noting that these subcultures exist in changeable relations of dominance, subordination and latency relative to each other ... these subcultures being a mix of social/cultural and material/technical concepts" (Bloomfield 2012, pp. 452–53).

Bloomfield also attempted to rationalize the interpretivist and positivist divide. He did this by repositioning this debate, arguing for a melding of both positions whereby strategic culture is not operationalized alongside material variables, but rather through a "social understanding" of the nature and character of the international system that "give[s] meaning to the material variables under consideration" (Bloomfield 2012, p. 454). In Bloomfield's view, this approach overcomes issues of overdetermination in either continuity or change and allows for some modicum of predictability about potential changes in the dominance of different subcultures. Thus, his model takes the contextual approach from Gray and the goal of a (somewhat) falsifiable theory from Johnston (Bloomfield 2012, p. 456).

In applying this approach to Australian strategic culture, Alex Burns and Ben Eltham in particular emphasized the role of norm entrepreneurs, both groups and individuals, in promoting these competing subcultures (Burns and Eltham 2014, pp. 187–210). One of the most interesting areas of their discussion is the intersection of strategic culture in Australia with what can be called a national security culture. Burns and Eltham correctly describe the concentration of national security policymaking power in the executive arm of the Australian government and the role of policy elites in formulating and prosecuting the dominant Australian strategic subcultural divide. However, where their analysis falls short is in a lack of knowledge of the evolution of Australian strategic policy that leads them to make some rather superficial, and at times factually incorrect, conclusions.

The most significant problems in Burns and Eltham's article are, however, at the same time the most interesting conceptually. The authors have attempted to move beyond a strategic cultural approach — that is in relation to the use or threatened use of force in international affairs — to a broader "national security" culture approach — one that encompasses much broader areas such as economic, monetary, energy, environmental, military, political, energy, and natural resources security. Their major problem is a lack of discipline in the application of these differing concepts, as well as their inability to accurately and coherently identify material and cultural drivers for their case study. Nonetheless, the approach is helpful in articulating ideas that are enhancing strategic culture, especially the analysis of norm entrepreneurs in the promotion of the competing subcultures within a strategic/national security community.

Overall, what Gray's traditional first generation, and largely strategy studies-based, approach to strategic culture and Bloomfield's fourth generation amalgamation emphasize are the importance of using strategic culture as a way to put policy decisions in context. This is critical in the understanding of these decisions, in circumstances that form the settings for ideas and behaviour that are essential in both understanding security communities, and also in assessing possible future directions and policy decisions.

STRATEGIC CULTURE IN THE ASIA-PACIFIC

To explain characteristic patterns in policy and war-fighting, strategic culture scholars go beyond the structure of the international environment and the raw indices of national power — population, technological development, and economy. Instead, they utilize a cultural approach that considers a diverse range of local, specific factors including national identity, geography, military organizational culture, historical experience, and political culture. Given this emphasis on the local, specific and idiosyncratic, the strategic culture discipline is well-suited to build security policy from the ground up. The question then arises — how well understood are the strategic cultures of the Asia-Pacific region? Where are the gaps? Below we survey the state of strategic studies for countries in the Asia-Pacific region.[4]

It was not until after the Cold War that strategic scholars began to focus on Asia.[5] One of the first Asian strategic culture studies was George Tanham's 1992 account of Indian strategic culture. India's strategic culture was shaped, according to Tanham, by its subcontinental geography, its view of time and destiny, its experience of centrifugal political forces, and its exposure to the strategic thought of the British Raj. This produced a land-oriented and non- aggressive strategic culture based around the concept of the subcontinent (Tanham 1992). Tanham's work was the beginning of a steady stream of scholarly output on Indian strategic culture. Following India's 1998 nuclear tests, Rajesh M. Basrur (2001) sought to explain the restraint, stability, and minimalism of Indian nuclear policy using strategic culture. Rashed Uz Zaman (2006) examined the influence of the ancient Indian thinker Kautilya on Indian strategic culture. Runa Das' more recent article (2010) nominally takes Indian nuclear policy as its subject. However, it is as much a theoretical analysis of the concept of strategic culture from a constructivist perspective as it is a study of Indian strategic culture.

Although India is of increasing interest, China has attracted the most sustained and intense attention, especially from U.S. academics. Alistair Iain Johnston's 1995 landmark study of China's strategic culture, *Cultural Realism*, remains one of the most significant strategic culture works in the field (Johnston 1995*a*). Johnston aimed to "explicate a research strategy that [could] credibly measure the effects of strategic culture on the process of making strategic choices" (Johnston 1995*a*, p. 30). He constructed his model of Chinese strategic culture by looking for consistent preferences in Chinese textual material, in particular a set of Chinese writings on strategy, statecraft, and war called the *Seven Military Classics* (Johnston 1995*a*, p. 46). These had been used in Chinese military education, thereby providing a means of cultural transmission. He found more than one strategic cultural preference, including one that extolled non-violence and others that conveyed a "parabellum", realpolitik lesson — "if you want peace, prepare for war".

Other U.S. writers on Chinese strategic culture include Thomas Mahnken and Andrew Scobell. Scobell holds a similar view to Johnston: while China's self-image of its strategic culture is Confucian, in actual fact, it is a fusion of Confucian and realpolitik strands. The outcome is a "cult of defence" where elites can portray their strategic culture as defensive, pacifist, and non-expansionist but, at the same time, justify nearly any use of force, including first use of force (Scobell 2002). Thomas Mahnken proposes a Chinese national strategic culture that has three tenets: that China is culturally superior; that China's natural position is that of the Middle Kingdom; and that China must be unified internally and free from external meddling (Mahnken 2009).

Chinese scholars have also studied Chinese strategic culture.[6] Tiejun Zhang concedes a significant difference between traditional Confucian strategic culture and the strategic culture of the modern Chinese state. But Zhang (2002) characterizes these differently to Johnston, as respectively, "cultural moralism" and "defensive realism". He agrees with Scobell that the presence of Confucianism is a lesser element in modern day Chinese strategic culture. Instead, the notion of Comprehensive National Power is dominant, including in matters of defence.

Japan and South Korea are other Northeast Asian states that have received significant attention. Written years before Japan's current incremental moves to normalization, Thomas Berger sought to explain why Japan had not adopted a more militarily assertive posture in line with its post-World War II economic success. He argued that fundamental shifts in norms towards armed force took place in the aftermath of Japan's defeat and these became embedded in national institutions (Berger 1996). Forrest Morgan's book on Japanese strategic culture uses the Triple Intervention of 1895 as a case study. He seeks to explain why representations from Russia, Germany, and France induced Japan to give up significant territorial gains after its war with China. Morgan explains Japanese behaviour by referring to Japanese ethics that control behaviour within groups, families, and organizations (Morgan 2003). More recently, Andrew Oros (2014) has argued that there is evidence that Japan may be developing a "fourth" state strategic culture, following its cultures of isolationism, militarism, and post-World War II domestic anti-militarism. His evidence includes constitutional reinterpretation to allow collective self-defence, the creation of a National Security Council in 2014, and the development of new operational concepts such as "dynamic defence". However, Oros considers that a distinctive anti-militarist "security identity" will continue to constrain significant expansion of Japan's role as a military actor in the Asia-Pacific.

Work on South Korea includes Victor Cha's explanation of why the South Korean government robustly maintained a weapons acquisition programme focused on force projection capabilities in the wake of the 1997 Asian financial crisis. Cha (2001, pp. 106–7) argues that strategic culture — rather than levels of affluence or the disappearance of the bipolar strategic environment — best explains South Korean strategy. Although the post-Cold War period was his analytic focus, he saw South Korea's strategic culture as the product of its longer history of victimization by larger powers, including 900 invasions. Jiyul Kim (2014) shares with Cha a view that experiences of colonization and victimization drive a strong desire for self-determination in South Korea. A narrative of South Korean nationalism, the vision of a strong and prosperous nation able to withstand the pressures of great powers (*puguk kangbyong*), interweaves the pillars of South Korean security policy. These include the alliance with the United States and the need to counter the existential threat from North Korea.

The first Southeast Asian strategic culture study was Dewi Fortuna Anwar's 1996 study of Indonesian strategic culture. Anwar (1996, p. 10) considered Indonesia's intentionally devised doctrines of Nusa Tenggara (Archipelagic Concept) and Pancasila as part of Indonesia's strategic culture. Anwar placed significant emphasis on the effect that the quest for social stability and national unity has had on Indonesia's strategic culture. Three years later, Ken Booth and Russell Trood considerably expanded the canon of Southeast Asian strategic culture studies with their book *Strategic Cultures in the Asia-Pacific Region* (1999). For the first time, the strategic cultures of Thailand, Vietnam, Myanmar, the Philippines, Malaysia, and Singapore were explored. While Trood and Booth's book was a landmark, it perhaps should have opened — rather than closed — the doors for future studies. Their anthology omitted studies of Cambodia, Laos, and Brunei. Also, in covering the entire Asia-Pacific in one volume, the authors admitted that there was an unavoidable "sacrifice of depth for breadth" (Booth and Trood 1999, p. x.).

However, since the publication of *Strategic Cultures in the Asia-Pacific Region*, the amount of work published on Southeast Asian strategic cultures has remained limited. Given the rising geopolitical importance of Southeast Asia as a locus straddling key sea lines of communication between China and India (within a region comprising a growing proportion of the global economy), this is unfortunate. In 2015, a special issue of *Contemporary Security Policy* focusing on strategic cultures of the Asia-Pacific helped, although more remains to be done. This issue contained a new assessment of Philippine strategic culture by Renato Cruz De Castro. Cruz De Castro (2014, pp. 249–69) argues that an emphasis on internal security is part of Philippine strategic culture and reflects the preferences of the elites who have dominated Philippine local politics since independence in 1946. This preference will inhibit plans of the current administration to adopt a more outward-looking defence posture despite new security imperatives, including the rise of tensions with China over territories in the South China Sea.

Australia has also been examined by analysts of strategic culture. Famously characterized by Samuel Huntington as a "torn" country with respect to its Anglo-Celtic cultural roots and attempts to integrate more closely with Asia, Australia remains indisputably part of the Asia-Pacific by virtue of location (Huntington 1997, p. 139). Like Southeast Asia, it is positioned at the fulcrum of the Indian and Pacific oceans, in a region of increasing global and geopolitical significance. Graeme Cheeseman's early piece in Booth and Trood's book emphasizes the influence of Australia's origins as a harsh penal colony and a "frightened country" who perennially seeks security by sending its forces abroad in support of great and powerful benefactors (1999, pp. 279–98). In a more recent article, Jeffrey S. Lantis and Andrew A. Charlton (2011) use Australia as a case study to advance a model for incremental change in strategic culture. Their study of Australian defence policy change between 1990 and 2010 argues that events — including the 1999 East Timor Crisis, Islamist terrorism since 2001 and the rise of Asian economies and militaries — have constituted "learning pressures" on elites. As a consequence, Australian strategic culture has undergone a transition from a continental outlook represented by the Dibb 1987 Defence of Australia White Paper, to a "regional security plus" outlook which gives greater licence for armed interventions regionally and further abroad (Lantis and Charlton 2011, pp. 291–315).[7]

Finally, we might consider the state of work on common traits across the strategic cultures of the Asia-Pacific, or indeed the notion of an "Asian strategic culture". This is a contested area; many writers emphasize that strategic cultures emerge from unique histories, cultural inheritances, and political systems, and so are highly distinctive. With respect to Southeast Asian countries, for example, John Girling has written that many experienced a:

> fusion of Western political-economic forms of expansion with indigenous attitudes and institutions. The resulting synthesis in Thailand differed from that in other countries in Southeast Asia because the impact of the West differed in each country.... In addition, the geography, politics, history and social structure of each country – or what was left of each country after colonization or semi colonization – also differed. (Girling 1966, p. 61)

Nonetheless, there is a small body of work on this topic, some of it dating back to the earliest period of studies of strategic culture of Asian states. Desmond Ball's work on common strategic cultural traits across the Asia-

Pacific is an example. Asians, according to Ball (1993), tend to prefer informality and personal connections in negotiations, take a long view of history, and have a comprehensive view of security. They also prefer bilateral to multilateral partnering and accept the military in internal security roles. Frank Miller (2003) also sees merit in a pan-Asian view of strategic culture. Miller speculates that the strategic cultures of Southeast Asia manifest a strong concern with internal security, an outcome of their ethnic and linguistic diversity. Ramesh Thakur proposes an "ASEAN way" in security whose core idea is:

> [The] idea of comprehensive security, which emphasizes links across the several dimensions of security (military, political, economic, societal, cultural and environmental). The key element is national resilience which puts the internal and external stability of states at the centre of security concerns. (Thakur 1999, p. 245)

The observation that Asian countries with relatively recent histories as unitary modern states will be, above all, concerned with the internal stability of that state is an important one. Modernizing Asian countries are frequently as concerned with *building* a strong state capable of withstanding internal pressures as they are with *protecting* the state from malign external actors. In 2002, Mohammed Ayoob criticized mainstream international relations theorists whose focus on nuclear weapons, bipolarity, and superpower rivalry in the twentieth century had overlooked what he argued to be equally significant developments; firstly, the entry of large numbers of postcolonial states into the international system, and secondly, "the continuing attempt by these new members of the system to replicate the European trajectory of state making and nation building in a vastly different international setting where the postcolonial states are much more vulnerable to physical and normative intrusion from outside" (Ayoob 2002, p. 33).

Ayoob's point is a clue as to where to find elements common to Asian strategic cultures. It is also a useful reminder that the differing role of militaries in many non-Western countries, including their involvement in politics and development, requires careful consideration. In particular, the possession of an internal security role does not mean a military's external security role is purely symbolic, or that this internal role will necessarily be progressively or quickly retracted as those countries develop economically, politically, and socially.

A NEW RESEARCH AGENDA FOR
STRATEGIC CULTURE IN THE ASIA-PACIFIC

As outlined, strategic culture offers a range of potential research areas in the Asia-Pacific that can enrich our understanding of the strategic dimensions of the region and provide insights into potential developments. We strongly recommend the commencement of research agendas around areas such as: the under-researched countries of Southeast Asia — notably Indonesia, Myanmar, Laos, and Cambodia, and the Pacific Islands amongst many others; a reconsideration of Desmond Ball's notion from the 1980s of a pan-Asian strategic culture; and the development of studies on subregion groundings, such as Southeast and Northeast Asia or Theravada Buddhist states (Myanmar, Thailand, Cambodia, Laos), maritime Islamic states (Malaysia, Brunei, Indonesia, or even groupings such as those that would include the southern Philippines), and the former British colonial states. Another key area for development is looking at strategic cultural influence in traditional areas of strategic studies research, including force structure development, crisis management, defence budgeting, and the balance between domestic security and international security concerns. We also believe there is a great deal of fruitful study and beneficial insights to be gained from bringing together strategic studies concepts and detailed empirical studies in local languages and discourse.

Those undertaking such a research agenda do, however, need to be wary of the common pitfalls in the study of culture and strategy. As Tom Mahnken has outlined:

> strategic cultures may share features. For example, just because a belief in the efficacy of deception is a feature of Chinese strategic culture, it does not follow that such a belief is uniquely Chinese. Other cultures, such as that of Persia (Iran), also put great weight on stratagem. Similarly, just because culture is influential, it is not necessarily determinative. (Mahnken 2011, p. 6)

Furthermore, simplistic approaches to strategic culture can easily lead to reinforcing stereotypes (Stone 2006, p. 2), and to those stereotypes replacing risk assessment and strategy (Porter 2007, p. 46). These pitfalls should not, however, be allowed to become an obstacle to the study of strategic culture. Overall, the potential rewards far outweigh the risks and both those in academic and policy communities (building security policy from the ground up) would benefit greatly from looking anew at this concept.

Notes

1. For an account of the "classical canon" of strategic studies, see Colin S. Gray, Appendix B, "General Strategic Theory, the Classical Canon", in *The Strategy Bridge* (New York: Oxford University Press, 2010), pp. 264–66.
2. For a detailed description of the differences inherent in the first three "generations", see Uz Zaman, "Strategic Culture: A 'Cultural' Understanding of War", *Comparative Strategy* 28, no. 1 (2009): 74–82. This division has also been referred to as the three "waves" of scholars, although "generation" is the standardized nomenclature; see Elizabeth Stone, *Comparative Strategic Cultures: Literature Review (Part 1)* (prepared for the Defense Threat Reduction Agency, Advanced Systems and Concepts Office, 31 October 2006, p. 1).
3. See Desmond Ball, *Strategic Culture in the Asia-Pacific Region*, Working Paper 270, Strategic and Defence Studies Centre, The Australian National University, 1993; Thomas G. Mahnken, *United States Strategic Culture*, Defense Threat Reduction Agency, 13 November 2006.
4. This chapter considers the countries of South Asia, Southeast Asia, North Asia, and Australasia. Although the United States is a Pacific power, it is not included in this survey as it is also an Atlantic power and a global power whose strategic culture has received extensive analysis. Australia is included because while it is palpably not Asian in culture, as with Southeast Asia, it is located close to the pivot point of South and North Asia.
5. Globally, strategic culture begins with Jack Snyder's pioneering 1977 work on the Soviet Union's strategic culture. His essay emphasized the importance of history and culture in Soviet nuclear decision making. Snyder's work shared, with other scholars in strategic studies and strategic culture in this period, a focus on the key protagonists of the Cold War superpower nuclear rivalry, Russia, and the United States.
6. See also Shu Guang Zhang, *Deterrence and Strategic Culture: Chinese-American Confrontations, 1949–1958* (Ithaca and London: Cornell University Press, 1992) and Huiyan Feng, *Chinese Strategic Culture and Foreign Policy Decision-making: Confucianism, Leadership and War* (New York: Routledge, 2007).
7. Other studies of Australian strategic culture include Michael Evans, *The Tyranny of Dissonance: Australia's Strategic Culture and Way of War* (Canberra: Land Warfare Studies Centre, 2005).

SECTION IV
Policy and Practice

12

SECURING THE LOCAL AND THE GLOBAL: THE STORY OF POLICY ENGAGEMENT

Michael Wesley[1]

Ours is a hyper-vigilant age. Our journey through life is cushioned and buffeted by a constant stream of warnings, prohibitions and exhortations intended to make us safer. Every accident, attack, fatal disease, or tragedy is followed by a flurry of post-mortems about what went wrong and recommendations about what should be done to make sure such an event cannot happen again or at least will be much more unlikely. We refuse to be comforted by the statistics that tell us we are, on average, leading longer, healthier lives, that crime and accident rates are falling, or that extremist attacks remain very rare, and fewer and fewer of our fellow citizens can remember the last time our countries were involved in a prolonged fight to the death between powerful countries. Meanwhile, our governments believe their survival depends on reassuring us that they are doing everything they can to ensure our individual, community, and national security. And a whole ecology of research institutions — university centres, think tanks, consultants, intelligence agencies — thrive on the endless demand by governments and their citizens for reassuring research into the latest causes of their anxieties.

It is no coincidence that our hyper-vigilant age is also an age of hyper-research and hyper-information. Our society has more capacity to investigate itself and its preoccupations, and to share the results of those investigations, than ever before. Each advance in our safety and well-being yields to new anxieties and new subjects for research and risk reduction. Research into security is a major industry, an academic-policy complex that has taken its place alongside the military-industrial complex. The symbiotic relationship between security policy and security research has been much noted and discussed, though it would seem with little impact on either the research or the policymaking (Herman and O'Sullivan 1989). It is worth looking at this relationship anew, and from a different angle, to consider how security policy shapes security research and vice versa, and to make a couple of comparisons: how the research-policy nexus in the security realm compares to the research-policy nexus in the prosperity realm, and how these mutual relationships between research and policy differ from country to country. On the basis of these two brief comparative excursions, I conclude by suggesting a new, programmatic and potentially more productive relationship between research and policy in the security realm.

RESEARCH AND POLICY: SECURITY VERSUS PROSPERITY

We can learn much about security as a field of research by comparing it with the study of that other paramount human value: prosperity. The discipline of economics is older, more widespread and more prestigious (even having established its own Nobel Prize) than that of security, but this should not blind us to the sufficient parallels between the two that makes them an interesting comparison. Economics and security studies are both social sciences; both have a distinct policy focus; and both are concerned with the effects of interdependent choices among humans and their institutions. While the methods of economics have, on occasion, made a significant impact on security studies (the work of Thomas Schelling comes to mind) the opposite impact is much rarer. Intriguingly, economists and security researchers can look at the same event or trend — such as the rise of China or an Asian financial crisis — and draw diametrically opposed conclusions.

An obvious difference between economic and security research is the availability of data.[2] Economists rely on large volumes of data recording economic preferences and behaviour, allowing them to draw confident conclusions about the complex workings of economies. Security researchers have little or no data; even the most common security phenomena, such as terrorism, are too rare, singular and widespread to generate the same confident causal relationships as economists can (there are exceptions; for example Pape 2005). Economists study behaviour that occurs constantly and is increasingly recorded in large data sets, partly in the knowledge that it will be subject to economic analysis. Security scholars focus mostly on potentials: events that could happen but that should preferably be prevented. The confirmation of an economist's conclusions lies in the effectiveness of his or her regressions in mapping the key trends in the data; the true measure of a security researcher's wisdom lies in a conflict or crisis that does not happen thanks (he or she would like us to believe) to the acuteness of his or her analysis and the appropriateness of his or her suggestions for avoiding catastrophe.

Economists work on different human emotions and motivations than security scholars. Economics is a field of human behaviour that is governed by fairly simple motivations: self-interest and greed. While the simple behavioural models economists have built on these motivations have come in for some legitimate criticism, they do allow relatively elaborate behavioural models to be built and tested. Security scholars are attuned to a different set of human motivations: power, fear, and pride. These have allowed some modelling to be done (the security dilemma, power balancing, absolute and relative gains come to mind), but are in general, much harder to define and build into predictive frameworks. True, both economists and security scholars rely heavily on revealed preferences — using actual acquisitive or aggressive behaviour to infer actual intentions — but security scholars on the whole tend to be more tentative, because they are aware they are working with more complex motivations. Part of the problem is that economics follows overt behaviour and openly admitted preferences, while the world of security is replete with hidden motives and designs, deliberate deception, and no small amount of self-delusion and denial.

Ultimately, economics deals with a realm of human activity characterized by relatively constant preferences and competing choices. The things humans desire most are relatively similar across large numbers of people. Humans' material wants do change, but over long periods of time; from year to year, they tend to hold a fairly stable set of prosperity goals. Security, on the other hand, is concerned with both competing preferences and competing choices. Human fears are highly varied, both across space and time. What one person or group fears most can be very different from what others fear. Context has a major effect on human fears; the evolution of regional or global affairs can change security orderings relatively quickly, as a range of opinion polls can demonstrate.

These differences tend to make for a very different relationship between research and policy in the fields of economics and security. Economic research is routinely read and quoted in business, media coverage, and government policymaking. Generally, officials involved in the realms of economic policy have formal training in economics; many to a very high level. The exchange of information and analysis is regular and largely technocratic; because government and non-government economists are largely working on the same open data sets, the research-policy exchange tends to be much less prone to accusations of bias or partisanship. Non-government economists are afforded the roles of "experts": the possessors of advanced research techniques and unbiased perspectives on issues of the economy.

Security research is not routinely read by many outside of the field of security studies. Prominent security scholars and think-tankers have become prominent media commentators, a tactic that ensures they are read and listened to by policymakers; but there is little evidence that their ideas are naturally absorbed as part of the policymaking process. Where a closer relationship between researchers and policymakers does exist in the field of security, it tends to be a largely directive one — of policy agencies commissioning researchers or institutions to undertake specific tasks for them. Part of the problem for security researchers is information asymmetry; unlike in economics, they do not work on the same data sets or knowledge base as policymakers. The foundational role of secrecy in security policy means that security researchers are often working at a considerable disadvantage; and even when classified material is not relevant to a particular piece of security analysis, the presumption of information asymmetry tends to lead officials to discount the opinions of researchers. Whereas economists tend to be seen by policymakers as "experts", there is a tendency for security policymakers to see researchers as either critics or uninformed armchair generals.

Of course, these are broad generalizations. The work of some security scholars does become part of the discussion and debate over security policy, just as there are more than a few economists whose research goes unnoticed by policymakers. My point is that the more seamless dialogue of economic research and policy is the result of certain structural conditions of economics: richness of data; stability and predictability of preferences; the overt nature of the motivations and decisions around prosperity. These conditions do not exist in the security realm. The lack of data makes security a more subjective art form, unable to be structured and disciplined around incontrovertible evidence. The subjectivity of security makes it much more open to critique and debate, which, in turn, leads to a greater personal investment in security judgements and a greater defensiveness when confronted with alternative views. The pervasive secrecy in the security space creates enduring information asymmetries and the tendency to discount non-government perspectives, whether this is justified or not.

All of this is to suggest that there is a qualitatively different relationship between research and policy in economics and security. Because of the structural features of security, researchers who want to build consequential relationships with the policy community must establish specific understandings and trust with government agencies. I would contend that this necessity changes the nature of the security research, and perhaps the security policymaking, that results. A security scholar wanting to develop and nurture a consequential relationship with policymakers is necessarily constrained in what he or she can say and write, lest he or she be cast back into the undifferentiated swamp of the critical and uninformed. Policy, on the other hand, acquires a powerful shaping force once it admits researchers into its inner sanctums. Unlike in economics, where the formal training of officials often rivals that of researchers, security officials can feel intimidated by the researchers that have been allowed into inner policy sanctums.

RESEARCH AND POLICY:
NATIONAL DIFFERENCES, COMMON DILEMMAS

Despite the structural obstacles, most countries, to some extent, integrate non- or semi-governmental security research into their policy deliberations. This process dates from at least the 1940s, with the establishment of institutions like the RAND Corporation in the United States and various policy research institutes in the Soviet Union. Security research institutions have been a significant part of the remarkable growth in global numbers of research centres and think tanks since the 1970s. A significant portion of that dramatic growth has occurred in the Asian region, where research institutions can play a distinctive role in international and security policies of states. We can gain further insights into the relationship between research and policy in the security realm by looking comparatively at these relationships in the countries of Northeast and Southeast Asia.

The establishment of non-governmental research centres on international and security affairs in Asia dates from the 1950s. This was at a time when

China, facing isolation after the Sino–Soviet split, and Japan, looking to "normalize" its external relations after the Second World War, established institutions such as the China Institute for Contemporary International Relations (CICIR) and the Japan Institute of International Affairs (JIIA). Think tanks came later to Southeast Asia, but along with those in Northeast Asia, they all represented a revealed need within East Asian governments for much greater knowledge about the world in which they had to survive and prosper.

There is a marked variance in how these security research institutions relate to the policy process in different Asian countries. While many security research centres are government-funded, this does not imply a similar level of access or intimacy with the policy process for all. In Japan, institutions such as the National Institute for Defense Studies (NIDS) and, until recently, the JIIA are directly funded by government agencies, and their direct input into the policy process has been limited. According to one observer, Japan's research centres provide the "groundwork" for the foreign policy and national security community "on a quiet and persistent basis" (Nakayama 2012). At the other end of the spectrum are Chinese think tanks, many of which sit within the bureaucratic wiring diagram of the Chinese government, and which make use of a range of formal and informal (*guanxi*) connections to deliver their research to policymakers. Some Chinese think tanks have access to classified government material, which presumably reduces information asymmetries and enhances the credibility of their judgements in the eyes of policymakers (Tanner 2002). Southeast Asia's security research institutions are themselves varied, but tend to fall between the Japanese arms-length relationships and the relative intimacy of research and policy in China. The "ISIS" Institutes in ASEAN countries (the Centre for Strategic and International Studies in Indonesia; Singapore Institute of International Affairs; Institutes of Strategic and International Studies in Malaysia, Thailand, and Myanmar; the Institute for Strategic and Development Studies in the Philippines) have both formal and informal linkages to national elites and the state apparatus (Stone 2011).

One major impact on the security research-policy nexus appears to be the general political environment within which security is considered. In Japan, the political context is highly polarized, between strongly anti-militarist state universities and an increasingly right-wing commentariat that can be savagely sensitive to any critique of government policy. In a recent controversy, the JIIA ran afoul of this environment, when two of its English-language commentaries were savaged by a right-wing commentator, who accused the JIIA of using taxpayers' funds to bash Japan for foreign consumption (McNeill 2006). Such experiences have a deadening effect on independent views on foreign and security policy, as was demonstrated when the JIIA quietly removed the two pieces that had so enraged the right-winger. On the other hand, Chinese security research institutes, and many of their counterparts in Southeast Asia, operate in a culture of expected conformity or at least non-criticism of government policies. This means, according to one observer, that an overriding orthodoxy pervades their research but, at the same time, makes policymakers much more open to the views of such compliant research institutions (Shambaugh 2002, p. 579).

But this is not to say that less-than-independent research institutes cannot have a catalytic effect on policy development. China's "second generation" think tanks, established early in the post-1978 reform era by reformist leaders unhappy with the orthodox Marxist research of the first-generation think tanks, were used by their sponsors as places where new ideas could be incubated until the right opportunity arose to propose them as reformist policies (Tanner 2002, p. 560). Meanwhile, by using their think tanks as the vehicles for reformist ideas, leaders established a degree of distance and deniability from unorthodox policy proposals. Similarly, in Southeast Asia, the quasi-governmental ASEAN-ISIS think tank network emerged in the 1990s as a major driver of new thinking on regional cooperation and helping to build understanding of the benefits of cooperation among regional elites (Stone 2011, p. 242).

The key tension, for both research institutions and policymakers, lies along an independence-compliance axis. On the one hand, research centres need to be independent enough to be able to promote innovative policy ideas. On the other hand, the conservative nature of the policy process has only so much appetite for innovation; ideas that challenge too many policy shibboleths can be seen as either dangerous or irrelevant, or both. The temptation towards innovation can lead to an almost programmatic critique of policy by research centres, leading to a spiral of defensive closing of the policy process, in turn leading to even greater critique by excluded researchers. The opposite pathology can develop when the desire for access, relevance, and impact leads to unproductive levels of consensus and group think between policymakers and researchers. The result is an unhealthy shared consensus about innovation, where certain policy verities go unquestioned and "innovation" is proposed and tested within very narrow shared parameters.

Research centres can also be useful as mechanisms of outreach. Non-governmental research institutions are regularly used by Asian governments as instruments of diplomacy, dissemination, or information gathering. The JIIA and NIDS are explicitly used by the Japanese government to build Japan's engagement with external communities of research and opinion (Kurihara 2013). Chinese security think tanks are expected to perform the roles of gathering information and intelligence through interaction with foreign counterparts, testing foreign reactions to proposed policy innovations, building networks with foreign policy research institutes, and conveying messages not deemed suitable for expression through conventional diplomatic means (Casarini 2012). At its ultimate iteration, such international networking by security researchers finds its articulation in Track II diplomacy,[3] a phenomenon that has proliferated in Asia over the past quarter century. Track II diplomacy is expected to play a range of roles, including promoting and testing policy innovation, progressing discussions deemed too sensitive to explore through official channels, and promoting mutual understanding and confidence-building among security elites. More often than not, officials attend such dialogues in non-official capacities, converting such exercises into "Track One and a Half" dialogues; or, in the case of the Shangri-La Dialogue, an exercise in defence diplomacy where officials are the main players, and researchers are invited to provide leavening to the discussions (Capie and Taylor 2010).

Once again, however, it is far from clear that these activities genuinely have an impact on security policymaking. According to one observer, "Track II fatigue" set in across Asia in the aftermath of the 1997–98 Asian financial crisis, as officials began to question the value of these proliferating "talk shops" (Nakayama 2012). Perhaps the clearest example lay in the case of CSCAP, the Council for Security Cooperation in the Asia Pacific, originally designated as the "brain" of the official ASEAN Regional Forum (ARF) security body. However, as the ARF succumbed to its own internally-mandated paralysis, it became clear that CSCAP has been unable to generate sufficiently innovative ideas to move the ARF process forward, despite its success in arriving at an agreed definition of preventive diplomacy (Simon 2002). One close study of both the CSCAP and ASEAN-ISIS processes concluded that their influence on both institutions and policy had waned after the turn of the century (Capie 2010). Other scholars are not so ready to dismiss CSCAP, however. While conceding that CSCAP's close relations with government had a narrowing effect on its deliberations, one study found that CSCAP continues to play a valuable role in raising and discussing issues too sensitive for Track I discussions and has facilitated the emergence of "Track III", or civil society diplomacy, in the Asia-Pacific (Kraft 2000).

Another peril for research institutes that play quasi-diplomatic, information-gathering roles is that they will come to be seen as "captured" by the counterparts with whom they interact. The predominant method for conducting security-oriented research on other countries is to consult the writings and opinions of policy elites and researchers in those countries. Their resulting attempts to explain the security attitudes and policy settings of the countries they study can lead suspicious policymakers to see them not as unbiased researchers but as captured advocates for rivals' interests. Sinologists in the United States branded as "panda-huggers" by policymakers have much to commiserate about with their counterparts in China: the U.S. experts who are disparaged as "eagle-huggers" (Glaser and Saunders 2002, p. 609). In Canberra, Indonesianists believed to be too sympathetic to the Indonesian view of security issues were branded as part of a "Jakarta lobby".

A NEW APPROACH: DEEP SECURITY

Amid all of these differences and dilemmas of innovation and impact, there are perhaps even greater challenges stemming from the substantial evolution of the field of security itself. While guarding against the parochialism of the present, it is hard to deny that security in the second decade of the twenty-first century is a more variegated and complex field than it was in the middle of the twentieth. Commentators have noted the process of the diffusion of power away from a handful of advanced wealthy states to developing states, private corporations, and empowered individuals and movements since at least the early 1970s. The range of issues we list as security concerns has broadened considerably, incorporating now not just dangers to states and regimes, but a panoply of "human security" concerns, from environmental degradation to pandemic disease outbreaks to natural disasters. But, perhaps the greatest change is the evolution of global order towards a multipolar and multicultural order, as states that have never been Western nor Western-aligned become increasingly consequential security actors. In this world we are entering, surely the differences between how societies conceive of security and react accordingly, will become more and more important.

As we noted above, security is a realm governed by competing preferences and competing choices. Currently, in many countries in Asia, there is an active or nascent debate among security analysts over whether Islamic extremism, in the form of the Islamic State movement, is a greater threat and, therefore, demands greater priority, than the issue of the rise of China and the consequent rivalry over regional order. Ultimately, this debate is unresolvable, because the advocates of each prioritize different values. Those who worry more about the Islamic State threat place greater importance on the stability and cohesion of society at home; those who prioritize concerns over the effects of regional rivalry worry more about the stability and coherence of the international order. If such differences in threat perceptions and ordering exist within societies, it should not surprise us that substantial gulfs exist between societies' security perceptions.

While remaining aware that differences in security perceptions exist within national communities, the field of security studies should be increasingly attentive to the differences among national elites' security perceptions and responses, as structured by geography, history and domestic sociopolitical dynamics. Furthermore, security studies should pay greater attention to the non-trivial effects of these differences in security perceptions when states interact in the security space — either in moments of collaboration or crisis. Abundant anecdotal evidence exists to show that when states misunderstand or fail to acknowledge substantial differences in security perceptions and orderings, catastrophic consequences ensue: the invasion of Iraq and "light footprint" occupation and rebuilding; the nationalization of the Senkaku/Diaoyu Islands in the hope of de-escalating the dispute; the eastern expansion of NATO (North Atlantic Treaty Organization) as a confidence-building measure. Such missteps suggest that an innovation frontier that researchers can open up for security policymakers is that of building much greater understandings of the consequential variances between national elites' security perceptions and orderings and the dangers and opportunities that may arise when these different conceptions interact in the security realm.

This is the motivation behind the "deep security" research agenda being developed within the Coral Bell School of Asia Pacific Affairs at the Australian National University. Taking advantage of a community of scholars — comprising both experts in international relations and security studies and those with deep expertise in the societies and politics of individual states in Asia and the Pacific — the deep security agenda focuses attention on the processes through which national elites define, order and respond to security challenges; and on how these processes and conceptions affect these states' security interactions, regionally and globally. Deep country knowledge, combined with detailed empirical research in vernacular languages, married to broad security studies and international relations methodologies, offers a chance to take security studies in substantially new directions, including in the way in which security researchers interact with policymakers. For the most part, policymakers are unable to acquire and maintain detailed knowledge of the conditions and dynamics that shape security perceptions within societies. Researchers can do this; but before this develops into a new form of research-policy interaction, scholars must first convince policymakers that differences in security perceptions can have significant consequences, and that understanding different security perceptions is a necessary precondition to dealing effectively with other countries in regional and global contexts.

The deep security research agenda is currently progressing along two separate tracks. The first has assembled teams of scholars to study security "from the ground up" in four countries in Asia and the Pacific: Solomon Islands, Indonesia, Myanmar, and China. Each group has produced an essay on domestic security dynamics within the country being studied; an essay examining how this affects its security interactions regionally; and an essay considering how these domestic and regional dynamics affect global level security considerations. These essays have been published in a 2016 special issue of the journal *Asia and the Pacific Policy Studies*. Importantly, the workshops and seminars supporting the development of these essays have been able to engage substantial involvement from Australian government officials in both confidential and open sessions.

The second track takes a more systematic, empirical approach. It involves the harvesting of security-relevant opinion polling data from across ten countries in Asia with the intention of establishing where differences in security perceptions occur across six axes: whether societies have a more controlling or fatalistic attitude to risks; whether they prioritize intentional over contextual threats or vice versa; the rates at which risk orderings change; concerns about internal or external threats; whether they prioritize the eradication of the threat or building resilience to it; and whether responses tend to be channelled towards individual or collective responses. Once these empirical differences in risk perception have been established, the project will begin to hypothesize and test the effects of different "cultures of risk" interactions — both in terms of their impact on security negotiations as well as on behaviours and perceptions during crises.

CONCLUSION

Security scholars occupy a distinctive position in the policy firmament. The subject they study is the highest purpose of the state; and yet, the comparatively data-poor, secretive, and speculative nature of their subject of interest places them in a relationship of considerable tension with the policies they critique and try to influence. This means the relationship between security research and policymaking will never be as simultaneously independent and seamless as in economics or health policy. The ongoing dilemma of independence and innovation versus acceptance and impact plays out in different ways in different countries; certainly, the political context of security making and the particular nature of state-scholar relations in each society has a major impact on the ability of security researchers to be independent and impactful.

At the same time, the field of security studies is becoming broader and more diverse. The array of threats and challenges, and the subjects of states' security interactions is growing greater and more varied by the decade. As security disperses as a field, it is almost certain that the differences in how different societies perceive, order, and respond to security threats will become ever more consequential. In this context, the deep security approach — dedicated to understanding different security perceptions among different societies and how these differences affect their security interactions — becomes ever more important. The deep security approach promises to take security studies and policymaking away from its current reactive, programmatic, iterative approach. It is a perspective that emphasizes the interactive, inter-societal nature of security, and in doing so, challenges the self-referential, ethnocentric, and often hyper-judgemental settings of security policymaking.

Notes

1. My thanks to Tomohiko Satake, Amy King, Zhang Feng, and Ryan Manuel for their advice in preparing this chapter.
2. A point made by Hugh White during the *Asia and the Pacific Policy Studies* special issue seminar on China.
3. Track II diplomacy refers to policy-based discussions among scholars, and is distinguished from Track I diplomacy (discussions among officials) and Track III diplomacy (discussions among civil society groups). Track one-and-a-half diplomacy refers to discussions among scholars, to which officials attend and contribute in a non-official capacity.

13

MUDDY BOOTS AND SMART SUITS: PRACTICAL CONSIDERATIONS FOR RESEARCH IN THE TWENTY-FIRST CENTURY

Amy King and Nicholas Farrelly

NEW KNOWLEDGE

Creating new knowledge — the task at the heart of research practice — is almost never straightforward. Whether you are in a Hmong village in northern Thailand, a government office in Canberra, a dusty archive in Beijing, or a banquet hall in Singapore, there is no single, or simple, way that research in Asia-Pacific affairs should be done. For some researchers, their career is spent down in the dirt, where muddy boots may be symbolic of long commitments. Others spend their time among sharply-dressed officials and business people — the other end of the continuum. Lack of unanimity about preferred research tactics and techniques inspires us to consider the many different ways that researchers can successfully blend disciplinary, thematic, and geographical orientations to support their analysis about how the world works and why. In fact, it is this wide variety of research practice that helps to sharpen our understanding of politics at the local, national, regional, and global levels. Good research begins with a puzzle about how things happen. In this chapter, we reflect on the different practices of solving these research puzzles, and consider the conceptual, ethical, and practical challenges researchers face in their quest to understand some of the biggest questions in social, political, and economic life.

The practical challenges of research tend not to receive much everyday attention beyond methodology classes, which often narrowly emphasize mechanics rather than cultures.

This is partly the result of professional hesitation about revealing some of the many difficulties involved in effective and sustained research practice. Researchers often enjoy a life of flexibility in terms of research topic and approach, with a variety of intellectual entanglements that can be the envy of those in many other twenty-first century jobs. Researchers also face the perpetual struggle for positions, funding, and priority in academic political economies that can prove inhospitable, even for the best prepared. Entire subcultures of academic reflection are devoted to the gripes and grievances of those who imagine that a gilded age has recently vanished: much of this material is nowadays found online, a global common room. At the same time, most universities are caught in an ongoing series of reviews and revitalizations, all designed to help ensure space for new technologies, management techniques, and productivity improvements. Unenviable decisions need to be made about the allocation of resources in an atmosphere when some still assume that all academic activities should, and can, be supported. In practice, there are essential trade-offs, especially when it comes to the expensive and painstaking work of research.

How we each respond to these circumstances is an individual and institutional issue. In this chapter, we seek to explain the practical challenges and opportunities of research in Asia-Pacific affairs, drawing on our experience across a range of disciplines, geographies, and experience of both "muddy boots" and "smart suits". Like in many complex undertakings, the distance between theory and practice can be vast, and we are not suggesting that aspiring researchers look to this discussion as a "how to" guide. Instead, we hope to generate some new debate about the realities of research for those wondering about the next steps in their own work. The chapter begins with an overview of research work with which we are familiar with in the Coral Bell School of Asia Pacific Affairs at the Australian National University (ANU). This is followed by an analysis of field research practice today and then an interrogation of common challenges and constraints. These discussions lead to a conclusion on the best preparation for tomorrow's research careers and some suggestions about where the frontiers of such work are emerging.

RESEARCH IN THE CORAL BELL SCHOOL

There are at least two distinctive features of research practice in the Coral Bell School of Asia Pacific Affairs. The first is the marriage between disciplinary and Area Studies expertise. Our colleagues are engaged in research that draws on long-term immersion in the societies, culture, history, language, and politics of the Pacific, Southeast Asia, Northeast Asia, and South Asia. At the same time, they remain committed to producing research that engages with disciplinary theories and debates in anthropology, politics, history, international relations, and strategic studies. Bridging the divide between disciplinary and Area Studies has important pay-offs. As Peter Dean and Greg Raymond (this volume) suggest in their chapter, the concept of "strategic culture" has emerged and evolved precisely through the findings of in-depth empirical research on the Soviet Union and Ming China, which has required familiarity with the languages, politics, histories, and military behaviours of these societies. More recently, scholars of Indonesia, the Philippines, and Australia have added their findings to further hone the "strategic culture" concept and strengthen its generalizability. Similarly, as Cecilia Jacob (this volume) outlines in her chapter, long-term fieldwork with children and child protection workers in Myanmar, Cambodia, and Thailand allowed her to shed light on the "micro-dynamics" of armed conflict and the ways in which international norms and practices are mediated at the local level. Jacob's research thus makes an important contribution to a growing body of international relations literature which is seeking to "open up" the state and look beyond traditional, state-based accounts of armed conflict (Jacob 2014a). On a practical level, undertaking this kind of interview-based and ethnographic research requires second, and sometimes third and fourth, language skills; the ability to work for extended periods of time across multiple field sites; and sensitivity to the complex ethical requirements surrounding research with children and other potentially vulnerable victims of armed conflict.

Yet, working across the disciplinary and Area Studies divide also presents challenges. Scholarly journals in the social sciences still overwhelmingly reward the development of theoretical and generalizable studies over single case studies based on deep expertise of a particular country or region. And where these journals do favour area expertise, it is often Europe and the United States that are prioritized over the Asia-Pacific region. In political science and international relations, for example, a recent investigation of the top eight journals in the field showed that these journals were publishing only a small percentage of research on East Asia, as compared to research on Europe or the United States (Johnston 2012, pp. 54–55). This not only makes it difficult for scholars specializing in the Asia-Pacific region to succeed in publishing in the top journals but, more troublingly, has ensured that Asia is heavily under-represented in much theory building (Johnston 2012). There are great career rewards for those who succeed in bringing Asian cases to the most prestigious, theoretically-inclined journals and publishers. But researchers should not underestimate the effort, time, and persistence in the face of knock-backs that will be required to do so. Alternatively, researchers might pursue the potentially fruitful option suggested by Paul Kenny (this volume) and Charles Miller (this volume). Exciting new empirical and theoretical contributions can be made when Area Studies specialists partner with those who have expertise in quantitative and/or comparative methods.

The second distinctive feature of scholarship in the Bell School is that it is the product of a close relationship between policy practice and research. This interface between policy and research has always been at the heart of the ANU's role as a *national* university. Located in Canberra, alongside the Australian federal government and diplomatic community, Australian policymakers and foreign government representatives can often be found roaming the corridors of the Bell School. Meanwhile, many academics have joined the Bell School after years or decades of working in the Australian government service. As Julien Barbara (this volume) explains, this characteristic of the Bell School ensures that ANU scholars have frequently found themselves engaged not only in describing and explaining the significance to government of major policy issues, but also in helping to identify innovative solutions to policy problems. In many cases, it is the very experience of getting mud on their boots in the field that has made these researchers of such use to the policy world. From assessing the success of the Regional Assistance Mission to Solomon Islands (RAMSI) to explaining election dynamics in Myanmar and Indonesia, and from interpreting Chinese security behaviour to drafting Australian Defence White Papers, the government has frequently asked for the input of Bell School researchers in identifying and explaining policy challenges, in offering policy solutions and, occasionally, in critiquing and offering provocative challenges to existing policy settings. This relationship is vitally important, not least because as scholars whose research is supported primarily by public funding, we have an obligation to offer our hard-won insights back to the sources of those funds. Moreover, engaging with policymakers from time to time provides researchers with a healthy dose of reality and can curb the academic tendency to pursue increasingly narrow, esoteric concerns.

The relationship between policymaking and research offers its own set of challenges. As Michael Wesley (this volume) suggests, policymakers and researchers occupy different worlds, with different data sets, styles of writing, pace of output, and incentive structures. These differences mean that there is no guarantee that the product of academic scholarship will be valuable to the policy community. Policymakers quite rightly require quick responses to immediate policy challenges or questions, and have little or no interest in whether an academic's findings make a contribution to the scholarly literature. At the same time, researchers who are frequently called upon by the policy community to offer advice or explanation about their subject matter expertise can quickly find that this becomes an all-consuming activity. Academics, even if engaged in policy-relevant research, need distance from their subjects in order to observe, to think deeply, to write, and to consider policy challenges in their historical, cultural, political, or strategic contexts. In this regard, academics do something that policymakers simply cannot do, which is to undertake the slow, messy, painstaking process of research.

Moreover, this tension between policy and research is not just about a difference in habits of work. In the pursuit of policy-relevant research, we run the risk of losing sight of the importance of basic research and the language training, fieldwork, and in-depth country or regional expertise that takes years to develop. This risk was pointed out by Georgetown University Professor Charles King in an article in *Foreign Affairs* in 2015. As King argued, the build-up of U.S. government and philanthropic funding for the study of foreign languages, culture, politics, and history was intimately linked to the onset of the Cold War, and the realization that the United States needed to train linguists and area experts in order to understand its Cold War adversaries. In-depth country and regional expertise was not only crucial for producing good foreign policy, King argued, it was also a source of U.S. prestige and power in the world:

> The rise of the United States as a global power was the product of more than merely economic and military advantages. Where the country was truly hegemonic was in its unmatched knowledge of the hidden interior of other nations: their languages and cultures, their histories and political systems, their local economies and human geographies. Through programs such as Title VIII, the U.S. government

created a remarkable community of minutemen of the mind: scholars, graduate students, and undergraduates who possessed the linguistic skills, historical sensitivity, and sheer intellectual curiosity to peer deeply into foreign societies. Policymakers sometimes learned to listen to them, and not infrequently, these scholars even became policymakers themselves (King 2015).

However, as King went on to argue, there has been a decline in U.S. government funding for this basic research because of an increasing insistence that the value of research lies in its "immediate usefulness" to policymakers, military and business, and hence a desire to fund projects "with actionable ideas and measurable impact". Research that cannot demonstrate its "immediate usefulness" is much less likely to receive funding, and this, in turn, has led to a serious decline in investment in language training, in-country fieldwork, and Area Studies more generally. The basic research that King is referring to is the kind of research that does not make the news, until it does. It takes years of training, fieldwork, observation, thinking, and writing to develop expertise on a little-known island in the Pacific, an obscure border region between India and China, or the history of Australian military engagement in World War I. Researchers may pursue these subjects for years or decades with little interest from the policy community. But when a sudden military conflict, democracy movement, commemoration, or economic boom occurs, this research becomes a precious asset. We cannot predict when research will become "immediately useful" or "policy relevant", and it would be a folly to try and design a decades-long research career around a topic that is in the news right now. Policy relevance is important, and governments understandably need to be able to demonstrate value for money in funding expensive research. But academics — and governments — must also remember that research is about playing the long game. Meaningful policy-relevant pay-offs may only come a handful of times in the space of a career.

WHAT IS FIELDWORK TODAY?

Such long-term perspectives are essential to good research practice, especially when it comes to developing a deep appreciation of something specific: "the field". There is no single definition of "the field", especially in an area of scholarly enquiry as vast as Asia-Pacific affairs. Yet, whatever the interpretation, spending significant periods of time in "the field" has been a long-standing way of developing research aptitude and awareness of local cultural, political, and linguistic forms. For anthropologists, at least, there is no obvious substitute: part of their apprenticeship is a significant stint, often a year or two, immersed in a specific social context. Many political scientists, sociologists, historians, and international relations specialists are similarly motivated to spend long periods of time accumulating the research material that can support their work. While some determine that participant-observation serves their purposes, there is an increasing tendency to use mixed methodologies to best explore complex (and often unfamiliar) social and political terrains. Such methods can draw on interviews, archival work, textual analysis, surveys, and network exploration, among a wide range of other well-developed research techniques. Where these are marshalled to best effect is often at their intersections: the places where disciplinary and methodological fashions collide.

One of the reasons that this comfortingly eclectic approach to field research has gained status is that the world has shifted rapidly since the modern techniques of historical, anthropological, and political analysis were first set down. It no longer makes sense to imagine that the boundaries between academic disciplines are meaningful, or natural, demarcations for scholarly work. This can prove confronting for those trained in one set of research approaches. They are often forced to seek out new areas of focus and to develop fresh techniques for fieldwork and analysis (for an example, see Taylor, Farrelly, and Lee 2012). Nowadays, we all need to grapple with the constant change implied by the digital revolution and the upending of economic certainties that came with Asia's momentous rise as the engine of global growth. Over the past generation, it has become increasingly cheap and easy to stay connected with research sites overseas, with the real cost of air travel on an almost constant downward trajectory in the twentieth and twenty-first centuries (Thompson 2013). In living memory, the best a researcher could expect in terms of local source material was a month-old metropolitan newspaper, and perhaps access to a limited range of vernacular television and radio programming. Field visits were rare, requiring substantial planning, and heavy expenditure, particularly whenever there was long distance travel and the need to sustain research teams in distant locations. The availability of relatively inexpensive airfares has changed the equation in many respects, shifting the burden of expense in radical ways. It is now possible for researchers to travel frequently to their key field sites and, in other cases, to cultivate steady contact online. Many of our Bell School colleagues have taken advantage of these technological and economic changes to maintain increasingly close contact with their specific fields of study.

The Internet has shifted the terms of research interaction in other important ways. The infinite variety of news sources, opportunities to monitor events in real time via Facebook and Twitter, and increasingly effective tools for communication and translation present researchers with the problem of unprecedented immediacy. They can be on the front lines, almost all the time, saturated by a deluge of terabytes of shifting data. Making sense of it all is one problem which is unlikely to go away. Fortunately, new tools have emerged that make some aspects of the digital researcher's life more reasonable. Online mapping platforms, for instance, give researchers a chance to peek into places that might otherwise be inaccessible for political or geographic reasons. Taken together, this new array of ways to understand the world obliterates some of the cosy expectations about research practice. The ever-increasing volume of information that intelligence agencies call "open source" means that an entire research agenda can be designed around the consolidation and analysis of digital material. How this works in practice is often yet to be determined, mostly because the skills required to thrive as a full-time digital researcher are yet to be fully developed, or even imagined.

For such researchers, "the field" can be the screen on their phone or tablet, a portal to worlds of infinite variety, and where new ways of harnessing information are challenging old certainties about what "counts" as research. As one example, Des Ball's recent and meticulous studies of Asian security issues are based, in large part, on Internet resources (see Ball 2014a; 2014b). He takes what he can find online to paint a picture of security organizations and their operations, all coloured by his own on-the-ground observations and calculations. This careful ground truthing of Internet information requires a commitment to using digital information to support the surgical examination of sensitive subject matter. It is a style of digital detective work that remains largely untheorized. In some quarters, there is still an untested assumption that Internet research is easier or somehow less important than the type of exploration that happens "on the ground". The fact, as studies by our Bell School colleague Sarah Logan (2012; 2014) have shown, is that Internet-focused "fieldwork" can prove as challenging as anything that happens offline.

CHALLENGES AND CONSTRAINTS

In this evolving research environment, there are a large number of practical problems. To help explain some of the challenges facing today's researcher, we will outline five key areas where issues commonly emerge.

First, there are circumstances where access is imperilled: where a researcher may be banned from travelling to their field site(s). Sometimes this may be the consequence of previous illegal behaviour, but in most instances, it is the result of political sensitivities. Where researchers touch on local "redlines", there is always the risk that they will be barred from entry. Scholars take different approaches to this issue. With many foreign researchers banned from China when they critically examine issues in Tibet or Xinjiang, hard decisions need to be made about the appropriate risks to take. Opinions vary. In Southeast Asia, where local contentions often infect the academic debate, dozens of scholars faced long-term bans from military-ruled Myanmar. When the final list of banned individuals was released publicly, it included some of our colleagues (see Nyein Nyein 2012). The maintenance of such exclusions requires time and energy on the part of officials, few of whom are trained to keep track of the intricacies of academic debate (for context, see University of Sydney 2005). Where political sensitivities are heightened, like they are in Thailand with regard to the royal family, then researchers need to think carefully about what they publish, where, and for what purposes.

The Internet changes the dynamics in this sphere, making more academic work more available to wide audiences. This is especially true of the evolving quasi-academic spaces hosted by blogs, magazines, and journals. They can make research work, or its reinterpretation, or critique, available instantaneously in all parts of the world. The results can be powerful: amplifying academic content to audiences near and far, and offering a chance to hold the powerful to account. The corollary is equally important. Governments and individuals can constantly monitor the digital musings of those of us who contribute to such accessible public debates. There is no shield when an article can go anywhere, for any purpose, merely with the snap of a "retweet" or the thump of a "like". Misunderstandings can accumulate, precisely because the Internet struggles to convey the glimmer or the wink that supports the accurate transmission of so much other human communication. Getting the tone right is an eternal challenge for those who hope to contribute to Internet-enabled discussions. This has been a particular challenge over the past decade for researchers focused on Thai politics (see Walker 2011).

The conflict between deposed former Prime Minister Thaksin Shinawatra and his enemies in royal and military circles has infected the academic debate and constrained the research options for some foreign scholars. There are extra considerations for junior scholars and PhD students who, in many cases, will need to guard their access, especially if they have made heavy investments in language and cultural skills.

Unfortunately, where governments find themselves bumping against academic criticism, it may often feel easiest to shut the door. Certainly that has been an approach taken over the years in China, Indonesia, Thailand, Myanmar, Sri Lanka, and many other places. In most cases, foreign researchers can avoid gaol and other sanctions, often because such punishments would only further the embarrassment for local authorities. However, their local counterparts are often not as lucky, with many researchers and commentators arrested across the Asia-Pacific region for offering their views on political practices and policies. These are often trying situations which can test even the strongest personalities. There are, as such, responsibilities for researchers with good institutional backing and long traditions of defending free academic enquiry to support their colleagues under these circumstances, with prominent organizations like the Scholars at Risk network taking a leading role.[1] They do excellent work. In the best cases, their activism leads to improved conditions for those who face authoritarian governments in systems where there are only thin traditions of supporting scholarly criticism.

Second, in recent years, we have seen the opening up of access to books, documents, people, officials, and traditional and social media in the Asia-Pacific region in ways that earlier generations of researchers could not have imagined. Indeed, as Michael Wesley (this volume) suggests, we are now in the age of "hyper-information". Yet, even in a period in which we have unprecedented access to data, people, and documents, access can still be abruptly turned off by governments that are uncomfortable with the direction of academic research. This is particularly the case for historians and other researchers pursuing archival research. In China, for instance, the passage of the Archives Law in 1998 opened up access to vast swathes of county, provincial, and national-level archival documents from the pre- and post-1949 eras (Zhang 2007/8; Kraus 2016). The 2000s were, therefore, a very exciting time to be undertaking archival research in China, even if academics were still required to jump through multiple regulatory hoops to gain access to archives. However, since late 2011, there has been a general tightening, and even complete blocking, of access to archives across China. The precise reasons for this remain unclear, but are likely linked to the changeover in political regime from Hu Jintao to Xi Jinping, an unwillingness to continue the "thirty-year rule" of declassifying archives from the Cultural Revolution period (1966–76) and beyond and, in the case of the Chinese Foreign Ministry archive, discomfort with allowing access to historical archival sources that may complicate the government's current foreign policy agenda (King 2016c). Moreover, even when archives in Asia are open, they do not always operate on the same basis as those in Australia, the United States, or United Kingdom. Photocopying is frequently prohibited, access to particularly sensitive documents can be turned off at a whim, and the legal frameworks behind the declassification process are rarely transparent. This "selective declassification" means that researchers are faced with many "unknown unknowns" and have no ready mechanism to find out which files have not been declassified.

Third, practising research on the Asia-Pacific often demands maintaining proficiency in second, and sometimes third and fourth, foreign languages. Maintaining language skills is a lifelong project and one that requires frequent exposure — via travel, lessons, conversations with native speakers, and daily reading of newspapers and other foreign language source materials. Furthermore, field research requires a willingness and ability to spend extended periods of time in archives, field sites, international organizations, or conflict zones far from home. Dedicating months of time to overseas field research is a common experience for many PhD students, but becomes increasingly challenging in post-PhD life as the pressures of university administration, teaching, family, and other commitments erode into time that can be spent in the field. Field research can also pose serious risks to personal health and safety. Many of our colleagues have experienced frequent and often quite dangerous illnesses while undertaking research in developing countries, while others have had to delay or permanently defer overseas field research visits because they cannot access necessary medical facilities or safe drinking water.

Fourth, undertaking research in conflict zones is a further challenge. Sometimes, this can be done safely and easily from adjacent areas. A number of Bell School scholars have studied long-running civil wars in Myanmar's eastern borderlands from the vantage of border towns on the Thai side. Places like Mae Sot and Mae Sai have hosted significant researcher populations, many of whom have worked with local activist and political organizations seeking to draw greater international attention to humanitarian crises. Sometimes, researchers end up much closer to the front lines, especially where their work builds on the engagement of activist or social support organizations. Desmond Ball is the most famous scholarly exponent of borderlands research in such contexts. For the past quarter century, he has worked closely with ethnic, political, and media organizations in the Myanmar–Thailand borderlands, as explained by Farrelly (2012, pp. 140–43). Yet, as a country like Myanmar now becomes more accessible to researchers, such approaches are being looked at afresh. There are compelling reasons for new generations of scholars to get beyond the distortions that inevitably come with borderland refraction (see Farrelly 2015*b*).

Fifth, developing academic partnerships is another major issue. When done well, these can help generate exciting collaborations, secure new funding streams, and offer the chance to forge fresh multidisciplinary link-ups. The reality is that even the most successful arrangements require years of quiet initiative to build trust and create networks. Where there is a significant difference in the academic training or academic culture of the partners, then it can mean even more effort. Some of these challenges are embraced as part of the capacity-building mandate of education institutions. There is great satisfaction in supporting the creation of new academic capability, especially in countries where it has been lacking. Significant elements of the Australian government aid programme support educational development in the Asia-Pacific region. Supporting the creation of sustainable academic programmes is the work of decades, and usually requires waves of scholars to be trained in the appropriate methodologies. Walking the corridors of the Bell School, it is apparent that students have been drawn to Australia from all corners of the globe. Where there are fresh political dynamics, as there were in Indonesia in the early 2000s, or in Myanmar in the 2010s, then there is often a new wave of academic interaction. Sustaining these over the long-term requires constant effort and awareness that the investments make sense at both political and scholarly levels. During the presidency of Susilo Bambang Yudhoyono, three cabinet ministers were ANU alumni who had studied on our campus in decades past (see Nielson and Post 2013). Working with the Asia-Pacific's future leaders is one of the Bell School's ambitions.

TOMORROW'S RESEARCH

The links between such practical considerations and the thematic, theoretical, or empirical concerns of our research is worth considering in more detail. Some projects make sense because they offer a clear response to great social, economic, or political challenges. In other cases, they appear to be closely aligned with a researcher's own priorities or whims. Which is better? We need to keep an open mind about the direction that successful research will take. The distinction between "basic" and "applied" research, so often invoked in the scientific disciplines, is less relevant to social science and humanities research. But there is still a need to reconcile what might be theoretically attractive or affirming and what can deliver the greatest benefits for both future generations of scholars, and for those who fund the research. Finding this balance will be one of the prevailing challenges for researchers in the twenty-first century.

It is therefore prudent to offer some thoughts on what preparation is required for aspiring researchers. Those who want to do serious work in the social sciences and humanities should develop their language and other communication skills. These are the foundation on which so much other understanding can grow. Without an appreciation for linguistic subtleties, there are many risks for the unwary researcher. Being able to crisply and clearly communicate ideas, in all manner of settings, is similarly important. Today's researcher needs to be a jack-of-all-communicative-trades: long-form writing, opinion pieces, hour-long lectures, the three-minute-thesis, podcasts, the works. Without confidence in different environments, it is very hard for researchers to get their messages out to a wide audience. At the same time, grounding in a number of core academic disciplines, including those in adjacent areas of the social sciences and humanities, seems to be increasingly valued. This means that a narrow training in, for instance, anthropology may generate frustrations over the long term. While there are places where disciplinary boundaries are still diligently policed, they are becoming the exception for those of us with globalized and multifaceted research interests.

In the long term, the use of the Internet to pioneer new research techniques will further distinguish the value of research in Asia-Pacific affairs. How this manifests in the academic system is yet to be made clear, with "Internet Studies" still a niche area, far removed from the ordinary business of most political and social studies. Digital research is yet to garner the prestige often associated with the type of work that requires muddy boots or smart suits. These have become the established paradigms for research in the humanities and social sciences, but they will soon need to be joined by a generation of researchers who are, for the first time, genuine digital natives. Those who completed their undergraduate degrees in the

2000s will, before long, be taking on increasingly senior academic roles. They have little direct experience of the old research cultures, when manuscripts were typed without computational assistance, and when the Internet could not give a ready answer to so many key questions. Their ideas of research, and their expectations about its dissemination, will require institutional and individual adjustments. Many of the old rules will be rewritten.

Under these conditions, what tomorrow's researchers confront is an academic environment that will need to fully integrate the immense opportunities of the Internet age and the flood of information from the Asia-Pacific societies in which we work. This will mean the redefinition of "fieldwork" and a new appreciation for the potential of research collaboration with scholars and institutions around the world. There will be few excuses for avoiding global entanglements when the price of connection has become so low. But first-hand experience in the culture, history, language, and politics of Asia-Pacific societies will become increasingly valuable for researchers seeking to build these connections and navigate this flood of new data. Moreover, some old issues will become ever more important: the need to focus on answering the really important research questions; the pursuit of the highest standards of research quality and ethical practice in answering those questions; and the careful management of time in a world where there are limitless opportunities for information overload. Identifying new areas for research achievement in Asia-Pacific affairs will naturally mean working with the cultures of scholarship that have come before. But these will need to be adjusted to best incorporate new practices of research in an age of inversion and disruption. Whether getting muddy in "the field" or engaging with the smart suits of the policy world, it is an exciting time to be a researcher in Asia-Pacific affairs.

Note

1. See Scholars at Risk network, hosted by New York University <http:// scholarsatrisk.nyu.edu/>.

BIBLIOGRAPHY

Acharya, Amitav. "How Ideas Spread: Whose Norms Matter? Norm Localization and Institutional Change in Asian Regionalism". *International Organization* 58, no. 2 (2004): 239–75.

———. "Europe and Asia: Reflections on a Tale of Two Regionalisms". In *Regional Integration in East Asia and Europe: Convergence or Divergence?*, edited by Bertrand Fort and Douglas Webber. London: Routledge, 2006, pp. 312–21.

———. *The Making of Southeast Asia: International Relations of a Region*. Ithaca and London: Cornell University Press, 2012.

———. "Thinking Theoretically about International Relations in Asia". In *International Relations of Asia*, rev. ed., edited by David Shambaugh and Michael Yahuda. Lanham: Rowman & Littlefield, 2013, pp. 59–89.

Adler, Emanuel and Vincent Pouliot. *International Practices*. Cambridge: Cambridge University Press, 2011.

Adler-Nissen, Rebecca. "Introduction". In *Bourdieu in International Relations: Rethinking Key Concepts in IR*, edited by Rebecca Adler-Nissen. London and New York: Routledge, 2013, pp. 1–23.

Aggarwal, Vinod K. and Min Gyo Koo. "Beyond Network Power? The Dynamics of Formal Economic Integration in Northeast Asia". *The Pacific Review* 18, no. 2 (2005): 189–216.

Agung, Ide Anak Agung Gde. *Twenty Years Indonesian Foreign Policy 1945–1965*. Yogyakarta: Duta Wacana University Press, 1990.

Alagappa, Muthiah, ed. *Asian Security Practice: Material and Ideational Influences*. Stanford: Stanford University Press, 1998.

Allen, Matthew and Sinclair Dinnen. "The North Down Under: Antimonies of Conflict and Intervention in Solomon Islands". *Conflict, Security & Development* 10, no. 3 (2010): 299–327.

———. "Beyond Life Support? Reflections on Solomon Islands after the Regional Assistance Mission". *Asia and the Pacific Policy Studies* 3, no. 1 (2016): 6–15.

Allen, Matthew, Sinclair Dinnen, Daniel Evans, and Rebecca Monson. "Justice Delivered Locally: Systems, Challenges, and Innovations in Solomon Islands". The World Bank, August 2013. <http://documents.worldbank.org/curated/

en/353081468308114790/pdf/812990WP0DL0Se0Box0379833B00PUBLIC0. pdf> (accessed 14 November 2016). (accessed 10 December 2015).

Amsden, Alice H. *The Rise of "The Rest": Challenges to the West from Late-Industrializing Economies.* New York: Oxford University Press, 2001.

Anderson, Benedict R. *Language and Power: Exploring Political Cultures in Indonesia.* Ithaca: Cornell University Press, 1990.

———. *Imagined Communities: Reflections on the Origin and Spread of Nationalism.* New York: Verso, 1991.

Angrist, Joshua D. and Jörn-Steggen Pischke. *Mastering 'Metrics: The Path from Cause to Effect.* Princeton: Princeton University Press, 2015.

Annan, Kofi. "Two Concepts of Sovereignty". *The Economist*, no. 137 (16 September 1999): 49.

Anwar, Dewi Fortuna. *Indonesia's Strategic Culture: Ketahanan Nasional, Wawasan Nusantara, and Hankamrata.* Australia-Asia papers no. 75. Centre for the Study of Australia-Asia Relations, Griffith University, May 1996.

Ariely, Dan, Ximena Garcia-Rada, Lars Hornuf, and Heather Mann. "The (True) Legacy of Two Really Existing Systems". Munich Discussion Paper 2014-26 (2015).

Asahi Shimbun. "Murayama Fires Shot at Abe's War Anniversary Statement", 15 August 2015.

ASEAN. "Overview of ASEAN-US Dialogue Relations". <http://www.asean. org/storage/2016/01/4Jan/Overview-of-ASEAN-US-Dialogue-Relations-(4-Jan-2016).pdf> (accessed 14 November 2016).

Ashplant, T.G., Graham Dawson, and Michael Roper, eds. *The Politics of War Memory and Commemoration.* London: Routledge, 2000.

Aslam, Mohamed. "The Impact of ASEAN-China Free Trade Agreement on ASEAN's Manufacturing Industry". *International Journal of China Studies* 3, no. 1 (April 2012): 43–78.

ASPI (Australian Strategic Policy Institute). "Our Failing Neighbour: Australia and the Future of Solomon Islands". *ASPI Policy Report*, 2003. <https://www.aspi. org.au/publications/our-failing-neighbour-australia-and-the-future-of-solomon-islands/solomons.pdf> (accessed 10 December 2015).

Aspinall, Edward. "Elections and the Normalization of Politics in Indonesia". *South East Asia Research* 13, no. 2 (2005): 117–56.

———. "The New Nationalism in Indonesia". *Asia and the Pacific Policy Studies* 3, no. 1 (2016): 72–82.

Australian Government. *Australia and the Asian Century.* White Paper. Canberra: Commonwealth of Australia, 2012.

Autesserre, Severine. *The Trouble with the Congo: Local Violence and the Failure of International Peacebuilding.* New York: Cambridge University Press, 2010.

Avey, Paul C. and Michael C. Desch. "What Do Policymakers Want From Us? Results of a Survey of Current and Former Senior National Security Decision Makers". *International Studies Quarterly* 58, no. 4 (2014): 227–46.

Ayoob, Mohammed. "Inequality and Theorizing in International Relations: The Case for Subaltern Realism". *International Studies Review* 4, no. 3 (Autumn 2002): 27–48.

Ba, Alice D. "China and ASEAN: Renavigating Relations for a 21st-Century Asia". *Asian Survey* 43, no. 4 (2003): 622–47.

Bakonyi, Jutta and Berit Bliesmann De Guevara. "The Mosaic of Violence — An Introduction". *Civil Wars* 11, no. 4 (2009): 397–413.

Ball, Desmond. *Strategic Culture in the Asia-Pacific Region*. Strategic and Defence Studies Centre (SDSC) Working Paper No. 270. Canberra: SDSC, Australian National University, 1993.

———. *Tor Chor Dor: Thailand's Border Patrol Police (BPP). Volume 1: History, Organization, Equipment and Personnel*. Bangkok: White Lotus Press, 2014a.

———. *Tor Chor Dor: Thailand's Border Patrol Police (BPP). Volume 2: Activities and Prospects*. Bangkok: White Lotus Press, 2014b.

Ban, Ki-moon. "Renewing Our Commitment to the Peoples and Purposes of the United Nations". Speech by the UN Secretary-General, UN Headquarters, 22 November 2013.

Banchoff, Thomas. *The German Problem Transformed: Institutions, Politics, and Foreign Policy, 1945–1995*. Ann Arbor: The University of Michigan Press, 1999.

Banerjee, Abhijit, Esther Duflo, Nathanael Goldberg, Dean Karlan, Robert Osei, William Parienté, Jeremy Shapiro, Bram Thuysbaert, and Christopher Udry. "A Multifaceted Program Causes Lasting Progress for the Very Poor: Evidence from Six Countries". *Science* 348, no. 6236 (2015).

Barbara, Julien. "Antipodean Statebuilding: The Regional Assistance Mission to Solomon Islands and Australian Intervention in the South Pacific". *Journal of Intervention and Statebuilding* 2, no. 2 (June 2008): 123–49.

———. "From Intervention to Partnership—Prospects for Development Partnership in Solomon Islands after the RAMSI". *Asia and the Pacific Policy Studies* 1, no. 2 (2014): 395–408.

Barr, Michael D. *Cultural Politics and Asian Values: The Tepid War*. New York: Routledge, 2002.

Barrett, Chistopher B. and Michael R. Carter. "A Retreat from Radical Skepticism: Rebalancing Theory, Observational Data, and Randomization in Development Economics". In *Field Experiments and Their Critics: Essays on the Uses and Abuses of Experimentation in the Social Sciences*, edited by Dawn Langan Teele. New Haven: Yale University Press, 2014.

Baser, Heather. *Provision of Technical Assistance Personnel in the Solomon Islands: What Can We Learn from the RAMSI Experience?* ECDPM Discussion Paper No. 76. Maastricht: European Centre for Development Policy Management (ECDPM), September 2007.

Basrur, Rajesh M. "Nuclear Weapons and Indian Strategic Culture". *Journal of Peace Research* 38, no. 2 (2001): 181–98.

Beaman, Lori, Esther Duflo, Rohini Pande, and Petia Topalova. "Female Leadership Raises Aspirations and Educational Attainment for Girls: A Policy Experiment in India". *Science* 335, no. 6068 (2012): 582–86.

Beaumont, Joan. "Contested Trans-national Heritage: The Demolition of Changi Prison, Singapore". *International Journal of Heritage Studies* 15, no. 4 (2009): 298–316.

———. "Hellfire Pass Memorial Museum, Thai–Burma Railway". In *The Heritage of War*, edited by Martin Gegner and Bart Ziino. Abingdon: Routledge, 2012, pp. 19–40.

Beaumont, Joan and Andrew Witcomb. "The Thai-Burma Railway: Asymmetrical and Transnational Memories". In *The Pacific War: Aftermaths, Remembrance and Culture*, edited by Christina Twomey and Ernest Koh. Abingdon and New York: Routledge, 2015, pp. 67–87.

Becker, Sascha O., Katrin Boeckh, Chrita Hainz, and Ludger Woessmann. "The Empire is Dead: Long Live the Empire!: Long-run Persistence of Trust and Corruption in the Civil Service". IZA Discussion Paper No. 5584. Bonn: Institute for the Study of Labor (IZA), 2011.

Beeson, Mark. "ASEAN Plus Three and the Rise of Reactionary Regionalism". *Contemporary Southeast Asia* 25, no. 2 (2003): 251–68.

———. "East Asian Regionalism and the End of the Asia-Pacific: After American Hegemony". *The Asia Pacific Journal* 7, no. 2 (2009): 1–19.

Bell, Coral. *The End of the Vasco da Gama Era: The Next Landscape of World Politics*. Lowy Institute Paper 21. Sydney: Lowy Institute for International Policy, 2007.

Bell, Duncan, ed. *Memory, Trauma and World Politics: Reflections on the Relationship between Past and Present*. London: Palgrave Macmillan, 2006.

Berger, Thomas U. "Norms, Identity, and National Security in Germany and Japan". In *The Culture of National Security: Norms and Identity in World Politics*, edited by Peter J. Katzenstein. New York: Columbia University Press, 1996, pp. 317–56.

Betts, Alexander. "The Refugee Regime Complex". *Refugee Survey Quarterly* 29, no. 1 (2010): 12–37.

Bhavnani, Rikhil R. "Do Electoral Quotas Work After They Are Withdrawn? Evidence from a Natural Experiment in India". *American Political Science Review* 103, no. 1 (2009): 23–35.

Bigo, Didier. "Protection: Security, Territory and Population". In *The Politics of Protection: Sites of Insecurity and Political Agency*, edited by Jef Huysmans, Andrew Dobson, and Raia Prokhovnik. London and New York: Routledge, 2006, pp. 84–100.

———. "Pierre Bourdieu and International Relations: Power of Practices, Practices of Power". *International Political Sociology* 5, no. 3 (2011): 225–58.

Bisley, Nick. *Great Powers in the Changing International Order*. Boulder: Lynne Rienner Publishers, 2012.

———. "Theoretical Approaches to Asia's Changing Security Order". In *Changing Security Dynamics in East Asia: A Post-US Regional Order in the Making?*, edited by Elena Atanassova-Cornelis and Frans-Paul van der Putten. Basingstoke: Palgrave, 2014.

Blackburn, Kevin. "Nation Building and Public Representations of History: The Japanese Occupation as a 'Shared Past' in Singapore". *Public History Review* 9 (2001): 8–21.

———. "War Memory and Nation-Building in South East Asia". *South East Asia Research* 18, no. 1 (2010): 5–31.

Blackburn, Kevin and Karl Hack. *War Memory and the Making of Modern Malaysia and Singapore*. Singapore: NUS Press, 2012.

Blattman, Christopher, Julian C. Jamison, and Margaret Sheridan. "Reducing Crime and Violence: Experimental Evidence on Adult Noncognitive Investments in Liberia". Policy Research Working Paper no. WPS 7648. Washington, D.C.: World Bank Group, 2015.

Bloomfield, Alan. "Time to Move On: Reconceptualizing the Strategic Culture Debate". *Contemporary Security Policy* 33, no. 3 (December 2012): 437–61.

Bobbitt, Philip. *The Shield of Achilles: War, Peace and the Course of History*. New York: Random House, 2002.

Booth, David and Sue Unsworth. "Politically Smart, Locally Led Development". ODI Discussion Paper, Overseas Development Institute, September 2014. <http://www.odi.org/publications/8800-politically-smart-locally-led> (accessed 10 December 2015).

Booth, Ken and Russell Trood, ed. *Strategic Cultures in the Asia-Pacific Region*. London: MacMillan, 1999.

Bourdieu, Pierre. *Outline of a Theory of Practice*. Cambridge and New York: Cambridge University Press, 1977.

Braithwaite, John, Sinclair Dinnen, Matthew Allen, Valerie Braithwaite, and Hilary Charlesworth. *Pillars and Shadows: Statebuilding as Peacebuilding in Solomon Islands*. Canberra: ANU E-Press, 2010.

Breckon, Lyall. "China-Southeast Asia Relations: A New Strategic Partnership is Declared". Center for Strategic and International Studies, 2004. <http://csis.org/files/media/csis/pubs/0304qchina_seasia.pdf> (accessed 27 April 2015).

Brennan, Geoffrey and Gordon Tullock. "An Economic Theory of Military Tactics: Methodological Individualism at War". *Journal of Economic Behavior & Organization* 3, nos. 2–3 (June–September 1982): 225–42.

Broinowski, Alison. *Understanding ASEAN*. New York: St. Martin's Press, 1982.

Brown, Michael E., Owen R. Coté, Sean M. Lynn-Jones, and Steven E. Miller, eds. *The Rise of China*. Cambridge: MIT Press, 2000.

Bull, Hedley. *The Anarchical Society: A Study of Order in World Politics*. London: Macmillan, 1977.

Burns, Alex and Ben Eltham. "Australia's Strategic Culture: Constraints and Opportunities in Security Policymaking". *Contemporary Security Studies* 35, no. 2 (2014): 187–210.

Butterfield, Herbert and Martin Wight, eds. *Diplomatic Investigations: Essays in the Theory of International Politics*. London: Unwin, 1966.

Capie, David. "When Does Track Two Matter? Structure, Agency and Asian Regionalism". *Review of International Political Economy* 17, no. 2 (May 2010): 291–318.

Capie, David and Brendan Taylor. "The Shangri-La Dialogue and the Institutionalization of Defence Diplomacy in Asia". *The Pacific Review* 23, no. 3 (July 2010): 359–76.

Carr, E.H. *The Twenty Years' Crisis 1919–1939*. 2nd ed. London: MacMillan, 1946.

Cartwright, Nancy and Jeremy Hardie. *Evidence-based Policy: A Practical Guide to Doing It Better*. Oxford; New York: Oxford University Press, 2012.

Casarini, Nicola. "The Role of Think Tanks in China". Short-Term Policy Brief 33. Europe China Research and Advice Network (ECRAN), June 2012.

Cederman, Lars-Erik, T. Camber Warren, and Didier Sornette. "Testing Clausewitz: Nationalism, Mass Mobilization, and the Severity of War". *International Organization* 65, no. 4 (2011): 605–38.

Cha, Victor D. "Abandonment, Entrapment, and Neoclassical Realism in Asia: The United States, Japan, and Korea". *International Studies Quarterly* 44, no. 2 (2000): 261–91.

———. "Strategic Culture and the Military Modernisation of South Korea". *Armed Forces and Society* 28, no. 1 (Fall 2001): 99–127.

Chandler, David. *Empire in Denial: The Politics of State-Building*. London: Pluto Press, 2006.

Chatterjee, Partha. *The Nation and its Fragments: Colonial and Postcolonial Histories*. Princeton: Princeton University Press, 1993.

Cheeseman, Graeme. "Australia: The White Experience of Fear and Dependence". In *Strategic Cultures in the Asia-Pacific Region*, edited by Ken Booth and Russell Trood. London: MacMillan, 1999, pp. 273–98.

Cho, Il Hyun and Seo-Hyun Park. "The Rise of China and Varying Sentiments in Southeast Asia toward Great Powers". *Strategic Studies Quarterly* 7, no. 2 (Summer 2013): 69–92.

Christensen, Thomas J. "China, the U.S.-Japan Alliance, and the Security Dilemma in East Asia". *International Security* 23, no. 4 (1999): 49–80.

Christensen, Thomas J. and Jack Snyder. "Chain Gangs and Passed Bucks: Predicting Alliance Patterns in Multipolarity". *International Organization* 44, no. 2 (1990): 137–68.

Christia, Fotini. *Alliance Formation in Civil Wars*. Cambridge: Cambridge University Press, 2012.

Clemens, Michael A. and Erwin Tiongson. "Split Decisions: Household Finance When a Policy Discontinuity Allocates Overseas Work". Working Paper 324. Center for Global Development, 2014.

Clinton, Hillary. "America's Pacific Century". *Foreign Policy*, 11 October 2011.

Cohen, Dov, Richard E. Nisbett, Brian F. Bowdle, and Norbert Schwarz. "Insult, Aggression and the Southern Culture of Honour: An 'Experimental Ethnography'". *Journal of Personality and Social Psychology* 70, no. 5 (1996): 945–60.

Commonwealth of Australia. "An Effective Aid Program for Australia: Making a Real Difference — Delivering Real Results", updated June 2012. <http://dfat.gov.au/news/news/Documents/effective-aid-program-for-australia.pdf> (accessed 10 June 2015).

Cook, Malcolm. "Southeast Asia and the Major Powers: Engagement not Entanglement". In *Southeast Asian Affairs 2014*, edited by Daljit Singh. Singapore: Institute of Southeast Asian Studies, 2014, pp. 37–52.

Cooper, Andrew F., Richard A. Higgott, and Kim R. Nossal. *Relocating Middle Powers: Australia and Canada in a Changing World Order*. Vancouver: UBC Press, 1993.

Côté-Boucher, Karine, Federica Infantino, and Mark B. Salter. "Border Security as Practice: An Agenda for Research". *Security Dialogue* 45, no. 3 (2014): 195–208.

Craig, David and Doug Porter. "Political Settlement in Solomon Islands: A Political Economic Basis for Stability after RAMSI?" *State, Society & Governance in Melanesia*. Working Paper Series, 2013/1 (2014).

Cruz De Castro, Renato. "Philippine Strategic Culture: Continuity in the Face of Changing Regional Dynamics". *Contemporary Security Policy* 35, no. 2 (2014): 249–69.

Curtis, Adam. "The Trap: What Happened to Our Dream of Freedom?". BBC Television Series, 2007.

Das, Runa. "Strategic Culture, Identity and Nuclear (In)Security in Indian Politics: Reflections from Critical Constructivist Lenses". *International Politics* 47, no. 5 (2010): 472–96.

Davenport, Thomas H. and D.J. Patil. "Data Scientist: The Sexiest Job of the 21st Century". *Harvard Business Review* (October 2012).

Deaton, Angus S. "Instruments of Development: Randomization in the Tropics, and the Search for the Elusive Keys to Economic Development". NBER

Working Paper No. 14690. National Bureau of Economic Research (NBER), 2009.

Deng, Francis M., Sadikiel Kimaro, Terrence Lyons, Donald Rothchild, and I. William Zartman. *Sovereignty as Responsibility: Conflict Management in Africa*. Washington, D.C.: Brookings Institution Press, 1996.

Dinnen, Sinclair. *Law and Order in a Weak State: Crime and Politics in Papua New Guinea*. Honolulu: University of Hawai'i Press, 2001.

————. "A Comment on State-Building in Solomon Islands". *The Journal of Pacific History* 42, no. 2 (2007): 255–63.

————. "The Solomon Islands Intervention and the Instabilities of the Post-colonial State". *Global Change, Peace & Security* 20, no. 3 (2008): 339–55.

Dirlik, Arif. "'Trapped in History' on the Way to Utopia: East Asia's 'Great War' Fifty Years Later". In *Perilous Memories: The Asia-Pacific War(s)*, edited by T. Fujitani, Geoffrey M. White, and Lisa Yoneyama. Durham and London: Duke University Press, 2001, pp. 299–322.

Downer, Alexander. "Neighbours Cannot Be Recolonised". *The Australian*, 8 January 2003.

Dressel, Bjorn and Sinclair Dinnen. "Political Settlements: Old Wine in New Bottles?" *Development Policy Centre*. Policy Brief, February 2014.

Duffield, Mark. *Global Governance and the New Wars: The Merging of Development and Security*. London: Zed Books, 2001.

Dunning, Thad. *Natural Experiments in the Social Sciences: A Design-Based Approach*. Cambridge; New York: Cambridge University Press, 2012.

Dutton, Michael. *Streetlife China*. Cambridge: Cambridge University Press, 1998.

Duus, Peter. "War Stories". In *History Textbooks and the Wars in Asia: Divided Memories*, edited by Gi-Wook Shin and Daniel C. Sneider. Abingdon: Routledge, 2011, pp. 99–14.

EAVG (East Asian Vision Group). "Final Report of the East Asia Study Group". ASEAN+3 Summit, Phom Penh, 4 November 2002. <http://www.mofa.go.jp/region/asia-paci/asean/pmv0211/report.pdf> (accessed 14 November 2016).

EAVG II (East Asia Vision Group II). "Report of the East Asian Vision Group II (EAVG II)". Phnom Penh, 19 November 2012. <http://www.mfa.go.th/asean/contents/files/asean-media-center-20130312-112418-758604.pdf> (accessed 14 November 2016).

Edwards, Meredith. "Social Science Research and Public Policy: Narrowing the Divide". *Australian Journal of Public Administration* 64, no. 1 (2005): 68–74.

Emmott, Sue, Manuhuia Barcham, and Tarcisius Kabutaulaka. *Annual Performance Report 2010: A Report on the Performance of the Regional Assistance Mission to the Solomon Islands*, March 2011.

Eriksson, Kimmo. "The Nonsense Math Effect". *Judgment and Decision Making* 7, no. 6 (2012): 746.

Evans, Michael. *The Tyranny of Dissonance: Australia's Strategic Culture and Way of War 1901–2005*. Canberra: Land Warfare Studies Centre, 2005.

Evans, Paul, ed. *Studying Asia Pacific Security: The Future of Research, Training and Dialogue Activities*. North York: University of Toronto-York University Joint Centre For Asia Pacific Studies, 1994.

Fair, C. Christine. *Fighting to the End: The Pakistan Army's Way of War*. New York: Oxford University Press, 2014.

Farrelly, Nicholas. "Securing a New Frontier in Mainland Southeast Asia". In *Insurgent Intellectual: Essays in Honour of Professor Desmond Ball*, edited by Brendan Taylor, Nicholas Farrelly, and Sheryn Lee. Singapore: Institute of Southeast Asian Studies, 2012, pp. 132–46.

————. "Nodes of Control in a South(east) Asian Borderland". In *Borderland Lives in Northern South Asia*, edited by David N. Gellner. Durham: Duke University Press, 2013, pp. 194–213.

————. "Beyond Electoral Authoritarianism in Transitional Myanmar". *European Journal of East Asian Studies* 14, no. 1 (2015*a*): 15–31.

————. "Don't Overlook Myanmar's Urban-Rural Divide". *Nikkei Asian Review* 12 (February 2015*b*). <http://asia.nikkei.com/magazine/20150212-Xi-s-dragnet/Politics-Economy/Nicholas-Farrelly-Don-t-overlook-Myanmar-s-urban-rural-divide> (accessed 14 November 2016).

Fawcett, Louise. "Exploring Regional Domains: A Comparative Historical Regionalism". *International Affairs* 80, no. 3 (2004): 429–46.

Feng, Huiyan, *Chinese Strategic Culture and Foreign Policy Decision-making: Confucianism, Leadership and War*. New York: Routledge, 2007.

Fisman, Raymond and Edward Miguel. "Cultures of Corruption: Evidence from Diplomatic Parking Tickets". NBER Working Paper No. 12312 (2006).

Fitriani, Evi. *Southeast Asians and the Asia-Europe Meeting (ASEM): State's Interests and Institution's Longevity*. Singapore: Institute of Southeast Asian Studies, 2014.

————. "Europe and Southeast Asia: The Nature of Contemporary Relations". In *Europe in Emerging Asia: Opportunities and Obstacles in Political and Economic Encounters*, edited by Frederick Erixon and Krishnan Srinivasan. London: Rowman & Littlefield, 2015, pp. 65–84.

Fraenkel, Jon, Anthony Regan, and David Hegarty. "The Dangers of Political Party Strengthening Legislation in Solomon Islands". *State, Society & Governance in Melanesia*. Working Paper No. 2 (2008).

Freedman, Lawrence. *The Revolution in Strategic Affairs*. Adelphi Paper 318. London: Oxford University Press for International Institute for Strategic Studies (IISS), 1998.

Friedberg, Aaron L. "Ripe for Rivalry? Prospects for Peace in a Multipolar Asia". *International Security* 18, no. 3 (1994): 5–33.

————. *A Contest for Supremacy: China, America, and the Struggle for Mastery in Asia*. New York: W.W. Norton, 2012.

Fry, Greg and Tarcisius Tara Kabutaulaka, eds. *Intervention and State-Building in the Pacific: The Legitimacy of "Co-operative Intervention"*. Manchester: Manchester University Press, 2008.

Fujitani, T., Geoffrey M. White, and Lisa Yoneyama, eds. *Perilous Memories: The Asia-Pacific War(s)*. Durham and London: Duke University Press, 2001.

Fullilove, Michael. "RAMSI and State Building in Solomon Islands". *Defender* (Autumn 2006): 31–35.

Garcia, Fernando Martel and Leonard Wantchekon. "Theory, External Validity and Experimental Inference: Some Conjectures". *The Annals of the American Academy of Political and Social Science* 628, no. 1 (2010): 132–47.

Geddes, Barbara. "How the Cases You Choose Affect the Answers You Get: Selection Bias in Comparative Politics". *Political Analysis* 2, no. 1 (1990): 131–50.

George, Alexander L. *Bridging the Gap: Theory and Practice in Foreign Policy*. Washington, D.C.: United States Institute of Peace, 1993.

Gerber, Alan S. and Donald P. Green. *Field Experiments: Design, Analysis, and Interpretation*. New York: W.W. Norton, 2012.

Gintis, Herbert. *The Bounds of Reason: Game Theory and the Social Sciences*. Princeton: Princeton University Press, 2009.

Girling, John L.S. *Thailand: Society and Politics*. Ithaca: Cornell University Press, 1966.

Glaser, Bonnie S. and Phillip C. Saunders. "Chinese Civilian Foreign Policy Research Institutes: Evolving Roles and Increasing Influence". *The China Quarterly*, no. 171 (2002): 597–616.

Goh, Evelyn. "Great Powers and Hierarchical Order in Southeast Asia: Analyzing Regional Security Strategies". *International Security* 32, no. 3 (2007/08): 113–57.

⸻. *The Struggle for Order: Hegemony, Hierarchy, and Transition in Post-Cold War East Asia*. Oxford: Oxford University Press, 2013.

Goodfellow, Tom. "Rwanda's Political Settlement and the Urban Transition: Expropriation, Construction and Taxation in Kigali". *Journal of Eastern African Studies* 8, no. 2 (2014): 311–29.

Grant, Lachlan. "They Also Served: Why D-Day Matters to Australia". *Sydney Morning Herald*, 5 June 2014. <http://www.smh.com.au/comment/they-also-served-why-dday-matters-to-australia- 20140602-zrv0r.html> (accessed 5 November 2015).

Graves, Matthew. "Memorial Diplomacy in Franco-Australian Relations". In *Nation, Memory and Great War Commemoration: Mobilizing the Past in Europe, Australia and New Zealand*, edited by Shanti Sumartojo and Ben Wellings. Bern: Peter Lang, 2014, pp. 169–87.

Graves, Matthew and Elizabeth Renchiewski. "From Collective Memory to Transcultural Remembrance". *PORTAL Journal of Multidisciplinary International Studies* 7, no. 1 (January 2010): 1–15.

Gray, Colin S. *Modern Strategy*. New York: Oxford University Press, 1999*a*.

———. "Strategic Culture as Context: The First Generation of Theory Strikes Back". *Review of International Studies* 25, no. 1 (January 1999*b*): 49–69.

———. *Another Bloody Century: Future Warfare*. London: Weidenfeld and Nicolson, 2005.

———. *The Strategy Bridge*. New York: Oxford University Press, 2010.

———. "Strategy and Culture". In *Strategy in Asia: The Past, Present, and Future of Regional Security*, edited by Thomas G. Mahnken and Dan Blumenthal. Stanford: Stanford Security Studies Press, 2014, pp. 92–107.

Haines, Steven. "The Nature of War and the Character of Contemporary Armed Conflict". In *International Law and the Classification of Conflicts*, edited by Elizabeth Wilmshurst. Oxford: Oxford University Press, 2012, pp. 9–31.

Haley, Nicole, Julien Barbara, Kerry Zubrinich, Hannah McMahon and Kerryn Baker. "2014 Solomon Islands Election Report". State Society and Governance in Melanesia (SSGM)/Centre for Democratic Institutions (CDI), Australian National University, 2015.

Hall, Ian. "Is a 'Modi Doctrine' Emerging in Indian Foreign Policy?". *Australian Journal of International Affairs* 69, no. 3 (2015): 247–52.

Hameiri, Shahar. *Regulating Statehood: State Building and the Transformation of Global Order*. Basingstoke: Palgrave Macmillan, 2010.

———. "Mitigating the Risk to Primitive Accumulation: State-building and the Logging Boom in Solomon Islands". *Journal of Contemporary Asia* 42, no. 3 (2012): 405–26.

———. "Regulatory Statebuilding and the Transformation of the State". In *The Routledge Handbook of International Statebuilding*, edited by David Chandler and Timothy D. Sisk. New York: Routledge, 2013.

He, Baogang. "East Asian Ideas of Regionalism: A Normative Critique". *Australian Journal of International Affairs* 58, no. 1 (2004): 105–25.

Heginbotham, Eric, Michael Nixon, Forrest E. Morgan, Jacob L. Heim, Jeff Hagen, Sheng Li, Jeffrey Engstrom, Martin C. Libicki, Paul DeLuca, David A. Shlapak, David R. Frelinger, Burgess Laird, Kyle Brady, and Lyle J. Morris. *The U.S.-China Military Scorecard: Forces, Geography, and the Evolving Balance of Power, 1996–2017*. Santa Monica: RAND Corp, 2015. <http://www.rand.org/content/dam/rand/pubs/research_reports/RR300/RR392/RAND_RR392.pdf> (accessed 14 November 2015).

Henderson, Joan C. "Remembering the Second World War in Singapore: Wartime Heritage as a Visitor Attraction". *Journal of Heritage Tourism* 2, no. 1 (2007): 36–52.

Herman, Edward and Gerry O'Sullivan. *The "Terrorism" Industry*. New York: Pantheon Books, 1989.

Hettne, Bjorn. "Beyond the 'New' Regionalism". *New Political Economy* 10, no. 4 (December 2005): 543–71.

Heydarian, Richard Javad. "Xi Jinping: China's 'Game Changer'?". *The National Interest*, 16 September 2014. <http://nationalinterest.org/feature/xi-jinping-chinas-game-changer-11285> (accessed 14 November 2016).

Heyward-Jones, Jenny. "Australia's Costly Investment in Solomon Islands: The Lessons of RAMSI". Sydney: Lowy Institute for International Policy, May 2014. <http://www.lowyinstitute.org/sites/default/files/hayward-jones_australias_costly_investment_in_solomon_islands_0.pdf> (accessed 10 December 2015).

Hicks, George. *The Comfort Women: Japan's Brutal Regime of Enforced Prostitution in Second World War*. New York: W.W. Norton, 1997.

Hiesser, Dan. "The United States as a Power in Europe". In *Europe and the Superpowers: Essays on European International Politics*, edited by Robert S. Jordan. London: Pinter Publishers, 1991, pp. 27–47.

Higgott, Richard and Richard Stubbs. "Competing Conceptions of Economic Regionalism: APEC versus EAEC in the Asia Pacific". *Review of International Political Economy* 2, no. 3 (1995): 516–35.

High-Level Independent Panel on Peace Operations. "Uniting Our Strengths for Peace — Politics, Partnerships, and People". Submitted to the UN Secretary-General, 16 June 2015.

Holm, Hans-Henrik and Georg Sorensen. "Introduction: What Has Changed?". In *Whose World Order?: Uneven Globalization and the End of the Cold War*, edited by Hans-Henrik Holm and Georg Sorensen. Boulder: Westview Press, 1995, pp. 1–17.

Horiuchi, Yusaku and Jun Saito. "Rain, Elections and Money: The Impact of Voter Turnout on Distributive Policy Outcomes in Japan". Asia Pacific Economic Paper no. 379. Australian National University, 2009.

Huntington, Samuel P. "The Clash of Civilizations?". *Foreign Affairs* 72, no. 3 (1993): 22–50.

―――. *The Clash of Civilizations and the Remaking of World Order*. New York: Touchstone Books, 1997.

ICISS (International Commission on Intervention and State Sovereignty). *The Responsibility to Protect: Report of the International Commission on Intervention and State Sovereignty*. Ottawa: International Development Research Centre, 2001.

ICRC (International Committee of the Red Cross). "International Humanitarian Law and the Challenges of Contemporary Armed Conflicts". Report of the 31st Conference of the Red Cross and Red Crescent, Geneva, Switzerland, 28 November–1 December 2011.

Ikenberry, G. John. "The Rise of China and the Future of the West". *Foreign Affairs* 87, no. 1 (January/February 2008).

———. "The Future of the Liberal World Order: Internationalism after America". *Foreign Affairs* 90, no. 3 (May/June 2011): 56–68.

Ikenberry, G. John and Michael Mastanduno, eds. *International Relations Theory and the Asia-Pacific*. New York: Columbia University Press, 2003.

Imbens, Guido and Donald B. Rubin. *Causal Inference for Statistics, Social, and Biomedical Science: An Introduction*. New York: Cambridge University Press, 2015.

Jacob, Cecilia. *Child Security in Asia: The Impact of Armed Conflict in Cambodia and Myanmar*. London and New York: Routledge, 2014*a*.

———. "Practicing Civilian Protection: Human Security in Myanmar and Cambodia". *Security Dialogue* 45, no. 4 (2014*b*): 391–408.

———. "'Children and Armed Conflict' and the Field of Security Studies". *Critical Studies on Security* 3, no. 1 (2015*a*): 14–28.

———. "State Responsibility and Prevention in the Responsibility to Protect: Communal Violence in India". *Global Responsibility to Protect* 7, no. 1 (2015*b*): 56–80.

———. "Evaluating the United Nation's Agenda for Atrocity Prevention: Prospects for the International Regulation of Internal Security". *Politics and Governance* 3, no. 3 (2015*c*).

Jakobson, Linda. *China's Unpredictable Maritime Security Actors*. Sydney: Lowy Institute for International Policy, December 2014. <https://www.files.ethz.ch/isn/186518/chinas-unpredictable-maritime-security-actors_1.pdf> (accessed 14 November 2016).

John, Peter. "Field Experiments in Political Science Research". Contribution to Oxford Bibliographies Online: Political Science, University College London, 2013. Available at Social Science Research Network <https://papers.ssrn.com/sol3/papers.cfm?abstract_id=2207877> (accessed 14 November 2016).

Johnson, Chalmers. *MITI and the Japanese Miracle: The Growth of Industrial Policy, 1925–1975*. Stanford: Stanford University Press, 1982.

Johnston, Alastair Iain. *Cultural Realism: Strategic Culture and Grand Strategy in Chinese History*. Princeton: Princeton University Press, 1995*a*.

———. "Thinking about Strategic Culture". *International Security* 19, no. 4 (1995*b*): 32–64.

———. "What (If Anything) Does East Asia Tell Us About International Relations Theory?". *Annual Review of Political Science* 15 (2012): 53–78.

Jonsson, Hjorleifur. "Above and Beyond: *Zomia* and the Ethnographic Challenge of/for Regional History". *History and Anthropology* 21, no. 2 (2010): 191–212.

Kahneman, Daniel. *Thinking, Fast and Slow*. New York: Farrar, Straus and Giroux, 2011.

Kaldor, Mary. *New and Old Wars: Organized Violence in a Global Era*. 2nd ed. Cambridge: Polity, 2006.

Kalyvas, Stathis N. "The Ontology of 'Political Violence': Action and Identity in Civil Wars". *Perspectives on Politics* 1, no. 3 (2003): 475–94.

———. *The Logic of Violence in Civil War.* New York: Cambridge University Press, 2006.

———. "The Changing Character of Civil Wars, 1800–2009". In *The Changing Character of War*, edited by Hew Strachan and Sibylle Scheipers. Oxford: Oxford University Press, 2011, pp. 209–19.

Kang, David C. *Crony Capitalism: Corruption and Development in South Korea and the Philippines.* Cambridge; New York: Cambridge University Press, 2002.

———. "Getting Asia Wrong: The Need for New Analytic Frameworks". *International Security* 27, no. 4 (2003): 57–85.

Karstedt, Susanne. "Contextualizing Mass Atrocity Crimes: Moving Toward a Relational Approach". *Annual Review of Law and Social Science* 9, no. 1 (2013): 383–404.

Katzenstein, Peter J. "East Asia — Beyond Japan". In *Beyond Japan: The Dynamics of East Asian Regionalism*, edited by Peter Katzenstein and Takashi Shiraishi. Ithaca: Cornell University Press, 2006, pp. 1–36.

———, ed. *The Culture of National Security: Norms and Identity in World Politics.* New York: Columbia University Press, 1996.

Kenny, Paul D. "The Patronage Network: Broker Power, Populism, and Democracy". PhD dissertation, Yale University, 2013.

Kertzer, David I. *Ritual, Politics, and Power.* New Haven and London: Yale University Press, 1988.

Khong, Yuen Foong. "Primacy or World Order? The United States and China's Rise — A Review Essay". *International Security* 38, no. 3 (2014): 153–55.

Kim, Jiyul. "Strategic Culture of the Republic of Korea". *Contemporary Security Policy* 35, no. 2 (2014): 270–89.

King, Amy. "Where Does Japan Fit in China's 'New Type of Great Power Relations'?" *The Asan Forum*, 20 March 2014. <http://www.theasanforum. org/where-does-japan-fit-in-chinas-new-type-of-great- power-relations/> (accessed 4 November 2015).

———. *China-Japan Relations After World War Two: Empire, Industry and War, 1949–1971.* Cambridge: Cambridge University Press, 2016a.

———. "Reconstructing China: Japanese Technicians and Industrialization in the Early Years of the People's Republic of China". *Modern Asian Studies* 50, no. 1 (2016b): 141–74.

———. "Navigating China's Archives". *Asian Currents, Asian Studies Association of Australia*, 2 August 2016c. <http://asaa.asn.au/navigating-chinas-archives/> (accessed 5 August 2016).

King, Amy and Brendan Taylor. "Northeast Asia's New 'History Spiral'". *Asia & the Pacific Policy Studies* 3, no. 1 (2016): 111–19.

King, Charles. "The Decline of International Studies: Why Flying Blind is Dangerous". *Foreign Affairs* (July/August 2015). <www.foreignaffairs.com/articles/united-states/decline-international-studies> (accessed 14 November 2016).

King, Gary, Robert O. Keohane, and Sidney Verba. *Designing Social Inquiry: Scientific Inference in Qualitative Research*. Princeton: Princeton University Press, 1994.

Kissinger, Henry. *A World Restored: Metternich, Castlereagh and the Problems of Peace 1812–1822*. London: Weidenfeld and Nicolson, 1957.

Koh, Ernest. "De-historicising the Second World War: Diaspora, Nation and the Overseas Chinese". In *The Pacific War: Aftermaths, Remembrance and Culture*, edited by Christina Twomey and Ernest Koh. Abingdon and New York: Routledge, 2015, pp. 11–31.

Koo, Min Gyo. "Same Bed, Different Dreams: Prospects and Challenges for ASEAN+'X' Forums". *Journal of International and Area Studies* 19, no. 1 (2012): 79–96.

Kotler, Mindy. "Comfort Women and Japan's War on Truth". *New York Times*, 14 November 2014.

Kraft, Herman Joseph S. "The Autonomy Dilemma of Track Two Diplomacy in Southeast Asia". *Security Dialogue* 31, no. 3 (2000): 343–56.

Kraus, Charles. "Researching the History of the People's Republic of China". Cold War International History Project Working Paper no. 79 (April 2016).

Krugman, Paul. "The Myth of Asia's Miracle". *Foreign Affairs* 73, no. 6 (November/December 1994): 62–78.

Kurihara, Jun. "Think Tanks: Their Expected Role in the Current Crisis". *Japan Spotlight* (January/February 2013).

Lantis, Jeffery S. "Strategic Culture: From Clausewitz to Constructivism". Prepared for: Defense Threat Reduction Agency, Advanced Systems and Concepts Office, 31 October 2006.

Lantis, Jeffrey S. and Andrew A. Charlton. "Continuity or Change? The Strategic Culture of Change". *Comparative Strategy* 30, no. 4 (2011): 291–315.

Lantz, Brett. *Machine Learning with R*. Birmingham, UK: Packt Publishing, 2013.

Leach, Michael and Damien Kingsbury, eds. *The Politics of Timor-Leste: Democratic Consolidation after Intervention*. Ithaca, NY: Cornell Southeast Asia Program Publications, 2012.

Leifer, Michael. *Politik Luar Negeri Indonesia*. Jakarta: PT Gramedia, 1986.

Lemarchand, René. *The Dynamics of Violence in Central Africa*. Philadelphia: Pennsylvania University Press, 2009.

Lewis, Michael. *Flash Boys: A Wall Street Revolt*. New York: W.W. Norton, 2015.

Lim, Jie-Hyun. "The Second World War in Global Memory Space". In *The Cambridge History of World War II Volume III — Total War: Economy, Society and Culture*, edited by Michael Geyer and Adam Tooze. Cambridge: Cambridge University Press, 2015, pp. 698–724.

Lind, Jennifer. "Memory, Apology, and International Reconciliation". *The Asia-Pacific Journal: Japan Focus* 6, no. 11 (2008). <http://japanfocus.org/-jennifer-lind/2957/article.html> (accessed 18 November 2015).

———. "The Perils of Apology: What Japan Shouldn't Learn from Germany". *Foreign Affairs* 88, no. 3 (2009): 132–46.

Logan, Sarah. "Rausim! Digital Politics in Papua New Guinea". SSGM Discussion Paper 2012/9. Canberra: State Society and Governance in Melanesia Program (SSGM), Australian National University, 2012.

———. "Electoral Integrity, Citizens and ICT in Melanesia". In Brief 2014/9. Canberra: State Society and Governance in Melanesia Program, Australian National University, 2014.

Logan, William and Keir Reeves, ed. *Places of Pain and Shame: Dealing with "Difficult Heritage"*. Abingdon: Routledge, 2009.

Logan, William and Nguyen Thanh Binh. "Victory and Defeat at Điện Biên Phủ: Memory and Memorialization in Vietnam and France". In *The Heritage of War*, edited by Bart Ziino and Martin Gegner. Abingdon: Routledge, 2012, pp. 41–63.

Lunn, Ken. "War Memorialisation and Public Heritage in Southeast Asia: Some Case Studies and Comparative Reflections". *International Journal of Heritage Studies* 13, no. 1 (2007): 81–95.

Lyall, Jason, Graeme Blair, and Kosuke Imai. "Explaining Support for Combatants during Wartime: A Survey Experiment in Afghanistan". *American Political Science Review* 107, no. 4 (2013): 679–705.

Mahbubani, Kishore. *The New Asian Hemisphere: The Irresistible Shift of Global Power to the East*. New York: Public Affairs, 2008.

Mahnken, Thomas G. *United States Strategic Culture*. Prepared for the Defense Threat Reduction Agency, Advanced Systems and Concepts Office, 13 November 2006.

———. "Chinese Strategic Culture: Can the Past Inform the Future". Presentation at Lowy Institute for International Policy, Sydney, 18 November 2009.

———. *Secrecy and Stratagem: Understanding Chinese Strategic Culture*. Double Bay: Lowy Institute for International Policy, 2011.

Malešević, Siniša. *The Sociology of War and Violence*. Cambridge: Cambridge University, 2010.

Mastanduno, Michael. "Incomplete Hegemony: The United States and Security Order in Asia". In *Asian Security Order: Instrumental and Normative Features*, edited by Muthiah Alagappa. Stanford: Stanford University Press, 2003, pp. 141–70.

McCurry, Justin. "Japanese PM Shinzo Abe Stops Short of New Apology in War Anniversary Speech". *The Guardian*, 14 August 2015.

McKay, Derek and H.M. Scott. *The Rise of the Great Powers, 1648–1815*. London: Longman, 1983.

McMaster, H.R. *Dereliction of Duty*. New York: HarperCollins Publishers, 1997.

McNamara, Robert S. *In Retrospect: The Tragedy and Lessons of Vietnam*. New York: Times Books, 1995.

McNeill, David. "The Struggle for the Japanese Soul: Komori Yoshihisa, Sankei Shimbun, and the JIIA Controversy". *The Asia-Pacific Journal: Japan Focus* 4, no. 9 (5 September 2006). <http://apjjf.org/-David-McNeill/2212/article.html> (accessed 14 November 2016).

Mearsheimer, John J. *The Tragedy of Great Power Politics*. New York: W.W. Norton, 2001.

Melander, Erik, Magnus Öberg, and Jonathan Hall. "Are 'New Wars' More Atrocious? Battle Severity, Civilians Killed and Forced Migration Before and After the End of the Cold War". *European Journal of International Relations* 15, no. 3 (2009): 505–36.

Mietzner, Marcus. *The Politics of Military Reform in Post-Suharto Indonesia: Elite Conflict, Nationalism, and Institutional Resistance*. Washington, D.C.: East-West Center, 2006.

Miller, Frank L. "Impact of Strategic Culture on U.S. Policies for East Asia". Carlisle Papers in Security Strategy Series. Carlisle: Strategic Studies Institute, U.S. Army War College, November 2003.

Miller, John H. and Scott E. Page. *Complex Adaptive Systems: An Introduction to Computational Models*. Princeton: Princeton University Press, 2007.

Miller, Meredith. "China's Relations with Southeast Asia: Testimony for the U.S.-China Economic and Security Review Commission", 13 May 2015. <http://www.uscc.gov/sites/default/files/Miller_Written%20Testimony_5.13.2015%20Hearing.pdf> (accessed 27 June 2015).

Milner, Anthony. *Kerajaan: Malay Political Culture on the Eve of Colonial Rule*. Association for Asian Studies Monograph No. XL. Tucson: University of Arizona Press, 1982.

———. *The Malays*. Chichester: Wiley-Blackwell, 2008.

Milner, James. "Introduction: Understanding Global Refugee Policy". *Journal of Refugee Studies* 27, no. 4 (2014): 477–94.

Milstein, Jeffrey S. *Dynamics of the Vietnam War: A Quantitative Analysis and Predictive Computer Simulation*. Stanford: Stanford University Press, 1974.

Min, Pyong Gap. "Korean 'Comfort Women': The Intersection of Colonial Power, Gender, and Class". *Gender & Society* 17, no. 6 (2003): 938–57.

Mitchell, Melanie. *Complexity: A Guided Tour*. Princeton: Princeton University Press, 2009.

Mitter, Rana. "Behind the Scenes at the Museum: Nationalism, History and Memory in the Beijing War of Resistance Museum, 1987–1997". *The China Quarterly*, no. 161 (March 2000): 279–93.

MOFA (Ministry of Foreign Affairs) of Japan. "The Amended Chiang Mai Initiative Multilateralisation (CMIM) Comes Into Effect on July 17, 2014". Press Release, Tokyo, 17 July 2014.

Montgomery, Jacob M. and Brendan Nyhan. "Bayesian Model Averaging: Theoretical Developments and Practical Applications". *Political Analysis* 18, no. 2 (2010): 245–70. <https://doi.org/10.1093/pan/mpq001>.

Morgan, Forrest E. *Compellance and the Strategic Culture of Imperial Japan: Implications for Coercive Diplomacy in the Twenty-first Century.* Westport: Praeger, 2003.

Morgan, Stephen L. and Christopher Winship. *Counterfactuals and Causal Inference: Methods and Principles for Social Research.* 2nd ed. New York: Cambridge University Press, 2015.

Morgenthau, Hans J. *Politics Among Nations: The Struggle for Power and Peace.* New York: Alfred A. Knopf, 1948.

Morris-Suzuki, Tess. "Shinzo Abe Divides Our Region with a Rewrite of Japan's War History". *The Age*, 16 August 2015. <http://www.theage.com.au/comment/shinzo-abe-divides-region-with-a-rewrite-of-japans-modern-history-20150815-gizxev.html> (accessed 11 November 2015).

Müller, Jan-Werner, ed. *Memory & Power in Post-War Europe: Studies in the Presence of the Past.* Cambridge: Cambridge University Press, 2002.

Mundy, Jacob. "Deconstructing Civil Wars: Beyond the New Wars Debate". *Security Dialogue* 42, no. 3 (2011): 279–95.

Murong, Xuecun. "China's Television War on Japan". *New York Times*, 9 February 2014. <http://www.nytimes.com/2014/02/10/opinion/murong-chinas-television-war-on-japan.html?_r=0> (accessed 6 November 2015).

Nair, Depak. "Regionalism in the Asia Pacific/East Asia: A Frustrated Regionalism?" *Contemporary Southeast Asia: A Journal of International and Strategic Affairs* 31, no. 1 (2009): 111.

Nakayama, Toshihiro. "How to Enliven Japan's Foreign Policy Think Tanks". Nippon.com, 2012. <http://www.nippon.com/en/simpleview/?post_id=7540> (accessed 8 November 2015).

Narlikar, Amrita. "Negotiating the Rise of New Powers". *International Affairs* 89, no. 3 (2013): 561–76.

Nasar, Sylvia. *Grand Pursuit: The Story of Economic Genius.* New York: Simon and Shuster, 2012.

Nelson, Daniel N. "The Soviet Union and Europe". In *Europe and the Superpowers: Essays on European International Politics*, edited by Robert S. Jordan. London: Pinter Publishers, 1991, pp. 48–66.

Newman, Edward. "The 'New Wars' Debate: A Historical Perspective is Needed". *Security Dialogue* 35, no. 2 (2004): 173–89.

Nielson, George and Stacey Post. "Indonesian Cabinet Stacked with ANU Talent". ANU College of Asia & the Pacific, 24 May 2013. <http://asiapacific.anu.edu.au/news-events/all- stories/indonesian-cabinet-stacked-anu-talent> (accessed 8 November 2015).

Nozaki, Yoshiko. *War Memory, Nationalism and Education in Postwar Japan, 1945–2007: The Japanese History Textbook Controversy and Ienaga Saburo's Court Challenges.* Abingdon: Routledge, 2008.

Nutley, Sandra. "Bridging the Policy/Research Divide: Reflections and Lessons from the UK". Keynote paper presented at "Facing the Future: Engaging Stakeholders and Citizens in Developing Public Policy". National Institute of Governance Conference, Canberra, Australia, 23–24 April 2003.

Nyein, Nyein. "Burma Releases Names of Those Removed from Blacklist". *The Irrawaddy*, 30 August 2012. <www.irrawaddy.org/burma/burma-releases-names-of-those-removed-from-blacklist.html> (accessed 8 November 2015).

Nyers, Peter. "Abject Cosmopolitanism: The Politics of Protection in the Anti-Deportation Movement". *Third World Quarterly* 24, no. 6 (2003): 1069–93.

ODE (Office of Development Effectiveness). "Research for Better Aid: An Evaluation of DFAT's Investments". Canberra: Commonwealth of Australia, February 2015.

OECD (Organisation for Economic Co-operation and Development). "The Paris Declaration of Aid Effectiveness and the Accra Agenda for Action". Paris: OECD, 2008.

Öjendal, Joakim. "Back to the Future? Regionalism in South-East Asia under Unilateral Pressure". *International Affairs* 80, no. 3 (2004): 519–33.

Oldenburg, Philip. *India, Pakistan, and Democracy: Solving the Puzzle of Divergent Paths*. New York: Routledge, 2010.

Olken, Benjamin A. "Monitoring Corruption: Evidence from a Field Experiment in Indonesia". *Journal of Political Economy* 115, no. 2 (2007): 200–49.

Ong, Aihwa. *Neoliberalism as Exception: Mutations in Citizenship and Sovereignty*. Durham and London: Duke University Press, 2006.

Oros, Andrew L. "Japan's Strategic Culture: Security Identity in a Fourth Modern Incarnation". *Contemporary Security Policy* 35, no. 2 (2014): 227–48.

Panennungi, Maddaremmeng, Rahadjeng Pulungsari, Evi Fitriani, Lily Tjahjandari, and Padang Wicaksono. "Analysis of Issues Development in Asia-Pacific Economic Cooperation". *Asia Pacific Social Science Review* 14, no. 1 (June 2014): 1–20.

Pape, Robert A. *Dying to Win: The Strategic Logic of Suicide Terrorism*. New York: Random House, 2005.

Paris, Roland. "Ordering the World: Academic Research and Policymaking on Fragile States". *International Studies Review* 13, no. 1 (2011): 58–71.

Paul, T.V. "Soft Balancing in the Age of U.S. Primacy". *International Security* 30, no. 1 (2005): 46–71.

Pettersson, Thérése and Peter Wallensteen. "Armed Conflicts, 1946–2014". *Journal of Peace Research* 52, no. 4 (2015): 536–50.

Pollman, Mina. "Why Japan's Textbook Controversy is Getting Worse". *The Diplomat*, 8 April 2015.

Porter, Patrick. "Good Anthropology, Bad History: The Cultural Turn in Studying War". *Parameters* 37, no. 2 (Summer 2007): 45–58.

Pouliot, Vincent. *International Security in Practice: The Politics of NATO-Russia Diplomacy*. Cambridge: Cambridge University Press, 2010.

Pouliot, Vincent and Frédéric Mérand. "Bourdieu's Concepts". In *Bourdieu in International Relations: Rethinking Key Concepts in IR*, edited by Rebecca Adler-Nissen. London and New York: Routledge, 2013, pp. 24–44.

PwC. "The World in 2050: Will the Shift in Global Economic Power Continue?", February 2015. <http://www.pwc.com/gx/en/issues/the-economy/assets/world-in-2050-february-2015.pdf> (accessed 8 November 2016).

RAMSI (Regional Assistance Mission to the Solomon Islands). "People's Survey", 2007–13. <http://www.ramsi.org/media/peoples-survey/> (accessed 10 December 2015).

Raymond, Greg. "Thailand's Strategic Culture". PhD dissertation. La Trobe University, 2015.

Reid, Anthony. "Remembering and Forgetting War and Revolution". In *Beginning to Remember: The Past in the Indonesian Present*, edited by Mary S. Zurbuchen. Singapore: Singapore University Press, 2005, pp. 168–91.

―――. *Imperial Alchemy: Nationalism and Political Identity in Southeast Asia*. Cambridge: Cambridge University Press, 2010.

"Report of the Advisory Panel on the History of the 20th Century and on Japan's Role and the World Order in the 21st Century", 6 August 2015. <https://www.kantei.go.jp/jp/singi/21c_koso/pdf/report_en.pdf> (accessed 6 November 2015).

Reus-Smit, Christian and Duncan Snidal. "Reuniting Ethics and Social Science: The Oxford Handbook of International Relations". *Ethics and International Affairs* 22, no. 3 (2008): 261–71.

Reynolds, David. "Afterword: Remembering the First World War: An International Perspective". In *Remembering the First World War*, edited by Bart Ziino. Abingdon: Routledge, 2015, pp. 221–38.

Rodrik, Dani. "The New Development Economics: We Shall Experiment, But How Shall We Learn?" Faculty Research Working Paper Series (RWP08-055). Harvard Kennedy School, John F. Kennedy School of Government, 2008.

Rosenberg, Sheri P. "Responsibility to Protect: A Framework for Prevention". *Global Responsibility to Protect* 1 (2009): 442–77.

Rothman, Kenneth J. "Causes". *American Journal of Epidemiology* 104, no. 6 (1976): 587–92.

Rozman, Gilbert. "China's Changing Images of Japan, 1989–2001: The Struggle to Balance Partnership and Rivalry". *International Relations of the Asia Pacific* 2, no. 1 (2002): 95–129.

Ruggie, John Gerard. "International Regimes, Transactions, and Change: Embedded Liberalism in the Postwar Economic Order". *International Organization* 36, no. 2 (Spring 1982): 379–415.

Ruland, Jurgen. "ASEAN and the Asian Crisis: Theoretical Implications and Practical Consequences for Southeast Asian Regionalism". *The Pacific Review* 13, no. 3 (2000): 421–51.

Saaler, Sven. "Pan Asianism in Meiji and Taishô Japan: A Preliminary Framework". Working Paper 02/4. Tokyo: Deutsches Institute für Japanstudien, 2002.

————. "Pan-Asianism in Modern Japanese History: Overcoming the Nation, Creating a Region, Forging an Empire". In *Pan-Asianism in Modern Japanese History: Colonialism, Regionalism and Borders*, edited by Sven Saaler and J. Victor Koschmann. Abingdon and New York: Routledge, 2007.

Sadan, Mandy. *Being and Becoming Kachin: Histories Beyond the State in the Borderworlds of Burma*. Oxford: Oxford University Press, 2013.

Salter, Mark B. "The Practice Turn: Introduction". In *Research Methods in Critical Security Studies: An Introduction*, edited by Mark B. Salter and Can E. Mutlu. London and New York: Routledge, 2013.

Sand, Jordan. "Historians and Public Memory in Japan: The 'Comfort Women' Controversy". *History and Memory* 11, no. 2 (1999): 117–26.

Sanín, Francisco Gutiérrez and Elisabeth Wood. "Ideology in Civil War: Instrumental Adoption and Beyond". *Journal of Peace Research* 51, no. 2 (2014): 213–26.

Sarkees, Meredith Reid and Frank Whelon Wayman. *Resort to War 1816–2007*. Washington, D.C.: CQ Press, 2010.

Schelling, Thomas C. *Micromotives and Macrobehavior*. New York: W.W. Norton, 1978.

Scobell, Andrew. "China and Strategic Culture". Monograph, Strategic Studies Institute, US Army War College, May 2002.

Scott, James C. *The Art of Not Being Governed: An Anarchist History of Upland Southeast Asia*. New Haven: Yale University Press, 2009.

Seaton, Philip A. *Japan's Contested War Memories: The 'Memory Rifts' in Historical Consciousness of World War II*. Abingdon: Routledge, 2007.

Shambaugh, David. "China's International Relations Think Tanks: Evolving Structure and Process". *The China Quarterly*, no. 171 (September 2002): 575–96.

Shin, Dong-Ik and Gerald Segal. "Getting Serious about Asia-Europe Security Cooperation". In *ASEM, the Asia-Europe Meeting: A Window of Opportunity*, edited by Wim Stockhof and Paul van der Velde. London and Leiden: Kegan Paul International, and the International Institute for Asian Studies, 1999, pp. 73–83.

Signorino, Curtis S. "Strategy and Selection in International Relations". *International Interactions* 28 (2002): 93–115.

Silver, Nate. *The Signal and the Noise*. New York: Penguin, 2013.

Simon, Sheldon W. "Evaluating Track II Approaches to Security Diplomacy in the Asia-Pacific: The CSCAP Experience". *The Pacific Review* 15, no. 2 (2002): 167–200.

Slater, Dan. *Ordering Power: Contentious Politics and Authoritarian Leviathans in Southeast Asia*. New York: Cambridge University Press, 2010.

Smith, Rupert. *The Utility of Force: The Art of War in the Modern World*. London: Allen Lane, 2005.

Snyder, Glenn H. "The Security Dilemma in Alliance Politics". *World Politics* 36, no. 4 (1984): 461–95.

Snyder, Jack L. "The Soviet Strategic Culture: Implications for Limited Nuclear Operations". A Project Air Force Report prepared for the United States Air Force (R-2154-AF). Santa Monica: RAND Corporation, 1977.

———. "The Concept of Strategic Culture: Caveat Emptor". In *Strategic Power: USA/USSR*, edited by Carl G. Jacobsen. London: Palgrave MacMillan, 1990, pp. 3–9.

Soh, C. Sarah. *The Comfort Women: Sexual Violence and Postcolonial Memory in Korea and Japan.* Chicago: University of Chicago Press, 2008.

Sorensen, Camilla T.N. "Is China Becoming More Aggressive? A Neoclassical Realist Analysis". *Asian Perspectives* 37, no. 3 (2013): 363–85.

Stahn, Carsten. "Responsibility to Protect: Political Rhetoric or Emerging Legal Norm?". *The American Journal of International Law* 101, no. 1 (2007): 99–120.

Staniland, Paul. *Networks of Rebellion: Explaining Insurgent Cohesion and Collapse.* Ithaca: Cornell University Press, 2014.

Stern, Maria and Joakim Öjendal. "Mapping the Security-Development Nexus: Conflict, Complexity, Cacophony, Convergence?" *Security Dialogue* 41, no. 1 (2010): 5–30.

St. Michel, Patrick. "Japanese Demons and Crotch Bombs: The Tense State of Asian Cinema". *The Atlantic*, 9 September 2015. <http://www.theatlantic.com/entertainment/archive/2015/09/east-asian-films-wwii-anniversary/404152/> (accessed 2 November 2015).

Stone, Diane. "The ASEAN-ISIS Network: Interpretive Communities, Informal Diplomacy and Discourses of Region". *Minerva* 49, no. 2 (2011): 241–62.

Stone, Elizabeth. *Comparative Strategic Cultures: Literature Review (Part 1).* Prepared for the Defense Threat Reduction Agency, Advanced Systems and Concepts Office, 31 October 2006.

Strachan, Hew and Sibylle Scheipers, eds. *The Changing Character of War.* Oxford: Oxford University Press, 2011.

Straits Times. "China Raps Japan for War Shrine Visit by Abe's Wife", 22 May 2015. <http://www.straitstimes.com/asia/east-asia/china-raps-japan-for-war-shrine-visit-by-pm-abes-wife> (accessed 22 May 2015).

Straus, Scott. *The Order of Genocide: Race, Power, and War in Rwanda.* Ithaca: Cornell University Press, 2008.

Strauss, Ekkehard. "A Bird in the Hand is Worth Two in the Bush — On the Assumed Legal Nature of the Responsibility to Protect". *Global Responsibility to Protect* 1, no. 3 (2009): 291–323.

Sturgeon, Janet C. *Border Landscapes: The Politics of Akha Land Use in China and Thailand.* Seattle: University of Washington Press, 2005.

Suh, J.J., Peter J. Katzenstein, and Allen Carlson, eds. *Rethinking Security in East Asia: Identity, Power, and Efficiency.* Stanford: Stanford University Press, 2004.

Taleb, Nassim Nicholas. *The Black Swan*. New York: Penguin, 2007.

Tan, See Seng. *The Making of the Asia Pacific: Knowledge Brokers and the Politics of Representation*. Amsterdam: Amsterdam University Press, 2013.

Tanham, George. "Indian Strategic Culture". *The Washington Quarterly* 15, no. 1 (1992): 129–42.

Tanner, Murray Scot. "Changing Windows on a Changing China: The Evolving 'Think Tank' System and the Case of the Public Security Sector". *The China Quarterly*, no. 171 (September 2002): 559–74.

Taylor, Brendan, Anthony Milner, and Desmond Ball. *Track 2 Diplomacy in Asia: Australian and New Zealand Engagement*. Canberra: Strategic and Defence Studies Centre, Australian National University, 2006.

Taylor, Brendan, Nicholas Farrelly, and Sheryn Lee, eds. *Insurgent Intellectual: Essays in Honour of Professor Desmond Ball*. Singapore: Institute of Southeast Asian Studies, 2012.

Thakur, Ramesh. "Military-to-Military Cooperation: Pacific Community Issues". In *Strength Through Cooperation: Military Forces in the Asia-Pacific Region*, edited by Frances Omori and Mary A. Somerville. Washington, D.C.: National Defense University Press, 1999, pp. 241–71.

Thompson, Derek. "How Airline Ticket Prices Fell 50% in 30 Years (and Why Nobody Noticed)". *The Atlantic*, 28 February 2013. <www.theatlantic.com/business/archive/2013/02/how-airline-ticket-prices-fell-50-in-30-years-and-why-nobody-noticed/273506/> (accessed 8 November 2015).

Tohmatsu, Haruo. "Japanese History Textbooks in Comparative Perspective". In *History Textbooks and the Wars in Asia: Divided Memories*, edited by Gi-Wook Shin and Daniel C. Sneider. Abingdon: Routledge, 2011, pp. 115–19.

Tsing, Anna Lowenhaupt. *Friction: An Ethnography of Global Connection*. Princeton and Oxford: Princeton University Press, 2005.

Tudor, Maya. *The Promise of Power: The Origins of Democracy in India and Autocracy in Pakistan*. New York: Cambridge University Press, 2013.

Twomey, Christina and Ernest Koh. "Thinking About the Pacific War". In *The Pacific War: Aftermaths, Remembrance and Culture*, edited by Christina Twomey and Ernest Koh. Abingdon and New York: Routledge, 2015.

Unger, Jonathan. *The Transformation of Rural China*. New York: M.E. Sharpe, 2002.

United Nations. *Implementing the Responsibility to Protect: Report of the Secretary-General* (A/63/677). New York: United Nations, 2009.

————. *Responsibility to Protect: State Responsibility and Prevention* (A/67/929–S/2013/399). New York: United Nations, 2013.

————. *Fulfilling Our Collective Responsibility: International Assistance and the Responsibility to Protect* (A/68/947–S/2014/449). New York: United Nations, 2014.

United Nations Development Program (UNDP). *Human Development Report 1994: New Dimensions of Human Security*. New York: Oxford University Press, 1994.

University of Sydney. "Sydney's Leading Indonesia Expert Banned". *News*, 3 March 2005. <http://sydney.edu.au/news/84.html?newsstoryid=47> (accessed 8 November 2015).

US DoD (Department of Defense). *US Nuclear Posture Review April 2010*. <http://www.defense.gov/News/Special-Reports/NPR> (accessed 8 November 2015).

Uz Zaman, Rashed. "Kautilya: The Indian Strategic Thinker and Indian Strategic Culture". *Comparative Strategy* 25, no. 3 (2006): 231–47.

———. "Strategic Culture: A 'Cultural' Understanding of War". *Comparative Strategy* 28, no. 1 (2009): 68–88.

van Creveld, Martin. *The Transformation of War*. New York: The Free Press, 1991.

———. *The Changing Face of War: Combat from the Marne to Iraq*. New York: Random House, 2008.

van Schendel, Willem. "Geographies of Knowing, Geographies of Ignorance: Jumping Scale in Southeast Asia". *Environment and Planning D: Society and Space* 20, no. 6 (2002): 647–68.

———. *The Bengal Borderland: Beyond State and Nation in South Asia*. London: Anthem Press, 2004.

Voigtlander, Nico and Hans-Joachim Voth. "Persecution Perpetuated: The Medieval Origins of Anti-Semitic Violence in Nazi Germany". NBER Working Paper 17113. National Bureau of Economic Research (NBER), 2011.

Waldman, Thomas. "The Use of Statebuilding Research in Fragile Contexts: Evidence from British Policymaking in Afghanistan, Nepal and Sierra Leone". *Journal of Intervention and Statebuilding* 8, no. 2–3 (2014): 149–72.

Walker, Andrew. *The Legend of the Golden Boat: Regulation, Trade and Traders in the Borderlands of Laos, Thailand, Burma and China*. Richmond: Curzon Press, 1999.

———. "Should the International Conference on Thai Studies Be Held in Thailand?" *New Mandala*, 24 February 2011. <http://www.newmandala.org/should-the-international-conference-on-thai-studies-be-held-in-thailand/> (accessed 14 November 2016).

———. *Thailand's Political Peasants: Power in the Modern Rural Economy*. Madison: University of Wisconsin Press, 2012.

Walt, Stephen M. *Taming American Power: The Global Response to U.S. Primacy*. New York: W.W. Norton, 2006.

Waltz, Kenneth N. *Theory of International Politics*. Boston: McGraw-Hill; Reading, MA: Addison-Wesley, 1979.

Weatherbee, Donald E. *International Relations in Southeast Asia: The Struggle for Autonomy*. London: Rowman and Littlefield, Inc., 2009.

Weinstein, Jeremy M. *Inside Rebellion: The Politics of Insurgent Violence*. New York: Cambridge University Press, 2007.

Welsh, Jennifer. "The Individualization of War: Protection, Liability, and Accountability". Lecture at the Trudeau Foundation, Ontario, 25 March 2014.

Welsh, Jennifer and Maria Banda. "International Law and the Responsibility to Protect: Clarifying or Expanding States' Responsibilities?" *Global Responsibility to Protect* 2, no. 3 (2010): 213–31.

Wesley, Michael. *Restless Continent: Wealth, Rivalry, and Asia's New Geopolitics*. Melbourne: Black Inc. Books, 2015.

White, Geoffrey M. and Lamont Lindstrom, eds. *The Pacific Theater: Island Representations of World War II*. Honolulu: University of Hawaii Press, 1989.

The White House. "Joint Press Conference with President Obama and Prime Minister Abe of Japan". Press release, 24 April 2014. <https://www.whitehouse. gov/the-press-office/2014/04/24/joint-press-conference-president-obama-and-prime-minister-abe-japan> (accessed 8 November 2015).

White, Hugh. "Nuclear Weapons and American Strategy in the Age of Obama". The Lowy Institute for International Policy, September 2010. <http://www. lowyinstitute.org/publications/nuclear-weapons-and-american-strategy-age-obama> (accessed 8 November 2015).

———. "Power Shift: Rethinking Australia's Place in the Asian Century". *Australian Journal of International Affairs* 65, no. 1 (2011): 81–93.

———. *The China Choice: Why America Should Share Power*. Melbourne: Black Inc. Books, 2012.

Wikipedia. "World War II Casualties", 2015*a*. <https://en.wikipedia.org/wiki/ World_War_II_casualties#Total_deaths> (accessed 8 July 2015).

———. "List of War Apology Statements Issued by Japan", 2015*b*. <https:// en.wikipedia.org/wiki/List_of_war_apology_statements_issued_by_Japan> (accessed 4 November 2015).

Wilmshurst, Elizabeth. "Introduction". In *International Law and the Classification of Conflicts*, edited by Elizabeth Wilmshurst. Oxford: Oxford University Press, 2012, pp. 1–8.

Wilson, Dick. *China The Big Tiger: A Nation Awakes*. London: Abacus, 1997.

Wilson, Rob and Arif Dirlik, eds. *Asia/Pacific as a Space of Cultural Production*. Durham: Duke University Press, 1995.

Winichakul, Thongchai. *Siam Mapped: A History of the Geo-body of a Nation*. Honolulu: University of Hawai'i Press, 1994.

Wood, Terence. "Understanding Electoral Politics in Solomon Islands". CDI Discussion Paper 2014/02. Australian National University, 2014.

World Bank. "The East Asian Miracle: Economic Growth and Public Policy". New York: Oxford University Press, 1993.

Wyatt-Walter, Andrew. "Regionalism, Globalization, and World Economic Order". In *Regionalism in World Politics: Regional Organization and International Order*, edited by Louise Fawcett and Andrew Hurrell. New York: Oxford University Press, 1995, pp. 74–121.

Yang, Daqing. "Convergence or Divergence? Recent Historical Writings on the Rape of Nanjing". *The American Historical Review* 104, no. 3 (1999): 842–65.

———. "The Malleable and the Contested: The Nanjing Massacre in Postwar China and Japan". In *Perilous Memories*, edited by T. Fujitani, Geoffrey M. White, and Lisa Yoneyama. Durham and London: Duke University Press, 2001, pp. 50–86.

Yoshida, Takashi. *The Making of the "Rape of Nanking": History and Memory in Japan, China, and the United States*. Oxford: Oxford University Press, 2006.

Yoshimi, Yoshiaki and Suzanne O'Brien. *Comfort Women: Sexual Slavery in the Japanese Military during World War II*. New York: Columbia University Press, 2000.

You, Jong-sung. *Democracy, Inequality and Corruption: Korea, Taiwan and the Philippines Compared*. New York: Cambridge University Press, 2015.

Young, Crawford. "The Dialectics of Cultural Pluralism". In *The Rising Tide of Cultural Pluralism: The Nation-State at Bay?*, edited by Crawforfd Young. Madison: The University of Wisconsin Press, 1993, pp. 3–35.

Zakaria, Fareed. *The Post-American World*. New York: W.W. Norton and Company, 2009.

Zhang, Shu Guang. *Deterrence and Strategic Culture: Chinese-American Confrontations, 1949–1958*. Ithaca and London: Cornell University Press, 1992.

Zhang, Sulin. "The Declassification of Chinese Foreign Ministry Archival Documents: A Brief Introduction". *Cold War International History Project Bulletin* 16 (2007/08): 10–11.

Zhang, Tiejun. "Chinese Strategic Culture: Traditional and Present Features". *Comparative Strategy* 21, no. 2 (2002): 73–90.

Zhang, Yunbi. "Abe Won't Attend China's Commemorative Celebration". *China Daily*, 25 August 2015.

INDEX

Note: Page numbers followed by "n" denote notes.

www.ingramcontent.com/pod-product-compliance
Lightning Source LLC
Chambersburg PA
CBHW050426280326
41932CB00013BA/2002